CENSORSHIP IN ENGLAND

"What business have our young girls at the Theatre?"
                                        GOETHE.

"Imagine the celestial refreshment of having a pure decency in the place of sham; real flesh; a soul born active, wind-beaten, but ascending. Honourable will fiction and the drama then appear; honourable, a fount of life, an aid to life, quick with our blood."
                                        GEORGE MEREDITH.

Thomas Killigrew, the Stage Censor during the Restoration. Killigrew was himself the author of some witty plays, which were, however, by modern standards, extravagantly indecent.

Frontispiece.

CENSORSHIP IN ENGLAND

BY

FRANK FOWELL

AND

FRANK PALMER

BENJAMIN BLOM  New York/London

First Published 1913
Reissued 1969 by
Benjamin Blom, Inc., Bronx, New York 10452
and 56 Doughty Street, London, W.C. 1

Library of Congress Catalog Card Number 74-82828

Printed in the United States of America

PREFACE

In one of our royal palaces you may, after inquiry, be directed to a certain room whose prosaic furnishings call for no special mention. Here you shall— if your visit be well timed—discover a gentleman, equally prosaic, whose amiable and inoffensive features suggest nothing of the stupendous responsibility with which he is invested. This gentleman is popularly known as the Stage Censor, and his duty is understood to be that of guarding the morals of a great nation from the more or less insidious attacks of dramatists and theatre-managers. The ripest product of whatever genius our nation can boast must, in company with the merest paste-pot pantomime, pass under the mild eyes of this curious potentate, and be shorn at his command of whatever offends him.

What actually happens in that room? How and when did it come to pass that a chair and a table and a man were first provided for the censorship of plays? Upon what principle is this gentleman selected? What are his qualifications? What instructions are given to him? What rules does he follow; to what precedents must he conform? Above all, how, and by whom, and why were those rules and precedents created? And, finally, what sort of men have held this important office since its creation? Have they been of such a class as would conform to the recognised principle that an Englishman—even a dramatist—shall be judged by his peers?

This book has been written in an effort to answer some of these queries. With great difficulty the available details and records concerning the office have been brought together so as to form a connected narrative of the whole course of censorship in England. Unfortunately, the available records are of the scantiest description, and the labour of discovering and co-ordinating these will only be appreciated by those patient students who have been engaged on similar quests. So far as the early Censors are concerned, it is unfortunately now improbable that much further detail will ever become available, and the records of the ensuing period are disappointingly meagre. Nevertheless, sufficiently numerous instances have been collected to outline the general trend of the censorship. It is important to note that when dealing with recent interventions we have had the assistance of the authors or managers directly interested, and must make general acknowledgments to Mr George Bernard Shaw, Mr Granville Barker, Mr Frederick Whelen, and those other ladies and gentlemen, too

numerous to mention, who have kindly accorded
their help. The Lord Chamberlain very courteously
supplied the official numerical results of censorship
as shown in the Appendix, and grateful thanks are
also due to the officials of the British Museum and
the Clerk of the London County Council. The
interesting portrait of Sir Henry Herbert by Dobson
has never previously, we believe, been reproduced,
and our thanks are due to Lord Powis for the
permission so readily accorded.

Throughout this book, with its appendices, various extracts have been reproduced from the official Reports of Select Committees which met to consider aspects of dramatic censorship in 1832, 1866, and 1909. Permission to make use of these extracts was duly obtained from the Controller of His Majesty's Stationery Office.

CONTENTS

LIST OF ILLUSTRATIONS

CENSORSHIP IN ENGLAND

CHAPTER I

MAINLY OF ORIGINS

WE have had many diverting histories written for us,
but the yet unwritten history of PUBLIC OFFICES is
likely to surpass them all in its wealth of humorous
incidents and absurdities. When such a history is
completed it will be interesting to note the incredibly
slender origin of many of these great State posts.
Very frequently they had their birth in a little power
granted on some special holiday to a favourite
retainer. As often as not the posts, even then, were
sinecures with ceremonial rather than useful functions ; but the holders seem, one and all, to have
been ambitious and enterprising. The first change
was to secure increasing frequency and duration of
those brief periods of office, so that, by slow degrees,
the post became a permanent and salaried one.
Then, in course of time, some indulgent sovereign,
swayed by sentiments of gratitude (or more frequently,
love) would post-prandially be induced to give the
office a legal standing and grant a patent.

Thereafter the developments were swift and
amusingly uniform. We can trace the same eager-

ness for prestige, the same overweening rapacity, the same sly aggressions, with the object of widening the area of jurisdiction. Instead of the post remaining one in the Royal Household it was quietly extended to London, and, if no vigorous opposition was met, to the country at large. Fees, rents, and commissions were increased, and every device which greed could suggest and audacity execute, was made use of to inflate the power of the office and widen its scope.

There is something very amusing in tracing the tenuity of under-structure and the audacious encroachments, which are characteristic of the growth of most of these offices. The history of the office of Dramatic Censor is no exception to the rule. It is an office unique in the extent of the power it wields. The Censor can, if he choose, destroy the product of another man's labour and besmirch a reputation without the victim having claim to defence or appeal. Powers such as these are not paralleled in our constitution, and for that reason it will be particularly interesting to try to discover on what grounds the powers are claimed. No other public servant claims such autocratic privileges, and it is a healthy and natural thing that these pretensions should be challenged with increasing frequency.

It is among the men who catered for the pleasures of our early sovereigns that you will find the first thread-like roots of modern censorship. There were two offices to which reference must be made, those of the Master of Revels (the real Stage Censor of early times) and the Lord of Misrule. The office of Master of Revels may possibly have been the permanent form given to the ephemeral and irresponsible powers held by the Lords of Misrule who figured so prominently in the Christmas festivities of mediæval times. Stow tells us that there was in the king's house, wherever he might be, "a lord of misrule or master of merry disports, and the like had ye in the house of every nobleman of honour or good spirit, were he spiritual or temporal." These temporary rulers, who were also to be found in the retinues of the Mayor and sheriffs of London, "misruled" from All-Hallows' Eve till Candlemas, and the expenses of their short but extravagant reign figure heavily in the accounts of the time, until by an Act of Common Council (1555) they were curtailed.

A Puritan writer in 1583 gives us the following sketch of an election of a Lord of Misrule :

"First of all the wilde heades of the parish flocking togethir chuse them a graunde captaine of mischiefe, whom they innoble with the title of 'lord of misrule'; and him they crowne with great solemnity and adopt for their king. This king . . . chooseth forth twenty, fourtie, threescore or an hundred . . . like to himself to wait upon . . . and to guard his noble person. Then every one of these men he investeth with his liveries of green, yellow, or some other light colour. . . . They bedecke themselves with scarffes, ribbons and laces. . . . They tie aboute either twentie or fortie belles, with rich handkerchiefes in their hands. . . . Thus all things set in order, they have their hobbie horses, their dragons, and other antiquities, together with their . . . pipers and

thundering drummers. . . . Then march this
heathen company towards the church, their
pypers pyping, their drums thundering, their
stumpes dauncing, their belles jyngling, their
handkerchiefs fluttering aboute their heades like
madde men, their hobbie horses and other
monsters skirmishing among the throng : and
in this sorte they go to church, though the
minister be at prayer or preaching . . . with
suche a confused noise that no man can heare
his owne voyce. Then the foolish people they
looke, they stare, they laugh, they fleere, and
mount upon the formes, and pewes to see these
goodly pageants solemnized."

A similar post existed in Scotland until 1555,
though the Lord of Misrule was there known as the
Abbot of Unreason, a fitting enough post for our
modern Censor to have his authority from. However, it is difficult to trace the origin and growth of
this old office. It was, in all probability, dramatic
rather than administrative, in which particular it
differed entirely from the office of Master of Revels,
though it certainly seems probable that the one
temporary office suggested the other permanent
one.[1]

---

[1] The following are instances of the appointment of Lords of
Misrule. Under 16, 17, Henry VII., A.D. 1525-6, there is this entry in
the accounts of the corporation of New Romney :

"Paid in expenses, when the lorde of misrewle of Olde Romney
came to towne, 40d."—*Hist. MSS. Rep.*, vol. v. pt. i. p. 551a.

"Jan. 3, 1551.—Warrant from the Lords of the Council to
Sir Thomas Carden, Master of the Revels, for the speedy equip-
ment of the eight counsellors of the appointed lord of misrule for
the king's house."—*Rep.*, vol. vii. pt. i. p. 606b.

"Christmas day, 1551.—Warrant from the same to the same,

The Master of Revels was an official of varying dignity, whose duty it was to arrange and control the royal entertainments, disguisings, masques, and so forth on festive occasions. The earliest traced reference to such an office is dated 1347, when the provision of *tunicae* and *viseres* for the Christmas *ludi* of Edward III. at Guildford is to be found among the expenses of the wardrobe. Among Lord Burghley's papers is to be found a quaint account of the origin of the post, which is worth repeating :

"The Office of the Revelles, as it shoulde seeme by reporte, hath in tymes past bene in that order, that the prince beinge disposed to pastyme would at one tyme appoynte one persone, at sometyme an other, suche as for creditte, pleasaunte witte, and habilitye in learn-ynge he thought meete to be the master of the Revelles for that tyme, to sett fourthe suche devises as might be most agreable to the princes expectacion. The workes being fynyshed, It is thought that the princes Tayler, havinge the oversight of the Workemanshippe, brought in the Bill of charges and was payed for it, whereupon is gathered that John Houlte, yeoman of the Revelles, used to say Concerninge allowaunce of charges in the office of the Revelles, 'it hath bene but a Taylers Bill.'"

&c., from the recently appointed lord of mysrule to be in his highnes household for the twelve days."

"December 30.—Warrant &c., to provide apparel for George Ferrers, the appointed lord of mysrule in his Majesty's house, and for three pages, eight counsellors, one tumbler, and twenty-four servants."—*Ibid.*, p. 607*a*.

Some little time after the Guildford entry to
which we have referred, we read of John Lydgate
composing a set of verses for a Christmas feast in
Hertford Castle " at the requeste of the countrowlore
Brys," who was probably Comptroller of the Household.   References to organised entertainments or
revels do not, however, become common until the
time of Henry VII., when items of expenditure in
connection with Christmas and other merry-makings
are frequently met with.   The Master of the Revels
was apparently by this time a minor member of the
Household, and official recognition of him is to be
found in an ORDER FOR SITTING IN THE KING'S GREAT
CHAMBER, dated 31st December 1494 : " If the
master of revells be there, he may sitt with the
chapleyns, or with the esquires or gentlemen ushers."
As the character of the court changed the opportunities of the office increased, and from being an
insignificant (and probably temporary) appointment
at the court of Henry VII., it became, in the reign
of his light-hearted successor, a post of considerable
importance.

In 1510 we find the Earl of Essex acting as
Superintendent of the Revels, and a year later the
honour of amusement purveyor seems to have been
bestowed on Sir Henry Guildford, who, as Squire of
the Body and Standard Bearer, then as Master of
the Horse, and a little later as Comptroller of the
Household, made something of a figure in courtly
circles.   Other names, such as Lord Leonard Grey
and Sir Anthony Browne, are variously mentioned
between 1524 and 1539, and as the nominal salary of
the office was only some ten shillings for each day

of personal supervision, we may be sure that it was not long before a minor, and possibly permanent, official was appointed by the Superintendent of Revels, " both to his own ease and the prince's good service." It was no doubt found desirable to have a permanent official acquainted with the technical details of the post ; some one who could be deputed, in the time-honoured fashion, to execute the drudgery and detail, and accept such cuffs and curses as might not conveniently be taken by his superior. As a matter of fact, as the work of the office increased, several subordinate posts were created.[1]

Of the drudgery and detail to which reference has been made, there was, we may be sure, a sufficiency. Masks, dresses, stuffs, and ornaments had to be obtained, architects, builders, carpenters, tailors, and embroiderers to be engaged, and the actual performances chosen and piloted to an acceptable conclusion. A further source of anxiety was the thieving propensities of the royal guests, who revealed a marked partiality for the " properties " and costumes of the players,[2] and an embarrassing ingenuity in stealing them.

Without any of these complications, the duties of the post must have been onerous, for the masques, at that time much favoured by the court, were on the grand scale. One such entertainment given in 1575 to Queen Elizabeth by Dudley, Earl of

[1] See p. 49 f.
[2] In the Revels Inventory for 1560, against items relating to cloth of silver "with workes," and some "purple gold sarcenet," appears in the column headed "Remayne," the following comment: "Nil. for they were all taken away by the Straungers and lords that masked in the same."

Leicester, is reported to have lasted for seventeen days, at a cost to the earl of £1,000 per day, while the total cost has been computed at about £60,000 of our present currency. Another one, said to have cost £21,000, was presented in 1633 to Charles I. and his French queen. According to Thornbury the music was written by Milton's friend, Lawes, the libretto by Shirley. The procession set out from Ely House in Holborn on Candlemas Day in the evening. The four chariots that bore the sixteen masquers were preceded by twenty footmen in silver-laced scarlet liveries, who carried torches and cleared the way. After these rode a hundred gentlemen from the Inns of Court, mounted and richly clad, every gentleman having two lackeys with torches, and a page to carry his cloak. Then followed the other masquers—beggars on horseback and boys dressed as birds. The colours of the first chariot were crimson and silver, the four horses being plumed and trapped in parti-coloured tissues. The Middle Temple rode next in blue and silver, and the Inner Temple and Lincoln's Inn followed in equal bravery, one hundred of the suits being reckoned to have cost £10,000. The masque was "most perfectly performed" in the Banqueting House at Whitehall, the Queen dancing with several of the masquers and declaring them to be as good dancers as ever she saw.

Machyn tells us of one "sergantt Gybsun, sergannt of armes, and of the reywelles and of the kynges tenstes," who was presumably that Richard Gibson, who, during his period of office, had the honour of engaging Hans Holbein for the decoration of the Banqueting Hall at Greenwich. Gibson died

in 1534, and on 20th November of that year John
Farlyon was appointed Yeoman of the Revels, the post
then coming for the first time into independent existence. In Farlyon's patent he is described as "Yeoman
or Keeper of the King's vestures or apparel of
masks, revels, and disguisings and of apparel and
trappers of horses for justes and turneys," the post
carrying a wage of 6d. a day, with an allowance
of one livery coat. Five years later Thomas
Thacker wrote to Cromwell, "Last night John
Farlian, serjeant of the king's tents died," and on
21st October 1539 the post fell to John Bridges,
who resigned it on 1st April 1547.[1] The scope and
power of the two offices of the Tents and the Revels
is a little confusing; but this ambiguity was ended
by the establishment in 1544 of a new functionary,
with the title of Master, as chief officer alike of the
offices of Tents and Revels. Cawarden, the next
Master, held both offices by two separate patents.
The reason given for the creation of the new title
was that "sergeant" seemed hardly a dignified enough
appellation for one of Sir Thomas Cawarden's credit.

---

[1] Two items may fittingly be mentioned here relative to this period.
In 1537 games and unlawful assemblies were prohibited in Suffolk on
account of a seditious May-game which was "of a king, how he should
rule his realm," in which one of the characters said "many things
against gentlemen more than was in the play."

In 1543 a statute was passed entitled "an act for the advancement
of true religion and for the abolishment of the contrary," which said—

"It shall be lawfull to all and everye prsone and prsones to
sette foorth songes, plaies and enterludes, to be used and exer-
cysed within this Realme and other the Kinges Domynions, for
the rebuking and reproching of vices and the setting foorth of
vertue; so allwaies the saide songes, playes or enterludes meddle
not with interpretacions of Scripture, contrarye to the doctryne set
foorth or to be sett foorth by the Kinges Majestie."

Cawarden certainly wore his court dignities with some stiffness, and the fact that he was of the King's Privy Chamber is repeatedly insisted on. We read that he " beinge of the king*es* maiesties pryvie Chamber, beinge skilfull and delightinge in matters of devise, preferred to that office, did mislyke to be tearmed a Seriaunt because of his better countenaunce of roome and place beinge of the King*es* maiesties privye Chamber." The full title of the office, as set out in the patent is *Magister Iocorum Revelorum et Mascorum omnium et singularium nostrorum vulgariter nuncupatorum Revells and Masks*, the appointment being for life. Cawarden was granted all houses, mansions, rights, liberties, and advantages appertaining to the office, and a salary of ten pounds per year. The salary was not a very big one ; but the office was young, and already there were some compensations to be obtained. The Master of Revels secured as a personal perquisite all the cast garments and accessories used in the masques, which he sold, probably to the actors, and we read of subsequent masters bequeathing substantial accumulations of such property to their heirs. This right to all the discarded garments and properties must have been a valuable one, and we can imagine the increasing anxiety and watchfulness of the Master of Revels on the one hand, and the nervous eagerness of the guests on the other, as the revels neared an end and the time for plunder approached.

The phrasing of Cawarden's patent was adopted almost without alteration in the patents of later Masters, and we shall shortly find Sir Henry Herbert claiming that the rather vague terms gave him a licensing authority over all kinds of shows and performances throughout the kingdom. In Cawarden's time, however, the jurisdiction did not extend beyond the court, and the Master of Revels was occupied in devising such masques and shows as were required for the personal entertainment of his royal master. Even Cawarden, however, tried his hand at stretching the powers of office, and there is a little incident on record which says a good deal for the importance and authority of the Master of Revels. Finding himself under the necessity of providing a new storehouse for his department, he turned the parishioners of St Anne's out of their church, giving as a reason that it was required " to laye in his Maties pavylyons, tentes, maskes and reuels." He calmly walled the building off, unroofed it, and after turning one portion into a stable, built tennis courts on the site. In the meantime the aggrieved parishioners were by the King's orders granted a room to use in place of their church. In 1555, however, a bill of complaint against Cawarden was brought before Bishop Gardiner, who ordered him to reinstate the church and, what was more troublesome, saw that his orders were carried out.

Cawarden held office long enough to superintend Elizabeth's Coronation festivities, and on his death in 1559 was succeeeded by Sir Thomas Benger, during whose term of office the work fell more and more into the hands of subordinates, with disastrous effects both to the organisation and expenses of the department. By 1573, on Benger's death, the demoralisation had gone so far and the need for drastic reorganisation become so obvious, that Lord Burghley was instructed to make an investigation into the origin, powers, and condition of the post. Burghley obtained reports from three different officials in the Revels office, and these reports, which, with their suggestions for reform, are still in existence, throw a good deal of light on the situation as it then was. It is important to note that although the powers of the office were exhaustively defined, no mention was made of any authority whatsoever to interfere with the drama outside the court circle. It is true that the Master frequently called outside companies of actors before him and had them rehearse plays which might be suitable for court presentation, so that he might select the best. The whole process, however, was simply the one followed in the selection of any other goods intended for use at court. In the ordinary course of sampling the proposed entertainments he would commonly glance over plays in manuscript to judge of their merits, to cut them down to tolerable limits if necessary, and to purge them of any expressions which might reasonably be suspected of being offensive to the royal audience. The Master of Revels was held responsible for the inoffensiveness and general success of these court entertainments, and for his own credit's sake it was necessary for him to discriminate between good and bad plays.

At Queen Mary's accession, however, an attempt had been made to put a stop to the growing freedom with which certain sacrosanct subjects were being discussed. The prohibitions then issued were certainly comprehensive enough to sterilise the intellectual life of the town. The proclamation is interesting as being one of the first to mention written licences for acting.

" AND furthermore, forasmuche also as it is well knowen, that sedition and false rumours have bene nouryshed and maynteyned in this realme, by the subteltye and malyce of some euell disposed persons, whiche take vpon them withoute sufficient auctoritie, to preache, and to interprete the worde of God, after theyr own brayne, in churches and other places, both publique and pryuate. And also by playinge of Interludes and pryntynge false fond bookes, ballettes, rymes, and other lewde treatises in the englyshe tonge, concernynge doctryne in matters now in question and controuersye, touching the hyghe poyntes and misteries of Christen religion. . . . Her highnes therfore strayghtly chargeth and commaundeth all and every her sayde subiectes . . . that none of them presume from henceforth to preache . . . or to interprete or teache any scriptures, or any mane poyntes of doctryne concernynge religion. Neyther also to prynte any bookes, matter, ballet, ryme interlude, processe or treatyse, nor to play any interlude except they haue her graces speciall licence in writynge for the same, vpon payne to incurre her highnesse indignation and displeasure."

We may also mention here an extract from an order of the Council to the Lord President of the North, dated 14th February 1556, to guard against any risk of " disorder " arising from the performance of plays. The order demands that

" they doo in no wyse suffer any playes enter-

> ludes songues, or any such lyke pastymes whereby
> the people may any wayes be steryd to dis-
> ordre, to be used by any manner p'sonnes or
> under any coulour or pretence."

In the next year, too, 5th September 1557, we find
the Council directing the Mayor of London to prevent
the further performance of another "lewd play"[1]
called A Sacke Full of Newes, at the Boar's Head,
without Aldgate, to arrest the players and send their
play book to the Council. Such a course was not of
much avail, for there was no means of preventing a
player from introducing whatever variations he chose
in the play as originally set out in the "play book."
The disadvantage of so much freedom was no doubt
becoming apparent, and two years later, on 16th
May 1559, Queen Elizabeth issued a proclamation,
establishing a more definite licensing system, and
giving broad instructions to guide officials in their
censoring.

> "And for instruction to euery of the sayde
> officers, her maiestie doth likewise charge euery
> of them as they will aunswere : that they permyt
> none to be played, wherin either matters of
> religion or of the governance of the estate of
> the commō weale shalbe handled, or treated ;
> beyng no meete matters to be wrytten or treated
> vpon, but by menne of aucthoritie, learning and

---

[1] It is hardly necessary to point out that the word "lewd" may not
be interpreted as "lustful." The ancient meaning of the word was
entirely different : *belonging to the laity*. Its early use is illustrated in
a proclamation dated 23rd June 1592 : In fear of disorder servants are
to be kept within doors, "nor to have anye weapons yf they shoulde be
so lewdlie disposed to execute any evill purpose."

wisedome, nor to be handled before any audience but of graue and discreete persons."

The whole proclamation has a very determined tone; but it is to be feared that its practical effect was very limited.

In the Revels Account for 1571 we find a list of six plays and six masques given at the court during Christmas and Shrovetide, and acted by companies of men or children who were "apparrelled and furnished and provided with apt howses made of canvasse, fframed, ffashioned and paynted accordingly" by the Revells office. These plays were duly read and corrected, "all whiche vi plays being chosen owte of many and ffownde to be the best that then were to be had, the same also being often perused and necessarely corrected and amended by all thafforeseide officers." Thereafter the "perusing and reforming" of plays begins to appear with increasing frequency in the Revels Account.

As far back as 1573 the question of the qualifications of the Master of Revels had come up for discussion, and it is very interesting to note what were regarded in those days as desirable qualities in the holder of the office. It is not surprising to find that he ought to have "some skill in staging"; but there are other phrases in Lord Burghley's report which, in view of the subsequent quarrels over the censorship, make entertaining reading. According to Edward Buggin, Clerk Comptroller of the Revels,

"The connynge of the office resteth in skill of devise, in understandinge of historyes, in judgement of comedies, tragedyes, and showes, in sight of perspective and architecture, some smacke of geometrye, and other thynges ; wherefore the best helpe for thofficers is to make good choyce of cunynge artificers severally, according to their best qualitie, and for one man to allowe of an other mans invencion, as it is worthie, especiallye to understande the princes vayne, and to order it so that everye man may learne somewhat the more what service meaneth, and as everye officer maye be made the more able to serve. For whiche service there would be an order made, as nere as maye be, what should be everye mans charge within the office according to his skill and habilitye."

" For one man to allow of another man's invention as it is worthy " is decidedly good, as is also the astute suggestion that the Master of Revels should " especially understand the prince's vein." As we follow the history of censorship through its varying phases of severity and looseness, we shall frequently be reminded of that diplomatic phrase.

In the second report, drawn up by Thomas Blagrave, the Clerk of the Revels, it is laid down that—

> " The Mayster of the office, oughte to be a man learned, of good engyne, inventife witte, and experience, aswell for varietie of straunge devises delectable, as to waye what moste aptlye and fitleye furrnissheth the tyme, place, presence and state."

A further clause in the same report suggests that

the Master of Revels should not only be able to judge a good play, but able to write and stage one, a qualification which, though attractive in theory, has not always worked out well in practice, as we shall later have occasion to remark.

> "The seconde is that the Maister of the office be appointed and chosen, suche as be neither gallant, prodigall, nedye, nor gredye, for if any of theis, suerlie he will never be fullie lyhable to this order, but make waiste, sucke the Quene, or pynche the poore, or all thre; And that he also be of suche learning, wytt, and experience, as hable of hymselfe to make and devise such shewes and devises, as may best fitt and furnisshe the tyme, place and state with leaste burden, and to frame all other speciall appointementes to the best shewe with least chardge and most spede."

We have seen then the early beginnings of the Master's power to act as censor of, and to expurgate where necessary, all plays and performances intended for presentation at court. His effective jurisdiction over the amusements of the general public appears up to this date to have been very slight, in spite of the somewhat sweeping proclamations to which we have already referred. For all practical purposes those proclamations were inoperative.

We may perhaps mention at this point an earlier proclamation, made in the City on Edward III.'s departure for France in 1329, which was later to be revived as a weapon against dramatists who became too personal in their writing.

" We do also forbid that any person, denizen or foreign be so bold as to menace, malign or slander the great men of the land, or any other person, or to carry lies or bad news among the people, by reason whereof damage may arise in the City."

In 1574, however, a new situation was created by Queen Elizabeth granting a patent to the players belonging to her favourite, the Earl of Leicester, giving them under the Great Seal the right to perform in all cities and towns of the realm, even within London itself, without molestation from the local authorities, any previous act or proclamation notwithstanding. Power such as this had never previously been granted to anyone, and it became necessary to make some provision against its abuse in this instance. There was a risk of the players, so soon as they were out of the immediate supervision of the court, taking advantage of their freedom to present plays likely to provoke disturbance, or incite disrespect for the court. To guard against such risks the Master of Revels was instructed to deal with these outside performances as though they were for the court, and the actors were only to hold their patent on the condition that all their plays " be by the Master of our Revels for the time being before seen and allowed."

This was a substantial increase of the Master's authority, and one that was destined to result in wide-reaching developments ; but when Benger died [1] and

---

[1] After Benger's death, which occurred in 1572–3, there was some delay in filling his place, Thomas Blagrave taking over the duties temporarily until Tilney's appointment.

Edmund Tilney was appointed Master by the patent of 1579, no mention was made of the new powers conferred on him, as a result of the patent given to Leicester's company five years before. Tilney was the last Master to hold office under Elizabeth, and although he retained the post until his death on 20th August 1610, he had, after the accession of James I., a deputy in the person of his nephew, Sir George Buck, who had been granted the reversion of the Mastership.

With Tilney's appointment the court entertainments entered on a period of greater lavishness and splendour, and by a patent dated 24th December 1581, his powers were considerably extended, and he was empowered to commit recalcitrant persons to prison. According to this interesting document, Tilney had the power, under the notable penalty of commitment for disobedience,

"To warne comaunde and appointe, . . . all and every plaier or plaiers, with their playmakers . . . from tyme to tyme and at all tymes to appeare before him, with all suche Plaies, Tragedies, Comedies or Showes as they shall have in readines or meane to sett forth, and them to presente and recite before our said Servant, or his sufficient Deputie, whom wee ordeyne, appointe, and authorise by these presentes of all such Showes, Plaies, Plaiers and Playmakers, together with playinge places, to order and reforme, auctorise and put downe, as shalbe thought meete or unmeete unto himselfe or his said Deputie in that behalfe."

It will be seen that the powers granted by this Commission were somewhat vague, for although the first part might be taken as referring solely to court performances, the latter phrases might reasonably be interpreted as referring to the stage in general. It was no doubt in this light that Tilney chose to interpret it. Naturally the licensing powers vested in him carried the right to a licensing fee, and though these at no time approached the figure secured by later Masters, they must have formed a useful source of income to Tilney. What he probably did was to issue to properly chosen companies, of whose repertoire he approved, licences somewhat similar to those given during Benger's Mastership to Leicester's men, which constituted a sort of passport to the magistrates and local authorities.[1]

[1] 1583

	Tuesdaie the third daie of mche, 1583, certen

	playors whoe said they were the sūnts of the Quenes
Mr Mayor.	Maiesties Master of the Revells, who required lycence
Mr J. Tatā.	to play & for there auchthorytye showed fōth an Inden-
Mr Morton.	ture of Lycense from one Mr Edmonde Tylneye, esquier,
	Mr. of her Ma^ts Revells of the one pte, and George
	Haysell of Wisbiche in the Ile of Elye in the couñ of
	Cambridge, gentlemā on the other pte.

The wch indenture is dated the vjth daie of februarye in the xxvth yere of her Ma^ts raign &c.

In wch Indenture there ys one article that all Jastices, Maiores, Sherifs, Bayllyfs, Constables and all other her Officers, Ministers & subiects whatsoeu to be aydinge & assistinge vnto the said Edmund Tilneye, his Deputies & Assignes, attendinge & having due regard vnto suche parsons as shall disorderly intrude themselves into any the doings & accōns before menčoned not beinge reformed qualifyed and bound to the orders pscribed by the said Edmund Tyllneye. These shalbee therefore not only to signifye & geve notice vnto all & eny her said Justices &c. that noñ of there owne ptensed aucthoritye intrude themselves & presume to showe forth any such plays, enterludes, tragedies,

It must not be thought, however, that these enactments gave to Tilney undisputed authority over the drama. As a matter of fact he only appears as a minor figure in the long and bitter struggle then in progress between the friends and enemies of the stage. The shopkeepers in the City of London, though not necessarily hostile to the stage as a form of amusement, were irritated and inconvenienced by the interruption of business and the waste of time and money in which it involved their wives and apprentices. Then there were, of course, the Puritan preachers. For many years the stage had been a battle-ground for the settlement of dry theological problems. As soon as these religious controversies were suppressed, however, the Puritan preachers discovered that the stage, no longer interesting to them, was wholly evil in its tendency and reeked offensively of hell. It was a change of front that was very common, very human, and entirely contemptible.

On the other hand, the increasing frequency of the court entertainments and the growing demand for variety made it absolutely necessary that various troops of players should be in a position to maintain themselves by public performances not too far distant from the court. Elizabeth, and indeed the court party generally, were strongly attached to dramatic

comedies or shewes in any places wth in this Realm, w^thoute the ordlye allowance thereof vnder the hand of the sayd Edmund.

Nota.—No play is to bee played but suche as is allowed by the sayd Edmund, & his hand at the latter end of the said book they doe play.

The foresed Haysell is nowe the chefe playor &c.

(From "Kelly's Notices of Leicester": *Hall Papers*, vol. i. fol. 42.)

entertainments, and in the centre of this interesting
position stood the Privy Council with the court and
preferment on one hand, and the Puritans and shopkeepers on the other. Naturally the Privy Council
was tempted both by inclination and interest to
gratify the Queen's tastes as far as possible ; moreover,
the City shopkeepers had more than once lately made
a show of independence, and an opportunity of
exercising a little stern authority over them was
welcome. At the same time the Privy Council had
very well grounded dread of anything likely to give
rise to rioting, or calculated to incite the common
people to rebellion. They were not able to forget
that some plays, notably religious ones it is true, had
given rise to serious disturbances, while over and
above all was the risk of infection and disease in
crowded audiences.

The licensing powers of the Master of Revels
came, therefore, more and more into conflict with
very similar powers claimed and exercised by the
City authorities. Those powers were, as a matter
of fact, actually conferred by the Council itself. As
a result of the excitement aroused by certain religious
plays, an order had been issued on 16th May 155c
prohibiting any performance without a licence i
towns from the Mayor, or in country districts fr
the Lord Lieutenant or two Justices of the Pea
By fairly continuous exercise of these powers t
position of the Mayor of London, in particular, ha
become fairly established ; but his powers had lately
been rather seriously encroached on, first by the over-
riding licence given to the Leicester players in 1574,
and later by the extended powers granted to the

Master of Revels in 1581. The rivalry soon became acute and resolved itself into a struggle between the court and the representatives of the people for the control of the popular stage.

As a retort to the Leicester patent, which had brought troubles to a head, an Act of Common Council was passed in the autumn of 1574 regulating public performances, and making it compulsory for all companies of players, as well as playing places, to be licensed by the Corporation, and all plays "allowed" by persons appointed by them for that purpose.[1] Feeling ran high over the privileges claimed by the Leicester players during the next year or so, and an open contest of powers between the City and Council was probably only averted by Leicester's men being transferred in 1576 outside the jurisdiction of the City authorities. As a body the City authorities remained hostile to the theatre mainly on account of the disturbing effect it had on the business life of the City. For the next few years the war between opponents and patrons of the stage was waged hotly by pulpit and pamphlet, and the Corporation encouraged by the amount of antagonism shown to the theatre ventured, in 1582, to pass a fresh Act of Common Council, permanently prohibiting all plays in London.

For a time no noteworthy protest was raised, a

---

[1] A law passed in 1574 enacted "That no innkeeper, tavern-keeper, or other person whatsoever within the said liberties should permit such play to be performed within his house or yard, which should not first be perused and allowed by the lord mayor and court of aldermen," and bound all persons who were permitted to perform plays in a penalty to the Chamberlain of London. This law does not appear to have been very strictly enforced.

fresh outbreak of plague making the public congregation of citizens undesirable ; but immediately
this danger was thought to be over the Queen's
players, selected by Tilney in 1583, applied for leave
to practise by means of public performances, in
preparation for the Queen's entertainment for the
following Christmas.　So far as we know there is
no documentary evidence in existence recording the
defeat of the City authorities in this direct appeal
against their jurisdiction ; but the fact is sufficiently
proven by the continuance of plays in London.　The
rights of local self-government were not, however,
finally overridden, and plays were again prohibited
in 1584 ; but, as a result of a petition by the Queen's
players, a working arrangement was arrived at
whereby the players were allowed to perform, but
under more stringent control.　During the next year
or two, plays were again prohibited on various
occasions for short periods, chiefly on account of
the prevalence of plague ; but these prohibitions
are not sufficiently important to justify enumera-
tion.

In 1596, however, a fresh set of circumstances
ruled.　Lord Hunsdon, the Lord Chamberlain, died,
and was succeeded by Lord Cobham, whose tastes
were Puritanic in their severity and simplicity.　The
Lord Mayor, thinking to benefit by this fact, made
a tentative and rather futile effort to banish plays
again.　Unfortunately for the Lord Mayor's hopes,
however, Cobham died the next year, and the office
reverting to the son of his predecessor, the City
Council found their prohibitions regarded with very
much less sympathy.　Ultimately, despairing of a

final prohibition, the Corporation contented itself with putting such restrictions on the power and liberty of the players as were practicable. [1]

In the interval the fight for the control of the stage through censorship had quietly proceeded. In 1582 the Privy Council called upon the Mayor to appoint " some fitte persones who maie consider and allowe of suche playes only as be fitte to yeld honest recreation and no example of evell." Whatever measures the Mayor took in answer to this message do not appear to have been very effective, and the half-hearted censorship which resulted was, as might have been expected, regarded as unsatisfactory by the Council. No doubt the Mayor, who wished to see the stage abolished, was by no means concerned in helping to make it innocuous, a change which would rather tend to consolidate its position than otherwise. In 1589 a fresh and important stage was reached when, after the publication of an order for the " staie of all playes within the Cittie . . . in that Mr Tilney did utterly mislyke the same," the Council quietly gathered the reins into its own hands. In the first place a letter was

---

[1] In 1597 an Act was passed in which these words occur : " That all persons that be or utter themselves to be proctors, patent gatherers, or collectors for gaols, prisons, or hospitals, or fencers, bearwards, common players of interludes or minstrels wandering abroad (other than players of interludes belonging to any baron of this realm or any other honourable personage of greater degree, to be authorised to play under the hand and seal of such baron or personage), all jugglers, tinkers, pedlars, and petty chapmen wandering abroad, etc. These shall be adjudged and deemed rogues, vagabonds, and sturdy beggars, and punished as such." It must be noted, however, that the parenthetical clause covered practically all the players performing in London, and was mainly directed to "masterless" men, at all times looked on with suspicion.

issued from the Star Chamber to the Archbishop of Canterbury setting forth that—

> " There hathe growne some inconvenience by comon playes and enterludes in and about the Cyttie of London in (that) the players take uppon them to handle in their plaies certen matters of Divinytie and of State unfitt to be suffred, for redresse whereof their Lordships have thought good to appointe some persones of judgement and understanding to viewe and examine their playes before they be permitted to present them publickly."

The Archbishop was instructed to nominate " some fytt persone well learned in divinitie " to serve on the outlined Commission. The Mayor of London had already been called on to appoint such a representative, " a sufficiente persone, learned and of judgement." In conjunction with these two Tilney was instructed—

> " To call before them the severall companies of players (whose servauntes soever they be) and to require them by authorytie hereof to delyver unto them their bookes, that they maye consider of the matters of their comedyes and tragedyes, and thereupon to stryke oute or reforme suche partes and matters as they shall fynd unfytt and undecent to be handled in playes, both for Divinitie and State, comaunding the said companies of players, in her Majestie's name, that they forbeare to present and playe publickly anie comedy or tragedy other then suche as

they three shall have seene and allowed,
which if they shall not observe, they shall
then knowe from their Lordships that they
shalbe not onely sevearely punished but made
(in)capable of the exercise of their profession
forever hereafter."

This was asking the Mayor to make himself
useful at his own execution with a vengeance. The
object of the whole arrangement was, without doubt,
to get the City to invest its authority in a single
unimportant individual who might easily be overridden and have his power quietly filched from him.
The ostensible purpose of the Commission was probably to make Tilney the real Licenser, with the
other two as consulting experts in the respective
spheres of religion and civic well-being. The actual
effect of the Commission was to establish Tilney's
absolute power. The other two coadjutors soon
ceased to take an active share in Tilney's duties, and
we can easily imagine that such a conclusion was
not far different from what Tilney had hoped and
doubtless schemed for. In any case the practical
control of stage plays passed from the hands of the
City authorities. They had, of course, the right to
pass resolutions prohibiting all stage plays ; but in
the meantime Tilney was quietly licensing as many
plays as he wished, and no evenly-brained author
would have much doubt as to which authority it
was advisable to placate.

Tilney's work as Licenser of Plays does not seem
to have been altogether satisfactory to the City
authorities. In 1592 we find them writing to

Archbishop Whitgift, with melancholy complaint as to the abuses which had arisen in recent years. Whitgift, who had not walked through the court with his eyes closed, replied with a tactful suggestion of some " consideration " for Tilney, which might induce him to exercise his powers, in the City at any rate, in more acceptable fashion. Apparently the archbishop had discovered that Tilney, following an excellent example, had a friendly eye for the cheerful giver. The suggestion was canvassed, and a little later we find the court of the Merchant Taylors' Company discussing a proposal by the Lord Mayor for " the payment of one Anuytie to one Mr Tylney, mayster of the Revelles of the Queene's house, in whose hands the redresse of this inconviency doeth rest and that those plays might be abandoned out of this citie." But however serious the evils arising from " those plays " may have been, they were evidently not serious enough to induce the Taylors' Company to vote a refresher to the Court Licenser, and we read that " wayinge the damage of the president and enovacion of raysinge of anuyties upon the Companies of London," they refused to fall in with the scheme. After this somewhat disheartening collapse it is not surprising to find few complaints of the " inconveniency " caused by plays in the next few years.

Tilney had already begun to realise the profitable possibilities of his licensing powers. The fixed fee for " allowing " a play was at this time seven shillings a play, while the theatres themselves were subject to monthly licensing fees, ranging from forty shillings to sixty shillings. Altogether, including his licensing fees, his fixed salary, his perquisites, and the further allowance of a hundred pounds [1] a year made to him, Tilney must have done very well.

Thereafter for some years the office gradually became more important, though several attempts were made to dispute its authority and challenge its privileges. As Tilney grew old, Sir George Buck became more and more actively concerned in the management of the office, and is, indeed, referred to as Master, and not deputy, in a document dated 1607, though in actual fact Tilney retained the titles of the office till his death in 1610. Buck had much larger ideas than his predecessor as to the remunerative possibilities of the office. Previous to his time the licences granted by the Master of Revels were for public performance only and had nothing to do with the publication of plays in book form. Since 1559 pamphlets, plays, and ballads might only be printed after inspection by, and licence from, three Commissioners for Religion. A little later, by a decree dated 23rd June 1586, a licence by a bishop or an archbishop was a necessary formality, and we find that these clerical gentlemen appointed a number of official licensers to deal with this work. In practice the whole scheme does not appear to have been very efficient, and though we find one or two protests were made by the reverend gentlemen because the conditions of the decree had been ignored, it is doubtful if any very

---

[1] This allowance does not seem to have been made to later Masters, who, however, received very substantial sums for special attendance, "diet," lodging, and incidental expenses.

serious steps were taken to bring ordinary offenders to book.

Buck, however, did not like to see the rapidly broadening stream of literature flowing titheless past him, and began tentatively issuing licences for the printing of plays in 1606. The new policy was both successful and profitable, and to Buck, therefore, must be the credit of starting the practice which ended in every drama entered during the next thirty years in the Stationers' Register bearing the authorisation of the Revels office. We have no means of estimating what increase this new practice produced in the revenues of the office, but it certainly did not leave Buck indifferent to other windfalls, for we find him in 1613 selling a permit for the erection of a new theatre in Whitefriars for the substantial fee of £20.

In a letter to John Packer, secretary to Lord Chamberlain Somerset, dated 10th July 1615, and allowing Samuel Daniel to appoint a company of youths to perform tragedies and comedies in Bristol, Buck states that he has received no stipend since 13th December, and begs for payment of the arrears. Five years later a letter from the Lord Chamberlain mentions, "Old Sir George Buck, master of the revels, has gone mad." This may not have been a disqualification in itself, but two years later he had become too infirm to discharge his duties, and on 2nd May 1622 Sir John Astley was appointed Master in his stead. On 22nd May Buck, was formally superseded in a Privy Seal which directed that as he, "by reason of sickness and indisposition of body, wherewith it had pleased God to visit him, was become disabled and insufficient to undergo and perform his duties, the office had been conferred on Sir John Astley."

Astley's period of office was mainly notable for the extraordinarily bad bargain he made with his successor.

Reproduction from manuscript of a play entitled SIR THOMAS MORE, which was submitted to the Censor (Tilney), 1586–1596. The MS. is important as being a specimen of a play-book still for the most part in the state in which the author sold it to the players. The Censor's marks and comments remain in the margin, and at the commencement of the play he wrote :—

"*Leave out y*ᵉ *insurrection wholy, and the Cause thereoff, and begin with* SIR THO. MOORE *at y*ᵉ *mayors sessions, with a reportt afterwardes off his good service don, being shrive off London, uppon a meeting agaynst y*ᵉ *Lumbardes, only by a shortt reportt, and nott otherwise, att your own perrilles.—E.* TYLLNEY." The indistinctness of the play itself is due to the fact that, owing to the age of the MSS., it has been found necessary to cover each folio with a protecting layer of transparent paper.

CHAPTER II

HERBERT AND HIS FEES

In 1623 the most original and striking Master of Revels in England comes to our notice, in the person of Sir Henry Herbert. Everything that Herbert did shows discreditable originality. Even the manner in which he secured his appointment was, to modern views, unorthodox. Sir Henry, who had, we doubt not, cast calculating eyes on the office of Master of Revels in Sir George Buck's time, soon noticed that Sir John Astley showed a deplorable lack of initiative in his new post. So Sir Henry, who was neither a Jew nor a Scotchman, and was only suspected of being either by his intimates, approached Astley and made a sporting offer to pay £150 a year for the powers and perquisites of the Revels office. We have gravely misjudged Sir Henry if he did not leave Sir John Astley under the belief that this offer was a philanthropic one, only to be explained by the depth of Herbert's friendship. We shall see later how Herbert emerged from the transaction.

The new arrangement seems to have shocked no one. On the contrary, it was accepted as a perfectly legitimate rearrangement, entitled to every recognition, and in fact the King shortly afterwards received Herbert as the new Master of Revels. Herbert

was quickly impressed with the rather imprecise
wording of Cawarden's patent, and soon started on a
series of experiments with the object of ascertaining
how far those somewhat elastic privileges would
stretch.   Acting on the very safe principle that he
who resolutely takès a thing will, in nine cases out
of ten, go unchallenged and in time be able to accept
the challenge of the tenth, Herbert began to claim
the right to license every form of public show or
performance.   Rope-dancers, the strident salesman
of drugs and cure-alls, and a host of others had soon
been entered as profitable clients on Herbert's register.
" Making show of an elephant," displaying " a live
Beaver," " a musical organ with divers motions in it,"
" an outlandish creature called a Possum," "a glass
called the world's Wonder," for " two Dromaderies "
and a " camel " were all acceptable fish in his net,
while Chalmers mentions " certain freakes of charging and discharging a gun," for " teaching the art of
music and dancing," for " a show of pictures in wax,"
and for an exhibition of " tumbling and vaulting with
other tricks of slight of hand," as appearing in the
register.   Most of these licences were for the space
of a year and vary considerably in the size of the
fees.   The peripatetic dromedary dealer paid a pound
for his licence.   Nowadays we do not insist on
the teacher of music or dancing getting a licence,
and one may even make "show of an elephant"
without the Censor having apprehensive thrills as
to the moral effect of the performance upon the
spectators.   We trust these people to have an
adequate respect for the morals of their pupils or
audiences.   Perhaps when the dramatic author shall

have climbed to the honourable level of a dancing master or tight-rope walker he may hope to be accorded the same responsibility.

Before long Herbert was bleeding the stage on a bold scale for further fees. As the monthly fees for licensing play-houses had come to an end, he substituted an arrangement in 1628, whereby the King's company "with a general consent and alacrity" arranged to give him two benefit performances annually—one in summer and one in winter, "to be taken out of the second day of a revived play at his own choice." This arrangement lasted for five and a half years, Herbert's receipts averaging £9 or £10 per performance. Then in 1633 a fresh arrangement was made, under which the manager of the company agreed to pay him a fixed sum of £10 every Christmas and £10 every Midsummer, instead of his two benefits. Herbert's benefits, however, sometimes brought him in a good deal more than £10, for we find in some early notes on Beaumont and Fletcher's CUSTOME OF THE COUNTRYE the following entry quoted :

> "The benefitt of the winters day, being the second day of an old play called THE CUSTOM OF THE CUNTRYE, came to £17 10s. od., this 22nd of November, 1628. From the Kinges company att the Blackfryers."

We may be sure, however, that this was an exceptionally high sum,[1] for we have no other record

---

[1] When Herbert was pressing his claim in 1662 he stated that his profit for each benefit performance was £50—a characteristic exaggeration.

of Herbert coming to a fresh arrangement with his clients without making some appreciable gain on the transaction.

By order of the Council, stage performances were entirely prohibited during Lent, and during the prevalence of plague;[1] but after a time it was whispered that a manager who tactfully mislaid a sufficiently heavy purse in Herbert's office might get a special licence or dispensation. Before long, records of fees exacted under these circumstances made their brazen or gilded appearance in Herbert's register. These Lenten performances were, we may be sure, profitable to the players, who would be willing enough to pay for the privilege. A company, too, which had been prohibited from playing on account of the plague, might find the prohibition lasting

[1] Plays were frequently prohibited on specified holy days. We give herewith one such proclamation issued as early as 1418:

"PROCLAMATION at Christmas against Mumming, Plays, Interludes, and Visors, and that a lantern shall be kept burning before each house.

"6 Henry V. A.D. 1418.

"The Mair and Aldermen chargen on the Kynges byhalf, and this Cite, that no maner persone, of what astate, degre, or condicioun that euere he be, during this holy time of Cristemes be so hardy in eny wyse to walk by nyght in eny manere mommyng, pleyes, enterludes or eny other disgisynges with eny feynyd berdis,[1] peyntid visers, diffourmyd or colourid visages in eny wise, up peyne of enprisonment of her bodyes, and macyng fyne after the discrecioun of the Mair and Aldremen; outake that hit be[2] leful to eche persone for to be honestly mery as he can with in his owne hous dwellyng. And more ouere thei charge on the Kynges byhalf, and the Cite that eche honest persone, dwellyng in eny hye strete or lane of this Citee, hang out of her hous, eche night, duryng this solempne Feste, a lanterne with a candell ther in, to brenne[3] as long as hit may endure, vp peyne to pay[4] ivd to the Chaumbre at eche tyme that hit failleth."

| [1] beards. | [2] except that it shall be. |
| [3] burn. | [4] upon pain of paying. |

unnecessarily long unless the treasurer of the company paid Herbert a friendly call. Such fees—"occasional gratuities" he called them—were entered at £3 or £3 10s. each.[1]

We note that Herbert had "a box gratis" at each of the theatres, and was also allowed a sum of twenty shillings weekly for a lodging. The regular fees which he received for the censorship and licensing of plays still, however, constituted the main source of his income. As a fee hunter Herbert was fertile in devices. Take the case of revived plays, for instance. In the ordinary way, revived plays which had previously been licensed by his predecessors were reallowed free of further charge. This seemed to Herbert unpleasantly like doing something for nothing ; but at the same time he was too cautious violently to demand a fresh fee. He laid his plans very skilfully. At first he would make a friendly arrangement with the player who brought an old play to be reallowed that he should get a book for his pains.[2] Custom soon gave this arrangement the force of a rule, and with the thin end of the wedge thus placed in position Herbert patiently waited a suitable opportunity to drive it home.

Such an opportunity came with the revival of THE TAMER TAMED in 1633. Some kindly disposed person was said to have laid a complaint to the court that the play contained objectionable matter, and on

[1] "From Mr Hemmings, for a courtesy done him about their Blackfriars house, £3."

[2] "Feb. 1625.—An olde play called THE HONEST MAN'S FORTUNE, the original being lost, was re-allowed by mee, at Mr Taylor's intreaty and on consideration to give mee a booke."

examination Sir Henry found this to be the case. He was therefore compelled to bring into force a new rule, under which the players submitting an old play for his inspection were ordered to pay a fresh fee of £1 per play. He defended it thus :

> " All ould plays ought to bee brought to the Master of the Revels, and have his allowance to them for which he should have his fee, since they may be full of offensive things against church and state, ye rather that in former times the poetts took greater libertie than is allowed them by mee."

The whole incident was neatly enough manœuvred.

To glance for a moment at the question of fees, we may note that these varied very considerably. Under Tilney the fee for reading and allowing a play was at first five shillings, then six shillings, and then six and eightpence. From 1598 to 1600 it was uniformly seven shillings per play ; but the figure thereafter steadily rose, and a year after his appointment we find Herbert acknowledging a regular fee of £1 for licensing Davenport's HISTORY OF HENRY I. ; but his fees appear to have been elastic, being, at any rate occasionally, based on the amount of work he felt called on to do. For instance, when he read THE HISTORY OF THE DUCHESS OF SUFFOLK in the same year, he demanded and obtained £2, giving as a reason that the play " being full of dangerous matter was much reformed by me." From what we know of Herbert it is not astonishing to find the higher fee became in time the regular one.

He established, too, another precedent. He

maintained that the fee was not for licensing a play, but to recompense him personally for his labour in reading and judging it. The fee, he said, "which belongs to me for reading itt over ought to be brought always with the booke"—a cautious provision against the risk of bad debts. The result of his new ruling was soon apparent, for in 1633 he records the fact that he duly received the fee for reading Massinger's BELIEVE AS YOU LIST, though its "dangerous matter" prevented him from licensing it. For the future, therefore, he was to have the comforting knowledge that his prohibitions were as valuable financially as his "allowances," or licences. In June 1642 there is a brief entry which no doubt caused the unfortunate author referred to a good deal more distress that it did Herbert. "Received from Kirke for a new play which I burnte for the ribaldry and offence that was in it, £2." This rather reminds us of the kindly Western custom of making the chief guest of a lynching party buy his own rope.

Presently a fresh inspiration came to Herbert. In those days the best copyright in a play was secured simply by guarding the copies of it. Rival players had no scruples against purloining any stray copy and thus securing a first performance. Several cases are on record of a copy of a play having been deliberately stolen and the play produced at a rival establishment, and in this fact lies the probable explanation of the comparative rarity with which early plays were printed. In these troubled waters Sir Henry Herbert dropped his net to advantage. Four years after the publication of Shakespeare's

dramas had made them easily available (1627), the
King's Company paid Herbert the respectable fee
of £5 " to forbid the playing of Shakespeare's plays
to the Red Bull Company."   Even the Lord Chamberlain himself was not always above taking a hand
in transactions of this kind ; but, so far as the Master
of Revels was concerned, such "extras" were only
very irregular sources of income.

We have already referred to Sir George Buck's
introduction of the system of licensing printed plays ;
though there is evidence that this rule was not very
strictly enforced toward the end of his Mastership.
But Sir Henry, who was as keen on increasing his
turnover as the owner of a New York "notion"
store, revived Buck's system with the utmost vigour,
and between 1628 and 1637 he issued licences and
received fees for every play entered in the Stationers'
Register.   In fact, he went further than this, and
stretched his fee-grabbing claws towards innocent
books of poems.   In October 1632 there are entries
of £1 and £1, 4s. for licensing verses by Lord
Brooks.   In another case we find him charging ten
shillings for two small pieces of verse by one Cowley.
Evidently he did not lack support in these new
charges so far as his right to make them was concerned, for when Donne's PARADOXES were printed,
Sir Henry was summoned before the Star Chamber
and told to " give account why he warranted " their
printing.

The reasons Herbert advanced to justify this
extension of his powers are worth preserving—

        " The   designe   is,   that   all   prophaneness,

oathes, ribaldry, and matters reflecting upon piety, and the present government may bee obliterated, before there bee any action in a publique Theatre.

"The like equitie there is, that all Ballads, songs and poems of that nature, should pass the same examinacion being argued a Majore ad Minus, and requiring the same antidote, because such things presently fly all over the Kingdom, to the Debauching and poisoning the younger sort of people, unles corrected and regulated."

To the rest of his activities Herbert occasionally added those of the lay lawyer, settling (for a consideration) litigation between parties, where the question in dispute was remotely associated with the theatre. In this connection it is worth noting that, however little his suggestions might commend themselves on the ground of equity, he had a variety of persuasive powers, including that of "committing to the Marshalsey." On such occasions his fees were doubtless computed according to the best traditions of lawyers.

Herbert made his last entry in the Register on the 8th June 1642, subsequently adding the words, "Here ended my allowance of plays, for the War began in August, 1642." After the Restoration, however, he came back to office in the expectation of exercising all his old powers.

In 1643, after the suppression of the theatres, Herbert made a note to the effect that the Crown owed him £2025 odd for "personal expenses, fees,

Diet, and boardinge," and the account he then prepared has a peculiar interest :

> " The Demandes of Sir Henry Herbert, knight, for his wages and boardwages, &c., as Master of the Revells to the late King :—

" Due to him to the last of October, 1638, as apeares by the Auditor's Bookes of Accountes, and by a Privy Seale, dated the sixthe of February, in the 16 yeare of the then Kinge Charles, the some of . . .	£1065	12	10
" Due to him for dyet and boardinges, as apeares by the Auditor's bookes of Accountes for 1639 . .	230	0	0
" Due to him for the lyke, for 1640, 1641, and 1642 being three yeares, the some of .	690	0	0
" Due to him for four yeares Fees at £10 per annum, to 1643	40	0	0
" Some is .	£2025	12	10 "

After reading the above account we are inclined to agree with Herbert's brother who once wrote of him, " He also hath given several proofs of his courage in duells, and otherwise, being no less dextrous in the ways of the Court, as having gotten much by it."

After the Restoration Sir Henry attempted to regain his lost authority, and even to extend it ; but, as we shall see, he never secured his original standing. According to Gildersleeve—

"After the Restoration Sir Henry Herbert, among suggestions for the confirmation and extension of the powers of the Revels Office, desired that it should have jurisdiction over all dancing schools, wakes or rural feasts,[1] and lotteries, and should even have the right to licence gaming, contrary to the law. He seems to have claimed authority also over billiards, ninepins, and cock-fighting—anything, in fact, over which his jurisdiction could possibly be stretched, and the licensing of which might be made a source of profit."

The Master's right to issue annual licences to bands of strolling players for country performances was pretty firmly established. In 1660, however, the Mayor and Recorder of Maidstone wrote suggesting with some frankness that Herbert's powers were simply confined to the court, and, in any event, did not extend so far as Maidstone. Herbert was much too astute to allow such a challenge to fall cold. He promptly sent a reply in the best official vein, threatening pains and penalties on the recalcitrant Mayor if he maintained his rebellious attitude. The original protest had been signed by " Richard Bills, Maior,"

[1] On 23rd July 1663 a messenger of the office was sent to Bristol Fair to investigate all showmen whatsoever, and see that they had commission from the Revels office. To what extent these powers were enforced prior to the Civil War is not known.

and " Lambarde Godfrey, Recorder." Herbert's reply was a judicious mixture of bluntness, tact, and postscript.

> " *Oct. 9th*, 1660
> from the Office of the Revelles.

" . . . You are the first Mayor or other officer that did ever dispute the authority or the extent of it ; for to confine it to the verge of the Court is such a sense as was never imposed upon it before, and contrary to the constant practice ; for severall grants have been made by me, since the happy restoration of our gracious sovereign, to persons in the like quality ; and seriously therefore admitted into all the counties and liberties of England, without any dispute or molestation. . . . But in case you doe delyghte in opposition and obstinacy to lawfull authority, and yet would be obeyed in yours without dispute, then you may take this from me, that I shall forthwith sende a message from his Majestie's chamber to fetche you and Mr Recorder Godfrey hither, to answer your disobedience to his Majestie's authority derived unto me under the great seale of England, and in exercise of the said powers by me for almost forty yeares, with exception only to the late times. And if you have endangered your charter by this refractoriness, and doe put charges and displeasures on your corporation and persons, you will remember that you were faierly invited to the contrary, and admonished thereof by your very affectionate friend,

" Henry Herbert."

" Respects to Mr Recorder Godfrey, of whom
I have hearde well by my cosen Lambert, and
for whom I have a particular kindnes."

Altogether Sir Henry Herbert's term of office
makes one of the most interesting and illuminating
chapters in the history of the British censorship.
There may have been other fields of revenue unex-
ploited by him, but they are not, so far, apparent to
us. Perhaps the best testimonial to his assiduity in
what it would be sarcasm to term the interests of
the public, is that provided by his income. He had,
as we have seen, purchased the office for a paltry
£150 a year. According to his own statement, his
income previous to the Civil War had risen to £4000
a year ! We cannot refrain from whispering again
his brother's restrained tribute to the effect that
Herbert was " dextrous in the ways of the Court, as
having gotten much by it."

There is one more characteristic incident which
must be mentioned. One Hayward, in the latter
days, purchased [1] from Herbert the deputyship of the
office. Unfortunately there are, so far as we are
aware, no figures in existence showing what sort
of a bargain Herbert struck with the new deputy-

[1] The custom of purchasing public offices is amusingly referred to
in a public advertisement made by Charles II.: " We must call upon
you again for a Black Dog, between a Greyhound and a Spaniel, no
white about him, only a streak on his brest and his tayl a little bobbed.
It is his Majesty's own Dog, and doubtless was stoln, for the Dog was
not born nor bred in England and would never forsake his Master.
Whosoever finds him may acquaint any at Whitehall, for the Dog was
better known at Court than those who stole him. Will they never
leave robbing his Majesty? Must he not keep a dog? *This Dog's
place is the only place which nobody offers to buy.*"

master. We find some confirmation of our suspicions, however, in a later statement that Hayward had not found the purchase a profitable one ;
we should have thought somewhat less of Herbert
if he had.

CHAPTER III

THE EARLY CENSORS AT WORK

WE have briefly outlined the history of the office of Public Censor, on its business side, down to the Civil War. It is now time to glance at its record from a literary and dramatic standpoint. By taking some characteristic instances of censorship we shall be able to see what were the actual, as apart from the theoretical, aims of the office. One of the first things it is necessary to emphasise is, that the motive underlying a large proportion of the activities of Master of Revels was undoubtedly personal gain. When Buck and Herbert began extending the scope of their office so as to make it include printed matter and freak side-shows, their motive had nothing whatever to do with the preservation of public morality or the control of licentiousness. It may have been on these grounds that they justified their aggressions ; but, to anyone who studies the position, it is hardly an arguable question as to whether preservation of public morality was the controlling factor or not. The result of the Licenser's activities was simply to bring an increasing number of citizens, ranging from dramatists to penny-show men, under their exactions, and we have no reason to suppose that this result was other than what was aimed at. The utter venality of the office

and the nature of the work finally licensed, is sufficient proof that the officials did not labour in any
rarefied atmosphere of austere morality. The atmosphere of the office was not that of a temple, but of a
rather mercenary lawyer's den.

It must not be forgotten that the functions of the
Master of Revels were, even theoretically, very different from those popularly attributed to the modern
Censor. It would be idle to claim for him any of
that moral anxiety which is supposed to animate his
modern prototype. He was, first and foremost, a
court official,[1] defending the powers and privileges
of the court, guarding the person and authority of
the King in one sphere,[2] precisely as the common
soldier at the palace gates did in another. The
appointment was not one likely to be given to a man
of Puritan tendencies. The Censor was a man who
moved in court circles, and usually had some literary
qualifications and pretensions. Sir Thomas Cawarden
was, we are told, "skilfull and delightinge in matters
of devise." Edmund Tylney was of good family, a
connection of Lord Howard of Effingham, and with
some literary achievement to his credit, including
The Flower of Friendship, dedicated to Elizabeth in
1568. Sir George Buck was author of various historical works and papers, including a treatise entitled
The Third University of England, and some commen-

[1] The primitive censorship exercised by the London Common
Council had been rather of a more moral and disinterested type. As
early as 6th December 1574 an order of the Common Council was
made against "unchaste, uncomely and unshamefaced speeches," evinc-
ing a desire for the moral purification of the stage, by no means so
evident in the labours of the Court Censor.

[2] See also Appendix for form of oath taken by Examiner of Plays
in 1824.

datory verses prefixed to Watson's *Hekatompathia*. Moreover, as he himself tells us, he wrote a long and particular commentary on *The Art of Revels*, which has been lost. He also, like Herbert, kept an office book, which was unfortunately burned.

Men such as these were not likely to have been at all hostile to the drama as seen from the dramatist's point of view. What Puritans thought of the stage and their horror at offences against decency and morality, interested the Master of Revels not at all. Indeed, unless human nature was a different thing, we may assume that the splenetic outbursts of the Puritans would only provoke him to greater tolerance toward the performances which gave them so much offence. We may be sure that the Master of Revels held the views of his own class and his own time. The idiosyncrasies of succeeding sovereigns, that "prince's vayne" which Masters were advised especially to understand, doubtless modified the Censor's activity and aggressiveness from time to time. But it is worth remembering that courts do not change so radically as kings, and to a large extent it would be the court tone that would be affected by the Censor.

Having hinted at these three sets of modifying influences, we may pass on to consider in what manner the office justified its existence. The Master of Revels had a certain minimum of official duties to the court,[1] and it will be interesting to examine the

---

[1] The Revels office, from very early times, had included, beside the Master, a Clerk-Comptroller, a Clerk, a Yeoman, and other minor offices. These were almost solely concerned with the preparation of court entertainments, the Master himself concentrating on the more profitable business of licensing public performances. It is only with the latter phase of his work that we are here concerned.

general principle which influenced him in the execution of those duties. We can gather a good deal of significant information from a study of the nature of the expurgations, emendations, and prosecutions of that period, as well as from the nature of the drama as finally censored.

The most obvious thing which attracts our attention is the indifference of the Censor to any nice points of propriety. Scenes and situations which would make a modern Censor squeal with horror and which to modern tastes would seem unnecessarily frank and offensive, were passed over in those early days without comment. It is not within our province here to discuss whether euphemism or *double entendres* indicate a higher standard of morality than existed in those days. Then, at any rate, habitual frankness left no excuse for hypocrisy. We will dodge the question of morals for the moment and simply say that the life and character of the times resulted in the production of a class of play which would, in these days, be regarded by many as derogatory to public morals. Discussions and incidents of the utmost intimacy were presented without offence, while entire freedom was granted to dramatists to deal with any phase of life or manners which appealed to them. The question of decency, as that tortured word is now interpreted, but rarely arose in the Censor's mind.

He was primarily concerned with the protection of the social order in its existing form. A dramatist could commit no graver offence than to write something tending to produce contempt for authority, whether of the Church or of the State. Ever since

Elizabeth's proclamation of 1559 it had been an offence to present upon the stage anything dealing with "matters of religion, or of the governance of the realm." Any attempt made to undermine the sources of authority were, on principle, suppressed, though it is not difficult to mention instances in which the Censor appears to have suffered from a temporary blindness. On the whole, however, the surest way of provoking the Master's ban was to present anything calculated to stir dissatisfaction in the common people, or to incite them to disorder and revolt. It was, in fact, not thought desirable that any scribbling play-maker should excite an intellectual inflammation in the national constitution.

Criticism of friendly foreign Powers was also forbidden, though naturally the severity of this injunction varied with the degree of friendliness officially extended to the Power in question. For a long time no reference was permitted to "modern Christian kings," but it was not always impossible to veil sufficiently clear references to particular personages under fictitious names. Finally, restrictions were at different times placed on the use of oaths and strong language, and here again the context sufficiently proves that the restriction was less in the interests of public decency than from fear of the possible results of too much freedom in thought and speech. For a long time the use of the word "God" was absolutely prohibited.

One of the earliest references made to drastic action in connection with a stage-play is to be found in the Commonplace Book of Charles, Duke of Dorset (the poet):

" Master of the Revells.—Sir Henry Herbert, in a tryall he had with my father to prove the antiquity of the Master of the Revells office, produced a very old man, who deposed that a long time since a small company of players represented a cobbler and his daughters upon the stage ; the cobbler complained in the Star Chamber ; the Master of the Revells, for licencing this, was fined, and put out of his office, and the players whipped. This I had from Mr C. K. M. R. and T. S."[1]

We have no other record of this incident, and have, therefore, no means of judging why the cobbler's protest was so extraordinarily effective. Possibly the cobbler or his daughters had some influential friend at court.

What is perhaps the earliest reference to a definite system of censorship is to be found in an Act of 1551 which contains a clause to the effect, " nor that any common players or other persons vpon like paines to plaie in thenglish tong, any maner Enterlude play or mattre, without they have special licence to shew for the same in writing vnder his maiesties signe or signed by vi of his highnes priuie counsaill." But the earliest intervention made by the Censor was in connection with the Martin Marprelate controversy in 1589. A number of plays were staged, violently inveighing against the Martinists, Puritan pamphleteers hostile to the Established Church. We may be sure that the authors were none

[1] The initials probably stand for Charles Killigrew, Master of the Revels, while T. S. probably means Thomas Skipwith, one of the patentees of Drury Lane Theatre, who died in 1710.

the less venomous because of the previous bitter attacks made by these same Martinists on the dramatic stage. In this instance, though the persons assailed were open adversaries of the Established Church, it was considered advisable to suppress the plays, as feeling was already running high and rioting was to be apprehended. One result of the incident was the appointment of the Commission to which we have already referred. The first suppression does not appear to have been effective, and some of the plays continued to make their appearance in one guise or another until 6th November, when the Council stepped in and suppressed all London plays. Here the motive for the action taken was perfectly simple. The offending plays were dealing with controversial matters of Divinity and State in a way calculated to provoke disorder. We have now no means of judging the precise nature of the plays under consideration ; but it is obvious that the objections taken were not to individual passages or the mode of treatment, but to any discussion of a dangerous question.

It may be as well to outline here what the routine of the Master of Revels' office at this time was. It was customary for the book-keeper of the company to prepare a fair copy of the play before its performance and submit it to the Licenser so that he might read it at his leisure. The latter would then strike out or alter such words or phrases as seemed objectionable to him, scrawling in the margin an intimation that certain scenes must be radically changed or omitted altogether. From a literary point of view the consequences were sometimes disastrous ; but that aspect of the question did not greatly concern him. It did not matter to him whether the offending scene was or was not the keystone to the whole play. If it displeased him, it must be deleted, even though the whole of the remaining manuscript was thereby reduced to wastepaper. But it is impossible to doubt that, to a large extent, the vigilance of this Argus was susceptible to golden anodyne. Men who had already proved themselves so expert at extracting good gold from other men's brains were not likely to be blind to the advantages of regulating their surgery according to their fees.

Be all this as it may, when the play had been finally read and corrected, the manuscript was endorsed on the back in some such way as follows :

> "This Second Maydens Tragedy (for it has no name inscribed) may with the reformacions bee acted publikely. 31 October, 1611.
>
> "G. Buc."

or

> "This play, called ye Seamans Honest Wife, all ye Oaths left out in the action as they are crost in ye booke and all other Reformations strictly observed, may bee acted, not otherwise. This 27th June 1633. Henry Herbert."

Since the licence to play was endorsed on the manuscript, it will be seen that the Censor's corrected copy remained in the players' possession, and, indeed, formed their sole warrant for acting it. In Herbert's time we find him occasionally requesting that a copy of the play should be left with him "that he may be able to shew what he hath allowed or disallowed."

He could then defend himself, if necessary, against any blame for improper interpolations made later, one such case actually arising over Jonson's MAGNETIC LADY. The alterations were then made by the book-keeper in the actors' various parts, and Herbert more than once insisted that the players ought not to study their rôles until the full text had been purged and licensed.

In general the procedure seems to have been very erratic. Sometimes a whole play would be confiscated and the author's work ruthlessly destroyed. At other times the Licenser nodded, or may possibly have got a coin in his eye, and would pass whole scenes of gross obscenity and disloyalty with hardly a single erasure. Sometimes, indeed, his errors of omission were so flagrant that they had to be redressed by the Lord Chamberlain or the sovereign in person. His errors of commission, of course, did not permit of redress. The poor author who found his lines hacked up, his rhymes wrecked, and his play mutilated, had to be humbly content to let his fragment of a play stumble into the world with what crippled grace it might.

Somewhere between 1586 and 1596, the exact date is a matter of controversy, SIR THOMAS MORE was censored. The scene in the play where More as Chancellor refuses to subscribe to the King's Articles, was scored out by Tilney, who made a marginal note "all altered," though the nature of the King's Articles was unspecified in the play. Against other portions which might be interpreted as provoking to discontent and rebellion, he wrote "mend y^t," while the part dealing with the insurrection of the citizens against the foreign residents seemed much too dangerous and inflammatory a topic, for he wrote at the beginning of the play : [1]

> "Leave out ye insurrection wholy, and the cause thereoff, and begin with Sir Tho. Moore at ye mayors sessions, with a reportt afterwardes off his good service don, being shrive off London, uppon a meeting agaynst ye Lumbardes, only by a shortt reportt, and nott otherwise, att your own perrilles.   E. TYLLNEY."

This manuscript, it may be mentioned, is particularly interesting, in so far as it is a specimen of a "book" still to all intents and purposes in the state in which the author sold it to the players.   It became, in fact, their official copy, which was duly sent to the Master of Revels to be censored, and it remains, with his comments in the margin, and his corrections, erasures, and substitutions, together with a number of added slips showing the way in which the suggested altera-tions were carried out.   Whether or not some of the alterations made in the manuscript were made by Shakespeare, is a problem which has afforded endless opportunities for discussion to Shakespeare enthusiasts.

That was one kind of censorship, and it is fairly obvious that no very high question of public morals was involved.   In 1597 we come across a different kind.   In that year Shakespeare had some passages with the Censor over HENRY IV.   The immediate source of the trouble was the full-bellied Falstaff. In the first instance the name of the historic fat knight

---

[1] An interesting reproduction is given at p. 32.

was Sir John Oldcastle. Some of the descendants of the famous Lollard martyr of that name chose to make impossible applications of the references in the play and protested with such energy that at last the Queen ordered Shakespeare to substitute another name for that of Oldcastle, "some of that family being then remaining." Had such a case occurred in modern times, Shakespeare would probably have been mulcted in some thousands of pounds under the blessed word "damages"; but in that less sophisticated age his offence was not recognised as having a cash value. We do not even read of him being punished, and we may be sure that any annoyance Elizabeth may have felt was quickly forgotten in the pleasure she found in following the amorous exploits of Falstaff, for whom she seems to have had an extraordinary and constant fondness.

Nash's Isle of Dogs came up for discussion in the Censor's office in 1599; but as this play has not survived the years, we cannot even conjecture the manner and extent of its offending. There is an entry in the Council Register for 15th August, gravely setting forth that The Isle of Dogs is "a lewd plaie . . . contanynge very seditious and sclanderous matter," and that in consequence "wee caused some of the players to be apprehended and comytted to pryson, whereof one of them was not only an actor, but a maker of parte of the said plaie." Nash's punishment, if he received any, must have been trifling, for very soon afterwards we find his company being singled out for special privileges by the Privy Council.

A little later Shakespeare's Richard II. came up

for notice, the scene of the king's abdication, particularly, arousing Elizabeth's apprehension. Those apprehensions were not altogether unfounded, for the Essex conspirators, thinking to encourage the common people to rebellion against Elizabeth, bribed the players with an offer of £2 to play the expurgated scenes at the Globe Theatre on 7th February 1601, one day before the date planned for the ill-fated rebellion. Here again the offence of the author and players seems to have been entirely overlooked.

By 1624 a prohibition against representing any modern Christian king in stage plays had come into force, an order the urgency of which may possibly have been suggested by the production in December 1604 of GOWRIE, and made still more imperative by Chapman's BIRON, in 1608. The play GOWRIE, performed by the King's own company of players, described the Gowrie plot[1] against James in 1600, and apparently gave great displeasure to the Councillors, and there was at any rate a threat to suppress it. Chapman's BIRON'S CONSPIRACY and BIRON'S TRAGEDY were not over-respectful to the French queen. Chapman had, it must be admitted, a somewhat rough hand in dealing with contemporary foreign history, and it is not surprising that Beaumont, the French ambassador, made several efforts to prevent the performance of the plays. He seems to have been partly successful; but in spite of his known influence with the court, the players persisted in

[1] John Ruthven, Earl of Gowrie, reckoning on the support of the boroughs and the kirk, conspired to dethrone James VI. of Scotland and seize the Government. The conspirators decoyed the King into Gowrie's house in Perth on 5th August 1600; but the plot was frustrated, the earl and his brother Alexander being killed on the spot.

acting the play as soon as the court had left town. As a result three of the players were arrested, Chapman, however, much to Beaumont's disgust, escaping. This was obviously a case where the play was more or less offensive to a friendly power, and its morality or decency were not in question.

It would appear that the French ambassador again secured the sympathy of the Master of Revels a little later, for when Chapman endeavoured to get a licence for the printing of his tragedy it was refused. The Privy Council had thrice given special permission for the performance of the two dramas, a fact which encouraged Chapman to make a bitter attack on the Censor, in record of which the following letter remains :

"S^r.,—I have not deserv'd what I suffer by your austeritie ; if the two or three lynes you crost were spoken ; my uttermost to suppresse them was enough for my discharge : to more then which no promysse can be rackt by reason ; I see not myne owne Plaies ; nor carrie the Actors Tongues in my mouthe ; The action of the mynde is performance sufficient dewtie, before the greatest authoritie, wherein I have quitted all your former favours, And made them more worthie then any you bestowe on outward observers ; If the thrice allowance of the Counsaile for the Presentment gave not weight enoughe to drawe yours after for the presse, my Breathe is a hopeless addition ; if you say, (for your Reason), you know not if more then was spoken be now written, no no ; nor can

you know that, if you had both the Copies :
not seeing the first at all :   Or if you had
seene it presented your Memorie could haredly
confer with it so strictly in the Revisall to
discerne the Adition ;   My short reason therefore can not sounde your severitie ;   Whosoever it were that first plaied the bitter Informer
before the frenche Ambassador for a matter so
far from offence ;   And of so much honour for
his maister as those two parts containe, perform'd it with the Gall of a Wulf, and not of a
man.   And theise hautie and secrett vengeances
taken for Crost and officious humours are now
more Politique than Christian ; which he that
hates will one day discover in the open ruin of
their Auctors ;   And though they be trifles he
yet laies them in the Ballance (as they concerne
Justice, and bewray Appetites to the greatest
Tyrannye) with the greatest ;   But how safely
soever Illiterate Aucthoritie setts up his Bristles
against Poverty, methinks yours (being accompanied with learning) should rebate the pointes
of them, and soften the fierceness of those rude
manners ; you know S^r ; They are sparkes of
the lowest fier in Nature that fly out uppon
weaknes with every puffe of Power ; I desire
not you should drenche your hand in the least
daunger for mee : And therefore (with entreatie
of my Papers returne) I cease ever to trouble you.
        " By the poore subject of your office for
                    the present."

A little later, with the assistance of friends at court,

Chapman induced the Censor to reconsider his decision, and mutilated editions of the plays were registered.[1]

The production of EASTWARD HOE, the joint work of Chapman, Marston, and Jonson, got the latter into more serious trouble. He was accused of "writing something against the Scots, and thrown into prison; but how often Jonson went to prison, and for how long, is very uncertain. In this case the Master of Revels did not take the initiative; the King himself seems to have taken action in the matter. His sensitiveness, in view of the changing relations with the Scotch people, is easily understood, and the royal intervention needs no further explanation. In the case of SEJANUS, however, and SIR GILES GOOSECAP, often attributed to the same author, some of the political, personal, and religious allusions were pounced on by the Master himself,

---

[1] " By an act of censorship, assuredly not so absurd or so arbitrary as in our own day has repeatedly exposed the direction of the English stage to the contempt and compassion of civilised Europe; which has seen at once the classical and the contemporary masterpieces of Italy and of France, and among them the works of the greatest tragic dramatist whom the world has seen since the death of Shakespeare, forbidden by the imperial mandate of some Lord Chamberlain or other Olympian person to corrupt the insular chastity of an audience too virtuous to face the contamination of such writers as Hugo or Alfieri; while the virtue thus tenderly guarded from the very sight of a Marion or a Mirra was by way of compensation—there is a law of compensation in all things—graciously permitted by leave of official examiners and under favour of a chaste Chamberlain to gloat upon the filthiest farces that could be raked from the sweepings of a stage whose national masterpieces were excluded from our own. But it is only proper that the public virginity which averts her eyes from the successors of Euripides or of Shakespeare should open her bosom to the successors of Wycherley and Mrs Behn. In the time of Chapman the Master of the Revels wielded with as fitful a hand as imperious an authority as any court official of later date. ALGERNON SWINBURNE."

without waiting for higher officials to remedy his own negligence.

A new phase of censorship is illustrated by the charge brought against Sir Edward Dymock in 1610, by Henry, Earl of Lincoln. It was asserted that Sir Edward and others had contrived and acted "a stage-play on a Sabbath day, on a Maypole green near Sir Edward Dymock's house, containing scurrilous and slanderous matter against the said Earl by name." After the play had been ended, an actor, "attired like a Minister, went up into the pulpit attached to the Maypole, with a book in his hand, and did most profanely in derision of the holy exercise of preaching, pronounce vain and scurrilous matter." As might be expected, such an offence was not in those days lightly overlooked. The three principal actors were sentenced to be pilloried and whipped at Westminster Hall and also in Lincolnshire, to pay a fine of £300 apiece, while Sir Edward Dymock was to be committed to the Fleet and fined £1000. The incident is instructive as showing how seriously such offences were regarded at that time.

With Tilney's death in 1610 Sir George Buck, as we have seen, became the Censor. A year later he was busily reforming the SECOND MAIDEN'S TRAGEDY, variously attributed to Middleton, Chapman, and Cyril Tourneur, and printed with Chapman's works among doubtful fragments. Buck carefully deleted a number of audacious passages describing and denouncing the royal lusts. Such references to vice in high places were, it may be assumed, a kind of disloyalty. A detailed reference to the censored passages would not be profitable here. In the main they reveal a comical concern and anxiety lest any disrespectful allusions to the gentry should escape uncensored. But however assiduous he may have been in shielding the royal peccadilloes from criticism, the play as expurgated sufficiently proves that no niggling love of decency or propriety guided his blue pencil.

Buck quickly came to regard himself as literary editor as well as Censor, and we find him deleting or subduing phrases that conflicted with his personal views and prejudices. Thus, when in the SECOND MAIDEN'S TRAGEDY he came across passages reflecting on women, such as "they'll rather kill themselves with lust than for it," he scored them carefully out. Similarly when (Act IV. Scene III.) the lady seeks refuge in death from the king's lawless passion, and the king says :

> " Hadst thou but asked the opinion of most ladies
> Thoud'st never come to this ! "

Buck carefully altered it to read

> " Hadst thou but asked the opinion of *many* ladies."

Surely there is some pleasure in imagining the prim Sir George Buck pursing his lips as he gravely made this niggling and gallant alteration.

Buck's corrections appear generally to have been made with an easy disregard for the needs of rhyme and metre, a failing which Censors have always shown, as for instance when Tilney, in reading SIR THOMAS MORE, taking offence at—

> " if he had the Maior of Londons wife
> He would keep her in despight of any Englishe,"

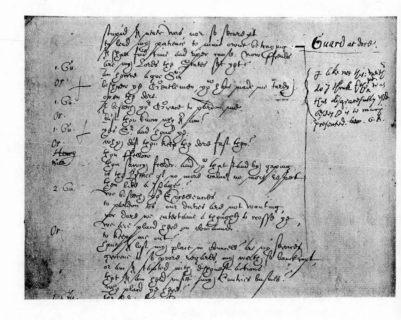

Reproduction from a manuscript play entitled Sir John van Olden Barnevelt, probably by Fletcher and Massinger, and now in the British Museum. The Censor objected to a great deal of the play dealing with revolt against tyranny, and to passages which might be interpreted as reflecting contemporary events. In Act I., Scene III., where the Guard refuses the Prince admittance to the Council Chamber, Buc wrote in the margin: "*I like not this: neither do I think that the pr. was thus disgracefully used, besides he is too much presented.—G. B.*"

crossed out "Englishe" and substituted "man." But this little failing of Buck's could not have been half so irritating to contemporary dramatists as his occasional fits of pink propriety. In spite of the broad manners and speech of the time, we find him on different occasions expunging such mild expressions as 'Sheart, Heart, 'Slife, Life, By th' Mass. This again was not by any means a censorship in the interest of public morals, and those who know the drama of the period will smile at the mere suggestion. The fact is that Buck evidently had his own idea of what were legitimate dramatic expressions, and was not able to resist the opportunity his post gave him of smoothing out contemporary dramatists under his little flat-iron.

About this time the office of Censor seems to have been generally looked on as a convenient means of enforcing personal views on the literature of the period. John Lilly (1554?–1606) was at one time eager to reform not only the stage but the English language, which, however, he miserably injured by substituting quaintness for simplicity, and bombast for wit. For many years he made the most persistent efforts to obtain the post of Master of Revels, so that he might impose his fanatic reforms on the drama of the period. We are told that "his aim was to become Master of the Revels, that through the medium of the stage he might promulgate his mad innovations." The incident throws an interesting sidelight on the popular conception of the post in those days.

During the next few years several unimportant cases of punishment for seditious plays are recorded.

These cases were in almost every instance either the result of unlicensed, and therefore fee-less, performances or controversial and disrespectful references to religion and nobility. In the corrections to SIR JOHN VAN OLDEN BARNEVELT, probably by Fletcher and Massinger, the same general motives may be traced—a timid desire to shield nobility from criticism and a determination to prohibit everything likely to arouse strong political feelings. In one case thirteen lines are scored out and are quite indecipherable. In Act I. Scene III., when the prince is refused admittance to the Council Chamber by the guard, Buck wrote in the margin :

> " I like not this : neither do I think that the pr. was thus disgracefully used, besides he is too much presented.   G. B."

One might almost conclude from this extraordinary comment that Buck thought himself responsible for the accuracy and proportion of the drama of his time. It is consoling to think that the period produced men who would not be mean antagonists to a man of Buck's calibre.

The gossipy office book of Sir Henry Herbert provides us with some good illustrations of the methods of the Censor in his day. Sir Henry was not, any more than his predecessor, addicted to extravagant Puritanism, nor, as we have already pointed out, was he working solely to protect a squeamish public from unchastity of tongue. At certain times (and with certain authors) Sir Herbert showed a somewhat finicky sensitiveness in the matter of small oaths, an attitude which doubtless

permitted aggravating as well as mollifying influences ; but even his sifted matter was a good deal
coarser than would be acceptable at the present time.
In his later and more arrogant days he took to
criticising the work of his predecessors.[1] There is
something pathetically humorous in his pompous
announcement that all old plays should be submitted
to him in case they should be " full of offensive
things against church and state ; yᵉ rather that in
former times the poetts took greater liberty than is
allowed them by mee." In Herbert's diary one can
trace without difficulty his lively appreciation of the
dignities of his post. The autocratic power of hack-
ing up the product of better men's brains no doubt
became pleasurable, and was exercised with some
eagerness and pride.

Middleton's GAME OF CHESS—a symbolical play
acted in August 1624, and dealing with Jesuitical
intrigue—caused Herbert a good deal of trouble.
Middleton, in his play, gave expression to the
popular satisfaction at the failure of the negotiations
regarding the proposed Spanish marriage. The
people were in fact tremendously inflamed on
account of James dallying with the Spanish court
under the astute guiding hand of Gondomar, the
Spanish Ambassador in London. The symbolical

---

[1] " The King's players sent me an oulde booke of Fletchers called
THE LOYAL SUBJECT, formerly allowed by Sir George Bucke, 16 Novemb.
1618, which according to their desire and agreement I did peruse, and
with some reformations allowed of, the 23 of Nov. 1633, for which they
sent mee according to their promise £1." (Added in the margin),
"The first ould play sent mee to be perused by the players."

" On tusday night at Whitehall the 10 of Decemb. 1633, was acted
before the King and Queen, THE LOYAL SUBJECT, made by Fletcher,
and very well likt by the King."

caricature of Middleton's play was scurrilous and bitter, and "they counterfeited his (Gondomar's) person to the life, with all his graces and faces, and had gotten, they say, a cast suit of his apparel for the purpose." Nevertheless, for some inexplicable reason or by a strange negligence, Herbert licensed the play, and it was acted nine times by the King's players[1] before any action was taken, Then, on the complaint of the Spanish Ambassador, Gondomar himself, the King intervened and the following indignant letter was sent, through Mr Secretary Conway, to the Privy Council :

"Rufford, 12*th August*, 1624.

"May it please your lordships :—

"His Majesty hath received information from the Spanish Ambassador of a very scandalous comedy acted publickly by the King's players, wherein they take the boldness and presumption, in a rude and dishonourable fashion, to represent on the stage the persons of his Majesty, the King of Spain, the Conde de Gondomar, the Bishop of Spalato, &c. His Majesty remembers well there was a commandment and restraining given against the representing of any modern Christian kings in those stage plays, and wonders much both at the boldness now taken by that company and also that it

---

[1] The play was acted with enormous success. On an old manuscript copy of the piece there is a note to the effect that in the nine days the actors took £1500. The public enthusiasm became a tradition of stage success.

"There's such a crowd at doors as if we had a new play of Gondomar." (PLAYHOUSE TO BE LET, 1663.)

hath been permitted to be so acted, and that the first notice thereof should be brought to him by a foreign ambassador, while so many ministers of his own are thereabouts and cannot but have heard of it. His Majesty's pleasure is that your lordships presently call before you as well the poet that made the comedy as the comedians that acted it. And upon examination of them to commit them, or such of them as you shall find most faulty, unto prison, if you find cause, or otherwise take security for their forthcoming ; and then certify his Majesty what you find that comedy to be, in what points it is most offensive, by whom it was made, by whom licensed, and what course you think fittest to be held for the exemplary and severe punishment of the present offenders, and to restrain such insolent and licentious presumption for the future. This is the charge I have received from his Majesty, and with it I make bold to offer to your Lordships the humble services of &c., &c."

The Privy Council, as may readily be imagined, was by no means eager to undertake the delicate and dangerous task of selecting all the offensive innuendoes from Middleton's play. They contented themselves therefore with sending the following diplomatic reply nine days later :

" 21st *August*, 1624.

" After our hearty commendations, &c.,
" According to his Majesty's pleasure signified to this Board by your letter of the 12th of Aug., touching the suppression of a scanda-

lous comedy acted by the King's players, we have called before us some of the principal actors, and demanded of them by what licence and authority they have presumed to act the same ; in answer whereto they produced a book, being an original and perfect copy thereof (as they affirmed) seen and allowed by Sir Henry Herbert, Knt., Master of the Revels, under his own hand, and subscribed in the last page of the said book. We demanding further, whether there were not other parts or passages represented on the stage than those expressly contained in the book, they confidently protested they added or varied from the same nothing at all. The poet, they tell us, is one Middleton, who shifting out of the way, and not attending the Board with the rest, as was expected, we have given warrant to a messenger for the apprehending of him. To those that were before us, we gave a round and sharp reproof, making them sensible of His Majesty's high displeasure therein, giving them strait charge and commands that they presumed not to act the said comedy any more, nor that they suffered any play or interlude whatsoever to be acted by them, or any of their company, until His Majesty's pleasure be further known. We have caused them likewise to enter into bond for their attendance upon the board whensoever they shall be called. As for our certifying to His Majesty as was intimated by your letter what passages in the said comedy we should find to be offensive and scandalous ; we have

thought it our duties, for his Majesty's clearer
information to send withal the book itself subscribed as aforesaid by the Master of the
Revels, so that either yourself or some other
whom his Majesty shall appoint to peruse the
same, may see the passages themselves out of
the original, and call Sir Henry Herbert before
you to know a reason of his licensing thereof,
who, (as we are given to understand,) is now
attending at court. So having done as much
as we conceive agreeable with our duties in conformity to his Majesty's royal commandments,
and that which we hope shall give him full
satisfaction, we shall continue our humble
prayers to Almighty God for his health and
safety, and bid you very heartily farewell."

Herbert, it will be seen, had very quickly got
into hot water, and the whole incident helps
to account for some of his drastic emendations in
later years. As Middleton had decamped, the
blame naturally fell on Herbert's shoulders ; but
it was probably child's play for him to secure the
intervention of his kinsman, the Earl of Pembroke,
who was then Lord Chamberlain. In any case,
though the play was prohibited for the future,
no one seems to have suffered much over the
incident.

Herbert doubtless became more wary after this,
and little of importance has to be recorded until
10th January 1631, when, according to his office book,
he refused to grant a licence for a play by Massinger
"because it did contain dangerous matter, as the

deposing of Sebastian, king of Portugal, by Philip II., and there being a peace sworn 'twixt the Kings of England and Spain." As we have already seen, however, he retained the fee. Massinger met Sir Henry's refusal by altering all the names and scenes, and in that form the play was ultimately passed, and appeared as BELIEVE AS YOU LIST, the revised draft in Massinger's handwriting, with the Master of Revels' licence, being still in existence.[1] Here again the objections taken were political. A year later THE BALL, by Shirley and Chapman, was under ban of displeasure. Various personages at court might, it was feared, take offence at some of the passages ; but finally, with these omitted, the play was licensed.

In May 1633 Jonson's TALE OF A TUB had to be modified, as Inigo Jones considered himself caricatured in the person of Vitruvius Hoop, and secured the Lord Chamberlain's sympathetic support. In the same year Herbert took offence at the occasional oaths in THE SEAMAN'S HONEST WIFE, a dry and drivelling puff of the East India Company, a kind of metrical advertisement. He returned the book with the following note added to the licence :—

"This play, called YE SEAMAN'S HONEST WIFE, all ye Oaths left out in ye action as they are crost in ye booke & all other Reformations strictly observed may bee acted, not otherwyse. this 27. June. 1633.
                                    "HENRY HERBERT."

[1] See illustration, p. 128.

"I commande your Bookeeper to present mee
with a faire Copy hereafter and to leave out all
oathes, prophaness & publick Ribaldry, as he will
answer it at his perill.   H. HERBERT."

It is interesting to note the Censor asking for a
corrected copy of the play to be deposited with him—
a practice which became fairly frequent in later days
when the play in question was of a dangerous
nature.

When Fletcher's TAMER TAMED was revived,
Herbert made a fresh complaint of these "oaths,
profaness, and publick Ribaldry," which, he added,
"I doe absolutely forbid to bee presented unto mee
in any play booke as you will answer it at your
perill."[1]   Nevertheless, essentially indecent though
the play was, it was acted a month later at court
and "was well liked."

In the same year we find in Herbert's office
book a long and patronising screed concerning
Shirley's YOUNG ADMIRAL, the reading of which had
given him much delight on account of its freedom
from "oaths, profaneness, or of Obsceanes." He
piously hopes that when other poets hear and
see Shirley's good success, they will "imitate the
original for their own credit, and make such copies
in this harmless way as shall speak them masters
in their art at the first sight to all judicious

[1] ". . . . Purge their parts, as I have the booke. And I hope
every hearer and player will think that I had done God good servise,
and the quality no wrong; who hath no greater enemies than oaths,
prophaneness, and publique ribaldry, wh^ch for the future I do absolutely
forbid to bee presented to mee in any play booke as you will answer
it at your perill."

spectators." There we have a classic definition of what the Censor regarded as revealing a master in dramatic art, and some of his successors have also shown this tendency to deify "harmlessness." As for Shirley's play, which aroused Herbert to so much enthusiasm, it has, in spite of its freedom from oaths, failed to keep its head above the tide of years, and the ordinary critical reader will admit that signs of its mastership are by no means conspicuous.

D'Avenant's Witts brought Herbert to the surface again with a fresh crusade against "profaness." The play itself is essentially indecent by modern standards; but Herbert's small comb was so quickly choked with the trifling stuff of oaths and so forth that it scraped harmlessly over the main plot and purpose of the play. Nevertheless, he lavished such care on trivial erasures that D'Avenant in despair took his mutilated and emasculated play to the chamber of the King himself and persuaded his royal patron personally to revise Herbert's corrections. This the King did and was "pleased to take faith, death, 'slight, for asseverations, and no oaths." Herbert had, of course, to submit to this ingenious distinction with what dignity he could. He entered the incident in his book with a protest against this kingly indulgence, insisting that he conceives the words in question, all royal sanction notwithstanding, to be mere oaths, "and enter them here to declare my opinion."

The Censor's tenderness on this matter of profane oaths, as he loved to call them, is worth illustrating from different plays. Here are a few of the ex-

pressions which he regarded as sacrilegious, together
with his suggestions for alternatives :—

By Jesu	became	Believe me.
Faith	,,	Marry, or Indeed.
By heaven	,,	By these hilts.
By the Gods	,,	And I vow, or By my sword, or By my life.
By the just Gods	,,	By Nemesis, or By all that's good.
The Gods	,,	My hopes.
Gods	,,	Pride.

Among other instances of censorial stupidity there
is one worthy of mention. The original clause in
the play was :

> "Strike the monuments
> Where noble names lie sleeping."

But to "strike monuments" sounded perilously like
insurrection and rioting, savoured of revolt against
the laws and irreverence for the nobler orders. The
monuments must at all costs be spared, so the lines
duly appeared :

> "Strike the mountains
> Where noble names lie sleeping."

We dare not spoil such a gem with comment.

We have already hinted at the frequency with
which over-sensitive individuals found innuendoes
in the stage-plays of the time. Private malice
seems to have made a business of searching for these
innuendoes, and, providing the offended person was
highly enough placed or otherwise worth considering,

the Censor was fairly certain to move in the matter. To have unearthed some unwitting insult was doubtless profitable, for the informer's honourable services would doubtless be rewarded by the slighted one in cash or hospitality. In the prologue to THE CUSTOM OF THE COUNTRY, by Massinger and Fletcher, we note the following lines :

> " So free this work is, gentlemen, from offence,
> That we are confident it needs no defence
> From us or from the poets. We dare look
> On any man that brings his table book
> To write down what again he may repeat
> At some great table, to deserve his meat.
> Let such come, swell'd with malice to apply
> What is mirth here, there for an injury."

We find the Church again soliciting protection in 1639, when the players at the Fortune were fined £1000 for setting up on the stage an altar, a basin, and two candlesticks, and bowing to them. The play was merely an old one, and the altar was only erected to heathen gods ; but the whole performance was held to be lacking in respect to the ceremonies of the Church. There is an entry in Herbert's office book relating to an incident two or three years earlier :

> " I committed Cromes, a broker in Long Lane, the 16th of February, 1634, to the Marshalsey, for lending a Church robe, with the name of Jesus upon it, to the players in Salisbury Court, to represent a flamen, a priest of the heathens. Upon his petition of submission and acknowledgment of his fault, I released him, the 17th February, 1634."

As we have already pointed out, nothing was more likely in those days to get the indiscreet dramatist into prompt trouble than something revealing disrespect for established authority. Society was banded together, then as now, to suppress all disruptive elements, and it was really only in this respect that the poor playwright was regarded seriously. One hardy scribbler of this period who ventured to make a character describe proctors as " arrant knaves," and at the same time assert that " the alderman is a base drunken, sottish knave," very quickly found himself in stirring trouble for his " insolence."

At the same time, although drastic action might very probably be taken over a dramatist's indiscretions, the orders of the Censor or of the court were carried out with very uncertain energy. Even orders to desist from acting were often ignored, and only in flagrant cases appear to have been enforced for more than a day or two. The varying interests of the officials and authorities themselves often produced some strangely erratic measures. For instance, the " king and queen's young company " produced a play at Drury Lane without a licence from the Master of Revels, and in spite of a general and specific prohibition against the playing of this or any other play, calmly continued their performances. But this was one of the orders intended to be taken seriously, and as an example Beeston was thrown into the Marshalsea. Four days later, however, on the personal request of the Lord Chamberlain, the company was allowed to resume its performances. Of the offending play in question, Herbert notes that he will

" keepe the booke, because it had relation to the passages of the king's journey into the Northe."

Summarising the censorship of this period we would point out that its general activities were directed to the suppression of political and profane references, and that public taste and morals were but rarely in the question. The Censor was primarily a court official, jealous in the defence of court life and court prestige, and in no sense whatever acting in the interests of the common people. His effect on the important drama of the period was probably slight. The references to which he took exception were of a topical and ephemeral interest, and though the abolition of the office would certainly have meant an increase of plays of this topical nature and of controversial religious ones, we may doubt if the real drama of the period would have been materially modified. The censorship really gave dramatic authors practically unlimited freedom in the selection and treatment of their subjects, so long as the existing order of things was not menaced. Fortunately Shakespeare and his contemporaries were primarily dramatists and not social reformers, and their personal inclinations are not likely to have been seriously thwarted by the existence of the censorship.[1] Although the censorship was as absurd then as now, its attitude to the stage was very different. It did not strike at the freedom and vitality of the contemporary dramatist, but merely insisted that he should kiss

[1] According to Mr Payne Collier in his NEW FACTS, Shakespeare's Company, as early as 1589, took occasion to commend themselves on this special account, " that they have brought into their plays no matters of state or religion unfitting to be handled by them, or to be presented before lewd (unlearned) spectators."

the hand of royalty and not rattle the people's chains on the stage.

In its way, the office was a fairly logical one. It existed to guard against certain practical and definite dangers to the court. It was perfectly frank in its intention to stifle criticism directed against existing institutions, and however much we may dislike the stifling of criticism as a theoretical policy, it could not, in those times, be called a reactionary process. It was perfectly in keeping with the other customs of the period and did not offend against anyone's sense of liberty, as liberty was in those days understood. It prevented an author throwing insults at the King in just the same way as it prevented any other citizen throwing stones at him, and in that light calls for neither vindication nor condemnation.

CHAPTER IV

SUPPRESSION AND REACTION

It is quite outwith the scope of the present book to follow the changing fortunes of the anti-stage war at this period. That war, interesting though it was, had little or no effect on the course of the censorship, although it may perhaps be held largely responsible for the reaction to laxness which followed its bigoted violence. For fifty years the war against the stage had gone on with varying success. A study of the pamphleteers of the period is a revelation of imprecation and invective; but no useful purpose would be served by a lengthy reference to the historic tirades of that time. Prynne's HISTRIO-MASTIX or PLAYER'S SCOURGE, published in 1632, cost him a pair of overnice ears; but certainly carried the Puritan war on the drama several stages forward. Bigoted, bitter works, such as Prynne's, came out in scores, and every village parson sat down to revile that stage, of which a little earlier he had been eager to avail himself. The Puritans marshalled themselves whole-heartedly behind that saying of the ancient Abbot Nilus:

" That he who is conversant in a multitude (especially at Stage playes) is affected with daily wounds ; for the countenance of women is a Dart, anoynted with poyson which wounds the soule and sends in venome, and by how much the longer it continueth so much the more the wound doth putrifie. He who desires to avoyde these wounds (pray marke it well) will absteine from publike Playes and Spectacles, neither will be conversant in such Assemblies. For it is better that thou abide at home, than that thou fall into the hands of the enemy whiles thou thinkest to honour such Solemnities."

England has, at all periods of her existence, been notable for breeding "a sort of sober, scurvy, precise neighbours that scarce have smiled twice since the king came in," and their temporary and inglorious supremacy over the stage need not be detailed here. With a stunted intelligence but a grotesquely enlarged conscience these fanatics steadily attacked the amusements of the common people. In 1642 an order appeared which, after a brief and solemn preamble, commanded

"that while these sad causes and set-times of humiliation do continue public stage-plays shall cease and be forborne."

In 1643 a mournful remonstrance was made by the players to the effect that they are reformed and poor, "so that were it not for our former providence we might be enforced to *act* our tragedies." Such a state of affairs as this was not likely to cause a thrill to the Puritan conscience, which doubtless traced in these sufferings the direct retribution of an offended

God.   How complete the Puritan domination was is
well summarised by Taine :

> " In 1644 Parliament forbade the sale of
> commodities on Sunday, and ordained ' that no
> person shall travel or carry a burden, or do any
> worldly labour upon penalty of ten shillings for
> the traveller and five shillings for every burden.
> That no person shall on the Lord's Day [1] use or
> be present at any wrestling, shooting, fowling,
> ringing of bells for pleasure, markets, wakes,
> church-ales, dancing, games or sports whatso-
> ever upon penalty of five shillings to every one
> above fourteen years of age.   And if children
> are found offending in the premises their parents
> or guardians to forfeit 12d. for every offence.
> If the several fines above cannot be levied the
> offending party shall be set in the stocks for the
> space of three hours.'   When the Independents
> were in power severity became still greater.
> The officers in the army, having convicted one
> of their quartermasters of blasphemy, con-
> demned him to have his tongue bored with
> a red-hot iron, his sword broken over his head,
> and himself to be dismissed from the army.
> During Cromwell's expedition in Ireland we

[1] It may be mentioned that, at one time, Sunday was the playgoer's
only chance of entertainment.   It was not, in fact, until 1579 that plays
were acted during the week.   In those early days, however, the theatre
was hedged in with rules of etiquette.   Ladies, for instance, were
supposed to be barred from play-going, yet the queen of them all broke
through the rule—Queen Elizabeth patronised Sunday plays at Oxford.
Another royal theatre-goer was James I., who gloried in Sunday shows.
Bishops, too, were not above patronising them.   We read of the
Bishop of London producing A MIDSUMMER NIGHT'S DREAM at his
town house on a Sunday evening in 1631.

read that no blasphemy was heard in the camp ; the soldiers spent their leisure hours in reading the Bible, singing psalms and holding religious controversies. In 1650 the punishments inflicted on Sabbath breakers were doubled. Stern laws were passed against betting, gallantry was reckoned a crime ; the theatres were destroyed, the spectators fined, the actors whipped at the cart's tail ; adultery punished with death : in order to reach crime more surely they persecuted pleasure."

For some time after the 1642 order was issued, dramatic entertainments of one kind or another seem to have been surreptitiously presented. In time the theatres were partly opened, and the general public appear to have responded eagerly to the renewed opportunity for amusement. In any case, the Puritan Parliament was roused to stricter measures and retaliated by a notable order passed 11th February 1647 for the destruction of all play-houses.

An Ordinance for Suppression of all Stage-Plays and Interludes

" Whereas the Acts of Stage-Plays, Interludes, and Common Playes, condemned by ancient Heathens and much lesse to be tolerated amongst Professors of the Christian Religion, is the occasion of many and sundry great vices and disorders tending to the high provocation of God's wrath and displeasure, which lies heavy upon this kingdome, and to the disturbance of the peace thereof ; in regard whereof this same hath been prohibited by Ordinance of this present Parliament and yet is presumed to be practised by divers in Contempt thereof ; Therefore for the better suppression of the said Stage-plays, Interludes, and Common Players, It is Ordered and Ordained by the Lords and Commons in this present Parliament assembled and by Authority of the same, That all Stage-players and Players of Interludes and Common Plays are hereby declared to be, and are and shall be taken to be Rogues and punishable within the Statutes of the Thirty ninth year of the Reign of Queen Elizabeth and the seventh year of the Reign of King James and lyable unto the pains and penalties therein contained, and proceeded against according to the said Statutes, Whether they be Wanderers or no, and notwithstanding any License whatsoever from the King or any person or persons to that purpose."

The Ordinance further directed the Lord Mayor, the Sheriffs, and the Justices of the Peace to " pull down and demolish . . . all Stage Galleries, Seats, and Boxes, erected and used for the acting and playing, or seeing acted or plaid, such Stage-Playes " in or about London. Any player proved to have acted in such performances, was to be " openly and publicly whipt," and bound by sureties never to act again, or in default of such security committed to jail. If he offended a second time, he was to be punished as an incorrigible rogue, according to the Statutes. All money taken as admission fees was to be forfeited to the churchwardens of the parish and devoted to the use of the poor, and every person present as a spectator was to be fined 5s. for each offence—this money to go also to the poor of the parish. It will be seen that, by this Act, actors, both licensed and unlicensed, were reduced to vagabonds, the whole system of patents and licences, controlled by the Master of Revels, being abolished.

Oliver Cromwell naturally had no tenderness toward actors and their art ; he would not even allow a verse of Shakespeare to be recited at the festivities of his daughter's marriage, a depressing ceremony which was no doubt concerned more with fecundity than fun.[1] The players took an honourable part in the Civil War, and at the close found both their military and dramatic vocations ended. Then came a period of struggle for the impoverished and unemployed artists, with the traditions of the stage maintained in various clandestine ways. Occasionally performances were held in private houses, and in this connection Holland House, Kensington, has an honourable record. The widow of the Earl of Holland arranged a series of performances there before a selected circle of friends, and a collection

---

[1] "Of importance it is to notice that though Oliver Cromwell refused to allow a single verse of Shakespeare to be recited on the festivities of his daughter's marriage, he hired buffoons to entertain the guests, and a great deal of fun was got out of the Great Protector himself snatching some one's hat and sitting on it to conceal it ; of importance because that attitude of contempt for the drama in its strenuous and serious aspect has survived through all the impertinence and scurrility of the Restoration : through all the intermittent brilliancy of the Hanoverian epoch down to the very moment in which we are living. Says Cromwell: 'Away with Shakespeare and his description of human passions. It offends against every commandment in the Decalogue. The kind of fun I like is the harmless joke of sitting on my hat.' A joke, by the way, that has not failed to amuse an English audience ever since."—Miss Gertrude Kingston, *Nineteenth Century*, vol. 64.

was made for the actors after the play. In such ways the life of the stage was maintained, the vigilance of the persecutors being foiled by various subterfuges. Sometimes a theatrical entertainment would be advertised as an exhibition of rope-walking ; sometimes the officer at Whitehall was flagrantly bribed, and, where other measures failed, chance performances were made in public with the risk of the soldiery interfering before the close.

The first glimmerings of reaction were seen in 1658, when we find Richard Cromwell ordering a report on a play of some kind which Sir William D'Avenant had ventured to present at Drury Lane. The poets and actors were to be arrested and strictly examined as to the nature of the play, while inquiry was to be made as to the authority given for its public performance. The play in question was probably " THE CRUELTY OF THE SPANIARDS IN PERU expressed by vocal and instrumental music and by art of perspective in Scenes, represented daily at the Cockpit in Drury Lane, at Three in the afternoon punctually, 1658 "—a fairly transparent evasion of the actual use of the word " play." According to *Censor Dramaticus*, this play was read and approved of by Cromwell, and as it contained " some very severe strokes on the Spaniards, with whom he was at variance," it would seem that Cromwell had been willing to condone even a stage-play for the sake of having Spain presented to the people in a humiliating light.

In another year or so the monarchy and the stage were restored together, and Sir Henry Herbert was once more wielding his pen as Licenser to the stage.

We even find him endeavouring to extend the powers of the Revels Office. He asked that the office should now have jurisdiction over all dancing schools, wakes, or rural feasts, and lotteries, and should even have the right to license gaming contrary to the law. Even billiards, ninepins, and cockfighting were not beneath his notice, and he was willing to claim authority over anything which his jurisdiction could possibly be stretched to cover, the licensing of which might be profitable.

He was never, however, to regain his old position. According to Gildersleeve :—

> " At the Restoration he resumed his former jurisdiction, but found that the recent times had given men new habits of reasoning, notions of privilege and propensities to resistance . . . he applied to the court of Justice for redress ; but the verdicts of juries were contradictory : he appealed to the ruler of the state ; but without receiving redress or exciting sympathy. . . . Like other disputed jurisdictions the authority of the Masters of Revels continued to be oppressive till the revolution taught new lessons to all parties."

In 1660 the practical control of the stage passed from Herbert by Royal warrant[1] to Sir William D'Avenant and Tom Killigrew,[2] who were made sole guardians of theatrical amusement in the metropolis. It may have been that the strictness of Herbert's

---

[1] See Appendix.

[2] Charles II. later granted a third patent to a man named Jolly, whose rights were, however, compounded, D'Avenant and Killigrew paying him £4 a week not to execute his patent.

taste was not altogether pleasing to Charles II. The " dilligent wisdom with which God had blest him " may have been too diligent to suit the taste of the new court. In the preamble to Killigrew's grant the reason for the new enactment was given as follows :

" Whereas we are given to understand that certaine persones in and about our citty of London, or the suburbs thereof, doe frequently assemble for the performing and acting of playes and enterludes for rewards to which divers of our subjects doe for their entertainment resort ; which said playes, as we are informed, doe containe much matter of prophanation and scurrility, soe that such kind of entertainments, which, if well managed, might serve as morall instructions in humane life, as the same are now used, doe for the most part tende to the debauchinge of the manners of such as are presente at them, and are very scandalous and offensive to all pious and well-disposed persons. We, takeing the premisses into our princely consideration, yet not holding it necessary totally to suppresse the use of theaters, because wee are assured, that, if the evill and scandall in the playes that now are or haue bin acted were taken away, the same might serue as innocent and harmless diuertissement for many of our subjects ; and hauing experience of the art and skill of our trusty and well beloued Thomas Killigrew, esq., one of the groomes of our Bedchamber and of Sir William Dauenant, knight, for the purposes hereafter mentioned, doe hereby giue and grante " etc.

It is amusing to reflect that the men who were specifically appointed to fit the stage for use " as morall instructions in humane life " actually led it to a level of dissoluteness not hitherto reached. The clause most germane to our subject is the one which authorises Killigrew and D'Avenant to expurgate the plays of earlier dramatists :

> " We doe hereby by our authority royal strictly enjoine the said Thomas Killigrew and Sir W^m D'Avenant that they doe not at any time hereafter cause to be acted or represented any play, enterlude, opera, containing any matter of prophanation, scurrility or obscenity : And wee doe further hereby authorize and command them the said Thomas Killigrew and Sir Wm Davenant to peruse all playes that have been formerly written, and to expunge all prophanesse and scurrility from the same before they be represented or acted."

The Act gave D'Avenant and Killigrew exclusive stage rights in the cities of London and Westminster, and there is something very entertaining in the idea of this couple being authorised to expunge the scurrility from previous plays. The situation has not, however, been without parallel in more recent days.

Herbert, as might have been expected, put up a vigorous fight to recover some at any rate of his previous rights and privileges, but he was thwarted at every step, and for the next two or three years he was engaged in innumerable quarrels both in and out of the courts in the vain hope of re-establishing his former autocracy. There is an entry on 30th July

1660 to the effect that he licensed at the Duke of
York's request a trial of skill with eight weapons
between two performers at the Red Bull play-house.
He received £200 for his expenses in October 1660,
and as late as 1663 claimed the right to license plays,
poems, and ballads for the press, even endeavouring
to secure a fee from the humble village wake.   He
was officially supported, too, for in 1661 he succeeded
in getting an order from the Lord Chamberlain
commanding all mayors, justices of the peace, etc.,
throughout the kingdom, to examine all players,
performers of shows, acrobats, etc., and discover
whether they " have a lycence from Sir Henry Herbert, master of his Majestys Office of the Revells."
If any other authority was shown, it was to be confiscated and sent to the office of Revels, while the
various shows in question were to be suppressed until
they had been duly authorised by Herbert.   But the
country was inclined to independence, and in the
mood to question some of these court claims.   We
have already referred to Maidstone's revolt from the
Master's authority.   In 1663 a similarly defiant
appeal came from Norwich, which resulted in the
King definitely withdrawing puppet and other shows
from Herbert's control, and doubtless there were
other similar cases.   All this time the real authority
behind the Censor was, of course, the Lord Chamberlain, and Sir Herbert very skilfully enlisted that
official's sympathetic aid.   Herbert may possibly
have hinted that these attacks on the Master of
Revels might be followed by similar attacks on the
hitherto unquestioned powers of the Lord Chamberlain himself.

But Herbert was long before this engaged in bitter and more serious quarrels with the chief London managers and actors. When Charles II. granted licences in 1660 to Killigrew and D'Avenant, Herbert promptly petitioned, and his case was referred to the attorney-general, Sir Geoffrey Palmer. D'Avenant openly defied Herbert, and Herbert brought two suits at law against him to recover arrears of fees due to the Revels office. He gained one action and lost the other, and D'Avenant was encouraged to appeal again to the King, with the result that Lord Clarendon and the Earl of Manchester, then Lord Chamberlain, were instructed to arbitrate between the two litigants in 1662. Herbert drew up an elaborate statement of the privileges which he had exercised, but the arbitrators seem to have decided against him. Meanwhile he endeavoured to close the Cockpit play-house in Drury Lane, which John Rhodes had opened without a licence from him, and also brought a successful action against Michael Mohun, Charles Hart, and other members of the King and Queen's Company, who obstinately ignored his claims.

At last Killigrew, more pliable, good-natured, or perhaps more lazy than D'Avenant, decided to come to terms with Herbert and terminate these incessant quarrels, and on 4th June 1662 an agreement was signed under which Killigrew agreed to pay before 4th August following, all monies due to Herbert. These financial arrangements form a fresh testimonial to Herbert's peculiar skill in negotiation. Herbert was to receive two years' dues from the King's and Queen's players " for the new plays at forty shillings a play, and for the revived plays at twenty shillings a play," while Killigrew was to assist Herbert in his office, the latter, in turn, helping in the control of the King's and Queen's players. The agreement carried costs and a solatium of £50 to Herbert for the damage he had suffered. Killigrew was formally to abjure D'Avenant and to support Herbert's authority, and on 15th January 1662–63, he received a second patent, identical with one given to D'Avenant at the same time. On Herbert's death, ten years later, Killigrew officially succeeded him as Master of Revels, though it is at least doubtful if his authority was in any way increased by the appointment.

The following note, taken from Warner's *Epistolatory Curiosities*, speaks for itself :

" Mr Killegrew's Promise to pay the Costes of Suite against the Players.

" *Julley* 14, 1662.

" I, Thomas Killegrew, doe by this presentes oblige myself to paey to Sir Henry Herbert all the costes and charges he shall apr, othe make apear, to be expendded in the sute betwixt him and the Kinges company of acters, in the axion of the caes which he had a verdict for against them in Ield Hall, woen (owing) ; and a part thereof, fortey pound, I hafe paid him. Witness my hand and seale the day and date over saide.

" Tho. Killigrew.

" *Witness*
 " Jo. Carew.
 " L. Kirke.
 " Walter Gyles."

By this arrangement Herbert's reign came practically to an end. To avoid further unprofitable quarrelling he leased out his office in 1663 to his insignificant deputies, Hayward and Poyntz. They were soon complaining volubly that they had lost heavily by the arrangement.

CHAPTER V

Tom Killigrew was a very decided change from the men who had previously held the office of Master of Revels. He had, as we shall see, plenty of faults for those in search of them, but gravity, pomposity, and rapacity were not among them. He was an easy, careless, brilliant man, with too keen a sense of humour to be greatly concerned over his official dignity. The fact that he was a great personal favourite of Charles II. is sufficient proof that he had no depressing sobriety of either manners or morals. In 1651 he had been appointed Resident to Venice ; but his careless debauchery and loose living there led to a complaint being made to the King by the Venetian ambassador in Paris. Killigrew was withdrawn, and his recall inspired Denham to the weak, but much-quoted lines :

> " Our Resident Tom
> From Venice is come,
> And has left all the statesmen behind him.
> Talks at the same pitch,
> Is as wise, is as rich,
> And just where you left him you find him."

After further continental travelling Killigrew returned home with a new wife, but unimproved

morals, and soon after, in 1660, he was made Groom
of the Bedchamber to the King, and subsequently
Chamberlain to the Queen. His travelling had given
him freedom and polish as a conversationalist, and he
was admitted into the King's society on terms of the
most unrestrained familiarity. Even when audience
was refused to the first ministers of the State, Killigrew
would be promptly admitted, nor were his visits refused on even the most important State occasions.

His audacity had an admirable side, however.
He was as ready to offend the King by blunt criticism
as to make him smile by a pointed personal jest.[1]
According to Warner, Charles was wholly occupied
with his pleasures and frequently in his mistress's
apartments when he ought to have been at the
Council Board. Noting this extreme negligence
Killigrew took on himself the thankless task of
admonishing it. He dressed himself in a pilgrim's
habit, invaded the King's chamber, and informed
him that he hated himself and the world ; that he
was resolved immediately to leave it and was at that
moment setting out upon a pilgrimage to Hell.
Entering into his humour the King asked him what
he proposed to do when he got there. " I shall speak
to the devil," said Killigrew, " and beg him to send
up Oliver Cromwell to take care of the English

---

[1] " Mr Cowley heard Tom Killigrew publicly tell the king that his
matters were coming into a very ill state, but that yet there was a way
to help all. Says he, ' There is a good, honest, able man that I could
name that if your Majesty would employ and command to see all well
executed, all things would soon be mended ; and this is one Charles
Stuart, who now spends his time in employing his lips about the Court,
and hath no other employment ; but if you would give him this employment he were the fittest man in the world to perform it.' The king
does not profit by any of this."—*Pepy's Diary*, 8th December 1666.

Government, as I have observed with regret that his successor is always employed in other business." On another occasion, when the Duke of Lauderdale was deploring Charles's continued absence from the Council Table, Killigrew offered to fetch him. Lauderdale, who probably knew something as to the nature of the King's occupation, wagered Killigrew £100 that he would not succeed, which wager Killigrew at once won by invading the Royal Chamber and persuading the King to attend on the Council immediately.[1] It is to Killigrew's conspicuous credit that he does not appear to have availed himself of his influence with the King to amass a personal fortune or to secure any particular position of influence or honour.

As we have seen, the patent granted to Killigrew and D'Avenant, giving them control of the London stage, was for some time hotly contested by Herbert ; but the quarrels were ultimately brought to an end and concluded by " a firme amity " signed 4th June 1662, and on the 29th March 1664, Herbert gave to Killigrew the following interesting manuscript directions concerning the duties of the office of Master of Revels :

> " The heads of what I gave to Mr Tho. Killigrew
> the 29th of March, 1664.

> " 1. To have a generall warrant for musick throughout England, which is practised already,

---

[1] Killigrew is said to have treated Louis XIV. with the same lack of ceremony. When Louis showed him at Paris a picture of the Crucifixion hanging between portraits of the Pope and himself, Killigrew is alleged to have remarked : " I have often heard that our Saviour was hanged between two thieves, but I never knew who they were till now."

GEORGE COLMAN.

George Colman, Examiner of Plays from 1824 to 1837. He was an extremely
witty author, but, by modern standards, a very coarse one.

but many are very obstinate, and refuse to take lycences especially in cities and townes corporate under the pretence of being freemen.

" 2. There being many complaints of abuses in dancing schooles, for want of a due inspection and regulation, an order is desired (as it is a most proper branch of the Revells) that I may bee impowered to lycence all the dancing schooles, and to bind them respectively against *mixt* dancing in the schooles, and other practises, which at present begette a scandalous report of them. This work is already began, and submitted to by some ; but it cannot bee done generally, unles countenanced by regall authority.

" 3. Touching wakes or rurall feasts (another proper branch of the Revells) which are observed in the greatest part of England, it is humbly desired, that some countenance may be putt upon the lycencing of them, by which means many disorders may bee prevented ; and though there bee but 1os. from the most eminent towns and 5s. from the meaner parishes (to bee paid annually by the churche wardens), it will not only bee a good advancement to the office of the Revells, but will much civilize the people, who are commonly dissordered at those feasts, which are constantly attended with revelling and musick.

" 4. All quack salvers and empyrickes, under the denomination of mountebankes, are properly belonging to the Revells, but will not come in (notwithstanding several summons) until compelled by regall authority.

" 5. The royall oake lottery, which is a modell or dumb shew, and sortition, and as cleerely belonging to the Revells, as the small lottery or pricking book, which have (*ab antiquo*) been commissioned by the office, the persons herein concerned are obstinate and will not come in, unles compelled by his Majestie's authority.

" 6. For gaming, though the justices throughout England, amongst other things, bind the victuallers in recognizances of £20 apiece, not to tolerate gaming in their houses ; yet, nevertheless under their noses, and to the knowledge of most justices, gaming is sett up and tolerated. Now, in regard it is against the letter of the law to lycence gaming, (though to do the same is consistent with the Master of the Revells' patent) it is desired, with some cautious lymitation, that his Majesty would countenance this particular, as to the lycencing all upon easy termes, by which meanes every victueller may bee bound to observe lawfull seasons and good orders, otherwise it will become a common custome to play on fast days, in time of divine service, and at other seasons prohibited ; and therefore some expedient to bee used that may please his Majesty, and support the power of the Revells, which hath been very much enervated, and weakened by the late times of trouble and distraction.

" 7. Though to grant lycences for gaming hath been practised ever since his Majesty's happy returne, by the porter, and Poyntz, yet as to my particular (who have not enjoyed the employment above nine months), I doe act under many feares, and with much tenderness, to those few who have submitted, least I should offend the law of the land ; and therefore once again humbly desire that some safe expedient may bee found out to reconcile the law and the King's prerogative."

Killigrew, like most of his predecessors, could claim literary qualifications ; qualifications which had been backed by substantial performance. He was the author of a number of plays, three of which had been acted before the Civil War ; but the remainder do not appear ever to have been performed. It must be admitted that Killigrew, who was so brilliant and witty in conversation, became dreadfully tedious when he sat down to write. His pen could not move fast enough to express the brilliant flashes of his wit, and at laboured performance he was simply futile. Consequently, when he was not prosy and dull he was unspeakably coarse, as in THE PARSON'S WEDDING which, though witty enough, would be regarded as flagrantly indecent by modern audiences. THE PARSON'S WEDDING was performed in October 1664, and again in 1672 or 1673. On both occasions it was acted by women only, presumably on account of its indecency ; Mrs Marshall speaking the prologue and epilogue in masculine attire. On 11th October 1664 Luellin remarked to Pepys, "What an obscene loose play this PARSON'S WEDDING is, that it is acted by nothing but women at the King's house ! " We had originally prepared one or two quotations to show what the Court Censor of 1660 regarded as fitting for public performance, but they have had to be excised from the later proofs as being much too coarse for inclusion.

Mr Bram Stoker once made the inspired assertion that " reticence was the highest quality of art." [1] By such a test the Court Censor of 1660 fell short of perfection.

When this merry gentleman, then, obtained control of the theatre, the inevitable happened, and the stage, far from being purged of plays " offensive to all pious and well-disposed persons," became grosser, coarser, and less restrained than ever. The new censorship not only failed to purify the stage, but neglected those duties which had under previous Masters been adequately performed. Instead of protecting the court it permitted blatant attacks on it, and in one case—Howard's CHANGE OF CROWNES —the abuse of the King was so violent as to give the greatest offence to Charles, who prohibited the

---

[1] Mediocrities have always attempted to chastise genius on this question of reticence. *The Nation* once pompously spoke of "that decent reticence which is an essential characteristic of the best art and good manners." Well, genius has been somewhat apt to overlook "good manners," and to leave that particular excellence to the care of butlers and drapers' assistants. So far as the "best art" is concerned, we can merely assert that the greatest artists and thinkers have never been conspicuous for their reticence. This fetish has been carried to such lengths that a writer in the *Nineteenth Century* once claimed that "the measure of the *ethics* of the artist is expressed in the reticence shown in his work," which is even worse than judging the *art* of the artist by his reticence. Perhaps the one thing which has characterised genius of all ages has been its lack of reticence, a lack which, as Ruskin has pointed out, has specially characterised all the greatest English writers. But this wail of jealous mediocrity, carried to its logical conclusion, stultifies itself. "Reticence," Mr Bram Stoker said, "is the highest quality of art; that which can be its chief and crowning glory." Then the supreme artistic level would be utter reticence, and the crowning glory of genius would be silence!

actors from further performance. Characteristically enough, however, this "silencing order" was partially rescinded a few days later.

Somewhere about this time Beaumont and Fletcher's THE MAID'S TRAGEDY was prohibited by an order from the Lord Chamberlain. Cibber tells us that for what reason this interdiction was laid upon the play the politics of those days have only left us to guess.

"Some said that the killing of the king in that Play, while the tragicall Death of King Charles I. was then so fresh in People's memory, was an Object too horribly impious for a Publick Entertainment. What makes this conjecture seem to have some foundation, is that the celebrated Waller, in compliment to that Court, alter'd the last act of this Play (which is Printed at the End of his Works) and gave it a new Catastrophe, wherein the life of the King is loyally saved, and the Lady's Matter made up with a less terrible Reparation. Others have given out, that a repenting Mistress, in a romantick Revenge of her Dishonour, killing the King in the very bed he expected her to come into, was shewing a too Dangerous Example to other Evadnes then shining at Court in the same Rank of royal Distinction, who, if ever their Consciences should have run equally mad, might have made frequent opportunities of putting the Expiation of their Frailty into the like Execution. But this I doubt is too deep a Speculation, or too ludicrous a Reason,

to be relied on ; it being well known that the
Ladies then in favour were not so nice in their
notions as to think their Preferment their
Dishonour or their Lover a tyrant : Besides,
that easy Monarch loved his Roses without
Thorns ; nor do we hear that he much chose
to be himself the first Gatherer of them." [1]

According to Langbaine (1691), " King Charles
II. for some particular Reasons forbid its further
Appearance during his Reign. It has since been
revived by Mr Waller, the last act having been
wholly altered to please the court."

Fletcher's PROPHETESS, produced in 1690, had
its prologue, written by Dryden, prohibited by the
Lord Chamberlain (Lord Dorset) after the first performance, the tone of some of its allusions being
thought offensive. The incident happened while
King William was prosecuting the war in Ireland,
and Cibber says of it, " It must be confessed that
this prologue had some familiar metaphorical sneers
at the Revolution itself, and as the Poetry of it was
good the offence of it was less pardonable."

Crown, taken with a sudden access of Protestant
fervour in 1681, introduced " a little viniger against
the Pope " in his FIRST PART OF HENRY VI. The
Romish faction at court was highly offended, and
Crown's tragedy was promptly suppressed. In his
dedication to the ENGLISH FRIER, Crown tells us :

" My aversion to some things I saw acted

---

[1] That the prohibition of THE MAID'S TRAGEDY did not immediately follow the Restoration is clear from the notices of performances in
November 1660 and February 1661.

there (at the Court) by great men, carried me against my interest to expose Popery and Popish Courts in a tragedy of mine called THE MURDER OF HUMPHRY, DUKE OF GLOUCESTER,[1] which pleas'd the best men of England, but displeas'd the worst ; for ere it liv'd long, it was stifled by command."

The SPANISH FRYAR or THE DOUBLE DISCOVERY, by Dryden, which appeared in 1681, figured pretty prominently in the records of the next few years. When it appeared, Dryden's enemies said that it was much too heavy on the Popish religion. His friends, equally censorious, said the play was mostly stolen from other authors. To these two criticisms Charles II. made an historic retort. Answering Dryden's enemies he said that knaves in every profession should be alike subject to ridicule. To Dryden's jealous friends he said : " God's fish ! Steal me such another play any of you and I'll frequent it as much as I do THE SPANISH FRYAR." During the whole of James II.'s reign the play was prohibited, the part of Dominick, the Spanish monk, offending James's new Romish sympathies. We read that the play was in the stock list, however, when William ascended the throne, and the Queen unwittingly ordered it for presentation. The King was at the moment in Ireland, the Queen being left Regent, and the allusions of the play caused her a good deal of confusion. Daniel Finch, second earl of Nottingham, wrote :

" The only day her Majesty gave herself the diversion of a play happened to be THE SPANISH

---

[1] A sub-title for the FIRST PART OF HENRY THE SIXTH.

FRYAR, the only play forbid by the late king. Some unhappy expressions put her into the greatest disorder, and frequently forced her to hold up her fan and often look behind and call for her palatine and hood, or anything she could think of."

Religious references were expunged with varying severity. When Shadwell introduced into LANCASHIRE WITCHES the Chaplain Smerk to ridicule Anglican pastors and especially their hatred of Dissenters, the Master of Revels passed the play with but few alterations, only a dozen lines or so being deleted. It was later, however, represented to him that the religious references were extremely offensive, and he called for the book again and violently censored the whole of Smerk's speeches. More than once our different Censors have seen no harm in a play until some fanatic, with an inflamed conscience, has made a protest. Then, instead of justifying his first decision, he has made an unthinking rush to change his opinion. Even in recent days we have had the humiliating spectacle of a Censor altering a play after it had been performed two hundred and forty-five times.

In 1681 a play was stopped at Dorset Garden because there was " too much talk of liberty in it." This was the LUCIUS JUNIUS BRUTUS of Nat Lee. Lee was accused of having too boldly vindicated republican principles. It was feared that the whole plan and sentiments of the play tended to inflame republican ideals among its auditors, and after the third presentation it was quietly suppressed.

We may briefly mention here two plays, THE

INNOCENT USURPER (1694), and CYRUS THE GREAT (1696), both of which were forbidden, though the latter was subsequently allowed. THE INNOCENT USURPER was forbidden because it was supposed to cast some reflections on Government, while CYRUS THE GREAT was, we are told, banned, "nobody knows why." It is difficult to see how THE INNOCENT USURPER could have contained any special attack on the Government of the day, because it was proved later that the play had been written ten years before, in 1684! The Censor had evidently made rather indiscreet application of some of the allusions. J. Banks, the author of both the above plays, was an indifferent writer, but had a knack of conducting his scenes "so that the venal, the unprincipled, and the vicious, got at length a knack of tingling at that imaginary rod which they fancied, while he depicted Nature, he held up to them."

It is unnecessary for us to emphasise or illustrate the utter demoralisation which fell on the English stage under Killigrew's censorship. There is no reason to suppose that, for the first part of the period at any rate, the liberties taken by dramatic authors were unwelcome to the mass of the people. In the violent reaction from the Puritan rigours the refreshing freedom of the stage would doubtless be palatable ; but toward the end of Charles's reign there were already signs that the pendulum of public opinion, after two violent oscillations, was swinging back toward its normal poise. Killigrew died on 19th March 1682–3, and was buried in Westminster Abbey, the office falling to his son, Charles Killigrew. We may mention here an interesting announcement

taken from the *London Gazette*, 3rd December to
7th December 1685 —

> " These are to give Notice, That all Rope-
> Dancers, Prize-Players, Strollers, and other
> Persons shewing Motions and other Sights, are
> to have Licenses from Charles Killigrew, Esq. ;
> Master of the Revels."

Then, with the death of Charles II. on 6th
February 1685, came the first hints of a changing
mood. It was, of course, the inevitable reaction, in
a nation naturally sober and phlegmatic, from the orgie
of unrestraint which had been indulged in for the past
twenty years. The people were, it would seem, tired of
too much naughtiness, and soon speakers and writers
were taking advantage of this chastened—or surfeited
—mood. In 1695 Richard Blackmore was vigorously attacking the theatre. In 1697 he came to
the attack again with a fresh outburst ; but, as Beljame says, " Blackmore n'avait pas les poumons assez
solides pour sonner la trompette de Jéricho." But, if
Blackmore lacked lung-power, there was one man
quietly preparing a blast against the stage, who certainly had no such disqualification. In 1697 Jeremy
Collier's SHORT VIEW OF THE PROFANENESS AND IM-
MORALITY OF THE ENGLISH STAGE made its paralysing
and devastating advent.

In the same year, too, we have to note an Order
issued by William III. and confirmed in the following
terms in 1698. This Order would seem to have been
largely inspired by Collier's book :—

> " His Majesty has been pleased to command

that the following Order should be sent to both playhouses :

" His Majesty being informed That notwithstanding an Order made 4th June 1697 by the Earl of Sunderland, then Lord Chamberlain of his Majesty's Household, to prevent the Profaneness and Immorality of the Stage (*note that these are the exact words of Collier's title*), several plays have lately been acted containing Expressions contrary to Religion and good Manners. And whereas the Master of the Revels has represented, That, in contempt of the said Order the Actors do often neglect to leave out such Profane and Indecent Expressions, as he has thought proper to be omitted These are therefore to signify his Majesty's pleasure, that you do not hereafter presume to act anything in any Plays contrary to Religion and good manners, as you shall answer it at your utmost peril. Given under my hand this 18th of February, 1698 In the 11th year of his Majesty's reign.

" An Order has been likewise sent by his Majesty's Command to the Master of the Revels, not to Licence any plays containing expressions contrary to Religion and good manners, and to give notice to the Lord Chamberlain of his Majesty's Household or in his absence the Vice-Chamberlain if the players presume to act anything which he has struck out " (*London Gazette*, 27th February 1698–9).

Collier's brilliant work was, as it happens, very much more than a personal expression of opinion.

As we have said, for some years before its appearance, there had been signs of an incipient reaction. Collier's pamphlet expressed with heat and sarcasm what a large number of people had been vaguely thinking.

Beljame says :—

"D'un autre côté, le public n'acceptait plus aussi aisément les gravelures qu'il avait tant recherchées autrefois. Tous ne passait pas sans protestation. Downes raconte que la comédie des GALANTES, de Granville, 'quoique extraordinairement spirituelle, et bien jouée,' offensa les oreilles de quelques dames 'qui prétendaient à la chasteté' et n'eut pour cette raison que peu de représentations. Le DON QUICHOTTE de D'Urfey et le DOUBLE DEALER de Congreve choquèrent aussi quelques spectateurs. Une pièce de Fletcher, qu'un nommé Scot, remit en 1697 à la mode de la Restauration, éveilla également les susceptibilités. La tragédie de Mrs Manley, dont il vient d'être question tout à l'heure, et la RECHUTE de Vanbrugh, ne furent pas non plus, si nous en croyons les préfaces de ces deux pièces, sans encourir quelques reproches d'immodestie. Aussi un épilogue de 1697 s'écria d'un ton mélancolique :

"'Autrefois les grasses plaisanteries plaisaient seules à la ville, mais maintenent (que le ciel vienne en aide à notre métier !) elles ne passent plus. Il semble du reste que les auteurs ne se sentaient plus aussi sûrs du terrain. Southerne n'osa pas faire représenter une certaine scène de

son Sir Anthony Love, singulièrement scabreuse
en effet, entre son abbé et son héroïne ; et Congreve, dédiant sa tragédie de la Fiancée Eplorée
à la princesse Anne, plaide pour la théâtre les cir-
constances atténuantes, en disant qu'il espère la
convaincre qu'une pièce "peut-être écrite de
façon à devenir un divertissement innocent et
même profitable." '

"Tout cela était l'annonce evidente d'un
changement prochain. On osait enfin, plus de
trente ans aprés la Restauration, prononcer les
mots de modestie et de retenue. C'était beau-
coup ; c'était encore bien peu. Les protestations étaient trop vagues et trop faibles encore
pour s'imposer, et la réaction anti-puritaine avait
été trop vive et trop vivace pour céder à des
attaques aussi indécises."

Collier savagely attacked the immorality of contemporary dramatists, collecting scores of illustrations
in support of his charges. Scenes and expressions
which, in their context, had seemed unimportant
and insignificant, became wholly abhorrent and
obscene when gathered into one noxious mass of
selections. The pamphlet had an enormous success
and enlisted the sympathy even of men who hated
Collier bitterly for his conduct in the matter of the
absolution, granted at the last moment at Tyburn to
Sir John Friend and Sir William Parkyns, convicted
of the attempted assassination of William in 1696.
Indeed, some of his bitterest opponents sent him
presents of money.

We need hardly say that Collier was not hitting

at the wind. The evils against which he protested had become obvious enough to every one. The licence granted to actors and dramatists had reached such a stage as to make the attendance of ladies at a first performance something of an adventure. The fair sex attended first-nights wearing masks to conceal the tell-tale blood which was supposed to flag wounded innocence. Only in this way could a woman, with any pretension to decency, face the fire of ribald wit on the stage.[1] Naturally enough, for a play to create any sort of stir in the fashionable world in this period, it had to outstrip its competitors in rank indecency, and Collier had not to search far to find a profusion of illustrations for his pamphlet. Dryden, Congreve, and their companions were bitterly lashed, and the most broad-minded critic will admit that a majority of the plays of the time were far from being models of virtue and modesty.

Of course, after the manner of most reformers, Collier ran wildly to excess. He waxed particularly indignant over the players abusing and ridiculing the clergy, which evoked Vanbrugh's cutting reply that " a clergyman is not, in any country, exempted from the gallows. A Hangman then may jerk him ; why

---

[1] " While our Authors took these extraordinary Liberties with their Wit, I remember the Ladies were then observ'd, to be decently afraid of venturing bare-fac'd to a new Comedy, 'till they had been assur'd they might do it, without the Risque of an Insult, to their Modesty; or if their Curiosity were too strong for their Patience, they took care, at least, to save Appearances, and rarely came upon the first Days of Acting, but in Masks (then daily worn, and admitted, in the Pit, the Side Boxes, and Gallery) which Custom, however, had so many ill Consequences attending it, that it has been abolished these many Years " (Cibber's *Apology*).

The wearing of masks in the theatre became in later years the privilege and hall-mark of women of easy morals.

not a Poet?" He found fault with Dryden for having lightly employed the name of Mahomet, and of speaking ill of Phœbus and Mercury. He did not even stop at this. In his retrospective zeal he complained that Aristophanes had shown a lack of respect for Neptune, Bacchus, and Hercules. Moreover, Collier roundly accused the stage of causing rather than reflecting the immorality of the period. One might conclude from Collier's book that he had never heard of vice but on the stage, and that the theatre had originally invented all the cardinal sins. Apparently Collier had wrought himself into a belief that England was peopled with innocent, candid souls, who would never have forsaken the paths of virtue, had not dramatic authors in sheer perversity pushed them nightly aside.

Without a shred of literary or artistic feeling he carried his onslaught so far as to correct the literary faults of his opponents—a display in which he did not figure to advantage. His indignation, being always in a violent shriek, became in time wearisome, and, as often happens, from constant searching, he soon became capable of finding evil even where it did not exist. Collier, with a good many of his companions, had developed a nose for truffles; but none of the obvious weaknesses of his book lessened its extraordinary success.

The King, whose tastes had never drawn him to the theatre, was immensely pleased with Collier's pamphlet and granted special favours to him, and, as we have seen, issued stricter regulations to the Censor, using the very words of Collier's title. The Master of Revels was bluntly informed that he must keep a keener watch on the morality of new plays, and the net result of Tom Killigrew's laxity was, therefore, to tighten the censorial authority and change it more definitely from a court protection to a moral supervision. *The Laureat* (p. 53) states that, soon after the publication of Collier's book, informers were placed in different parts of the theatres, on whose information several players were charged with uttering immoral words. Queen Anne, however, satisfied that the informers were not actuated by zeal for morality, stopped the inquisition. These informers were paid by the Society for the Reformation of Manners.

As might have been expected, Collier's attack did not pass unchallenged. The various authors who were accused took up defensive cudgels, though Dryden admitted that he at any rate had been to blame. Collier was, however, by no means disinclined to a pen war. As Johnson said, " contest was his delight ; he was not to be frighted from his purpose or his prey," and in spite of a host of retaliatory attacks, Collier undoubtedly remained in possession of the field. The dramatists, admitting a long-overdue change in public taste, began to delete the coarser expressions from their play, and, for instance, when Congreve's DOUBLE DEALER was revived, it had been carefully pruned.[1]   He also

" corrigea dans sa FIANCÉE EPLORÉE et dans sa comédie de AMOUR POUR AMOUR, des passages qui

[1] "This day was played a revived comedy of Mr Congreve's called THE DOUBLE DEALER. In the playbill was printed, 'Written by Mr Congreve: with several expressions omitted.' "—Letter from Dryden to Mrs Steward, 1698.

avaient choqué Collier ; Vanbrugh, dans sa
FEMME POUSSÉE À BOUT, remania une scène
dans laquelle Sir John Brute, courant les rues,
ivre, en costume d'ecclésiastique, se fasait menir
devant un magistrat qu'il édifiait médiocrement
par son langage ; dans la scène modifiée la robe
de prêtre est remplacée par une robe de femme.
En même temps les pièces nouvelles furent
faites d'après une nouvelle inspiration : Congreve
dans THE WAY OF THE WORLD, Vanbrugh dans son
PROVOKED HUSBAND, se montrèrent plus retenus
qu'ils ne l'avaient été jusque-là ; et petit à petit,
en passant par les dernières comédies de Farquhar
et de Vanbrugh, libres d'allure encore, mais où
l'entrain naturel et la franche gaieté emportent
dans leur courant ce qu'il y a parfois de trop vif,
le théâtre anglais se modéra, se calma, s'amenda
jusqu'au paisible CATON d'Addison, jusqu'aux
tragédies sentimentales et monotones de Rowe,
et aux comédies morales de Steele."[1]

It is difficult to specify precisely what share the
Master of Revels had in this work of reformation ;
but we may be sure that he acted somewhat along
the lines of the grave cold King's clerical protégé.
Charles Killigrew, who now held the office, was the
son of Thomas Killigrew by his second wife, and
was gentleman of the Privy Chamber to Charles II.,
1670 ; James II., 1685 ; and to William and Mary,
1689. Cibber tells us that after Collier's crusade the
dramatic writers were a great deal more restrained.
Indecencies were no longer justified by wit, and

[1] Beljame.

gradually women came again to fill the boxes on the first day of a new comedy with uncovered faces and without risk of any intolerable offence against their modesty. "Après Guillaume, le trône fut occupé par la reine Anne et par George I. ; et ce n'était pas une femme, surtout une femme parcimonieuse et bigote, ce n'était pas un prince de cinquante-cinq ans, ne parlant pas un mot de la langue de ses sujets, et bourgeois jusqu'en ses galanteries royales, qui pouvaient faire renaître les jours de la Restauration ; la tradition joyeuse de la cour de l'Angleterre se trouva ainsi interrompue, et pour toujours." [1]

Although there are not many particulars available as to Charles Killigrew's censorship, what few particulars we have indicate that he assisted the reforming movement with embarrassing energy. When a play offended his scruples he would, without compunction, strike out whole scenes, if he suspected them of having a vicious or immoral tendency. Even when vice had obviously only been introduced in order to be punished, he ruthlessly erased all references to it. He would not have a wound exposed even for the doctor to apply a remedy ; a policy which is, perhaps, not quite so beneficial to the patient as some people apparently believe.

Cibber's records are not always impeccable in tone, and are far from being infallible narrations of the events he deals with. But he has left us one instance of the Censor's surgery which seems stamped with accuracy on its face. When Cibber submitted his altered version of RICHARD III., the Censor expunged the whole first act without sparing a line

[1] Beljame.

of it ! Poor Cibber, contemplating the mutilated fragments with horror, despairingly begged the indulgence of one or two inoffensive speeches, so that, as he said, the other four acts might limp on with a little less absurdity. But the Censor, acting up to the true official traditions, replied that he *had not leisure* to determine what might be separately inoffensive ! Even a king, one would imagine, when shown a list of suggested guests, would deign to indicate what was "separately inoffensive," and not reject the whole list because of one unwelcome name. But more than once the English Censor has been contemptuously indifferent to the moderate example of a mere monarch.

The whole act, then, offended him, and, somewhat rashly, he gave one reason. The distresses of King Henry VI., who is killed by Richard in the first act, might, he said, put weak people too much in mind of King James, then living in France ! "In a word," adds Cibber, " we were forc'd for some few years to let the play take its fate, with only four acts divided into five ; by the loss of so considerable a limb may not one modestly suppose it was robbed of at least a fifth part of that favour it afterwards met with ? For tho' the first act was at last recovered and made the play whole again, yet the relief came too late to repay me for the pains I had taken in it."

One can hardly wonder that when a little later Cibber had a chance to " talk with my Oppressor in my Turn," he took full advantage of it. A patent granted 19th January 1715 by George I. to Sir Richard Steele and his assigns, of whom Cibber was one, made them, they claimed, sole judges of what plays might be proper for performance at their Drury Lane Theatre, without previous examination by the official Licenser. In defiance of this claim, the Master of Revels demanded his usual fee of £2 upon the actor's producing a new play, though, as Cibber tactfully puts it, " We had spared him the trouble of perusing it." Cibber was deputed to interview the Master of Revels, and bring the matter to an amicable settlement, and he adds grimly, " I confess I did not dislike the office."

Cibber therefore complacently strolled down to the Revels office and told Killigrew—

> " That I came not to defend even our own right in prejudice to his ; that if our Patent had inadvertantly superseded the grant of any former Power or Warrant whereon he might ground his Pretensions, we would not insist upon our Broad Seal, but would readily answer his Demands upon sight of such his Warrant ; any thing in our Patent to the contrary notwith-standing. This I had reason to think he could not do ; and when I found he made no direct Reply to my Question, I repeated it with greater Civilities and Offers of Compliance, till I was forc'd in the end to conclude with telling him, That as his Pretensions were not backed with any visible Instrument of Right, and as his strongest Plea was Custom, we could not so far extend our Complaisance as to continue his Fees upon so slender a claim to them. And from that time neither our Plays or his Fees gave either of us any farther trouble."

Steele's patent, on which he based his claim to exemption, was, however, by no means as perfect as he assumed, and would certainly have justified a challenge. It is, indeed, more than a little surprising that Killigrew should have succumbed so readily, but he was by this time a man of sixty-five, and, no doubt, wisely disinclined to war. We can imagine something of the flaming and desperate outburst which would have ensued had Sir Henry Herbert's pockets and privileges been similarly threatened at any time. We read that in 1725 Charles Henry Lee succeeded Killigrew as Master of Revels, and that "during nineteen years he exercised such authority as was not opposed, and received such fees as were willingly paid." Evidently the office was losing something of its autocratic glory.

It will not be out of place here to give a few particulars of the later Masters of the Revels. Charles Killigrew, who was one of the managers of Drury Lane Theatre, died in 1725. In the dedication to his translation of Juvenal's SATIRES, Dryden calls him his "ingenious friend." Charles Henry Lee was, as we have seen, appointed to the vacant office on Killigrew's death, and when Lee died in 1744 Solomon Dayrolle was appointed in his place. Dayrolle was an intimate friend and correspondent of the great Lord Chesterfield, and seems to have held a diplomatic appointment from this country at the Hague from 1748 to 1755. With him probably died the office of the Master of the Revels ; but in any case the ancient jurisdiction of the Revels Master had been transferred in 1737 to a legally appointed Stage Licenser.

On the back of his " Petition to Charles the
Second against the Grant to Killigrew and D'Avenant
To form two companies of Players," Sir Henry
Herbert wrote down the following list :—

"MASTERS OF YE REVELS.

Sir Richard Guilford	Not on record.
Sir Thomas Cawerden	(1544) 36 Henry VIII.
Sir Thomas Beneger	Not on record.
Sir John Fortescue	Not on record.
Edmund Tilney, Esqre.	July 24th (1578) 21 Eliz.
Sir George Buck	June 23 (1603) 1 Jac.
Sir John Astley	(1612) 10 Jac. I.
Benjamin Johnson	(1617) 15 Jac. I.
Sir Henry Herbert &	
Simon Thelwall, Esq.	August 21 (1629) 5 Car. I."

The inclusion of Benjamin Jonson's name in the
above list calls for some notice.   According to
Gifford's notes on Jonson, we learn that " he obtained from His Majesty, who seems to have been
unusually pleased with the MASQUE OF GIPSIES, in
which he bore a part, a reversionary grant of the
office of Master of the Revels."   The King, by letters
patent, dated 5th October 1621, granted him by the
style and addition of " our beloved servant Benjamin
Jonson, gentleman, the said office to be held and
enjoyed by him and his assigns, during his life, from
and after the death of Sir George Buc and Sir John
Astley, or as soon as the office should become vacant
by resignation, forfeiture, or surrender."   In con-
templation perhaps of his speedy accession to this
office James was desirous of conferring upon him the
honour of knighthood.   Jonson, for whom wealth

and title had no charms, and who was well aware that a distinction of this nature would exasperate the envy which pursued him from his earliest years, shrunk from the meditated kindness of his sovereign, and prevailed on some of his friends about the court to dissuade his royal master from his purpose. Jonson received no advantage from the grant specified above, as Sir J. Astley survived him : it appears, however, that finding himself incapable, during his last illness, of performing the duties of the office, supposing it to devolve upon him, he had been graciously permitted by Charles to transfer the patent to his son, who died in 1635. A passage in the SATIRO-MASTIX would suggest that Jonson had made some attempts to procure the reversion of the office of Master of Revels before the death of Elizabeth.

CHAPTER VI

THE THEATRES ACT 1737

THE first two decades of the eighteenth century furnish us with little documentary evidence regarding the working of the censorship. Something may be done in the course of time to bridge this gap in our records; but it is unlikely that anything which may be brought forward will materially modify our present views on the nature of the office. The tendency appears at this time to have been for the authority in connection with the general control of the theatre to revert to the Lord Chamberlain himself. The range of the Lord Chamberlain's powers was all the wider because the instrument conferring them, if indeed any such instrument ever existed, was unknown. His reign about this time was that of a more or less benevolent autocrat. The smallest details of organisation were liable to his interference.[1] At one time, for instance, he issued an order that no actor should leave one company to join another without a formal discharge from the first manager and the official per-

---

[1] On one occasion, at least, the Lord Chamberlain prohibited a play because another house had a play in prospect on the same subject. This play was Swiney's QUACKS or LOVE'S THE PHYSICIAN, produced at Drury Lane on the 18th March 1705, after being vetoed. Swiney, in his Preface, gives the above as a reason for the prohibition. (See Cibber's APOLOGY, ff. I. 247, Lowe ed.)

mission of the Lord Chamberlain. On one occasion
Powell the actor having left Drury Lane Theatre
and joined that of Lincoln's Inn Fields, became dis-
satisfied with the change and wished to return to
Drury Lane. But although this technical offence
had been overlooked in the first instance, he was not
allowed to repeat it, but was arrested by a messenger,
and confined for some days to the porter's lodge.
On another occasion the same actor having struck a
gentleman whose family had previously been associated with the play-house, complaint was made, in
the absence of the Lord Chamberlain, to the vice-
Chamberlain. The latter official promptly silenced
the whole company for having suffered Powell to
appear on the stage before he had given the offended
gentleman satisfaction. Among the Lord Chamberlain's records is a copy of a decree suspending all
performances at Drury Lane because Powell had
been allowed to play. The decree is dated 3rd May
1698. His offence was that he " had drawn his
sword on Colonel Stanhope and young D'Avenant."
The suspension was removed the following day ; but
on the nineteenth of the same month Powell was
forbidden to be received at either Drury Lane or
Dorset Garden.

The whole incident showed, of course, a flagrant
abuse of power on the Lord Chamberlain's part.
No tittle of justification can be offered for such out-
rageous interference, which is only explicable on the
assumption that subterranean influences were operating on the court official. It is pleasant to record
that this calm assumption of omnipotence did not
always pass unchallenged. On another occasion

Doggett the actor having attempted to change companies, found himself in trouble with the Lord Chamberlain, who had been applied to by the manager of the company. But doughty Doggett, "who had money in his pocket, and the cause of liberty in his heart," travelled back from Norwich to London in great style at his country's expense,[1] and then, arrived in town at the end of a very pleasant journey, formally applied to the courts and was promptly discharged. It will be seen, therefore, that Herbert's old prediction, that attacks would sooner or later be made on the powers of the Lord Chamberlain himself, was already being fulfilled.

THE ISLAND QUEENS, or THE DEATH OF MARY QUEEN OF SCOTS, by John Banks, had been printed in 1684, but, owing to the censorship, was not performed till twenty years later, when it made its appearance at Drury Lane as THE ALBION QUEENS. Cibber says of it, " The tragedy of MARY, QUEEN OF SCOTLAND, had been offered to the stage twenty years before it was acted. But from the profound penetration of the Master of Revels, who saw political spectres in it that never appeared in the presentation, it had lain so long upon the Hands of the Author ; who had at last the good Fortune to prevail with a Nobleman to favour his Petition to Queen Anne for Permission to have it acted. The Queen had the Goodness to refer the Merit of his Play to the Opinion of that

---

[1] Everyone knows that Rabelais, when he had not a sou in his pocket, contrived to feast sumptuously all the way from Provence to Paris by wrapping up brick dust in different papers and writing on them, "Poison for the King," "Poison for the Queen," "Poison for the Dauphin," by which stratagem he contrived to be conveyed at the expense of the government as a state prisoner.

noble Person, although he was not her Majesty's Lord
Chamberlain ; upon whose Report of its being every
way an innocent Piece, it was soon after acted with
success." Genest also tells us of another play, THE
PORTSMOUTH HEIRESS, or THE GENEROUS REFUSAL, the
author being unknown, which, in 1704, was refused
a licence " through an idle caprice of the Licenser."

In 1681 Tate, who remodelled the RICHARD II.
of Shakespeare, had to modify his characters, and
even then the piece was stopped on its second performance for political reasons. There was, however,
nothing that might reasonably be regarded as objectionable in the piece, the whole setting of the play
had been transferred to Sicily ; in fact it appeared
under the title of THE SICILIAN USURPER. Nevertheless, the Lord Chamberlain refused to look on Tate's
work with a charitable eye—the piece itself, we
cannot help but surmise, was only a pretext for the
satisfaction of personal resentments in some direction
—and the whole play was damned. In his introduction to the published play Tate says : " I fell upon
the new-modelling of this Tragedy (as I had just
before done on the History of King Lear), charm'd
with the many beauties I discover'd in it, which
I knew wou'd become the stage ; with as little
design of Satyr on present Transactions, as Shakespear himself that wrote this Story before this Age
began. I am not ignorant of the posture of Affairs
in King Richard the Second's Reign, how dissolute
then the Age, and how corrupt the Court ; a Season
that beheld Ignorance and Infamy preferr'd to Office
and Pow'r exercis'd in Oppressing, Learning, and
Merit ; but why a History of those times shou'd be

Supprest as a Libel upon Ours, is past my Understanding. 'Tis sure the worst Complement that ever was made to a Prince. . . . After this account it will be askt why this Play shou'd be supprest, first in its own Name, and after in Disguise? All that I can answer to this, is, That it was *Silenc'd on the Third Day.* I confess, I expected it wou'd have found Protection from whence it receiv'd Prohibition; and so questionless it wou'd, cou'd I have obtain'd my Petition to have it perus'd and dealt with according as the Contents Deserv'd, but a positive Doom of Suppression, *without Examination,* was all that I cou'd procure. . . . Every Scene is full of Respect to Majesty and the Dignity of Courts, not one altered Page but what breathes Loyalty, yet had this play the hard fortune to receive its Prohibition from Court." The whole incident showed the court control of dramatists at its contemptible worst.

In 1709 we find the Lord Chamberlain acting as arbitrator between the actors and patentees, and issuing a very peremptory silencing order warning the patentees at their peril to refuse the actors full satisfaction. Colley Cibber quotes the following from the Lord Chamberlain's record:

" PLAY HOUSE IN COVENT GARDEN SILENC'D.

" Whereas by an Order dated the 30th day of Apr^{ll} last upon the peti$\tilde{\text{c}}$on of sev^{ll} Players &c., I did then direct and require you to pay to the respective Comedians who had benfit plays last winter the full receip^{ts} of such plays, deducting only from each the sume of £40 for the Charges of the House pursuant to the Articles made wth y^m at y^e theatre in the Haymarkett and wch were promis^d to be made good upon their removall to the theatre in Covent Garden.

" And whereas I am inform^d y^t in Contempt of the said Ord^r y^u still refuse to pay and detain from the s^d Comedians ye profits of ye s^d benefit plays I do therefore for the s^d Contempt hereby silence you from further acting and require you not to perform any Plays or other Theatricall entertainm^{ts} till further Ord^r. And all her Maj^{ts} Sworn Comedians are hereby forbid to act any Plays at ye theatre in Covent Gardⁿ or else where wthout my leave as they shall answer the contrary at their perill. And &c., Given &c. : this 6th day of June, 1709, in the Eighth year of her Majesty's Reign (signed) KENT."

" To the Manager or Manag^{rs} of her Maj^{ts} Company of Comedi^{ns} for their Patentees."

Somewhere about this period Sir Richard Steele fell into the hands of the Lord Chamberlain. For some two or three years after obtaining his patent, in 1715, things ran smoothly enough ; but on the appointment of the Duke of Newcastle as Lord Chamberlain (13th April 1717), trouble began. Cibber tells us of a record among the office papers concerning a consultation with the Attorney-General as to whether Steele's original patent made him independent of the Lord Chamberlain's authority. Whatever the result of that consultation may have been, the Duke of Newcastle, soon after his appointment, demanded that Steele should resign his patent and accept an ordinary licence in its place. What probably lay at the bottom of this and succeeding incidents was the hostility aroused by Steele's vigorous opposition to Lord Sunderland's Bill for limiting the power of creating new peers. On 19th December 1719 an order was issued demanding the dismissal of Cibber, which duly took place, his suspension lasting till 28th January 1720. It need hardly be said that the Lord Chamberlain had no shadow of suggestion for any such demand, and Steele would have been entitled to resist this preposterous order by every means in his power. He shrewdly surmised, however, that this official zeal and intolerance was inspired and was to be regarded as an oblique attack on himself. He therefore wrote to two Ministers of State and presented a petition to the King in 1720, praying to be protected from the attacks of the Lord Chamberlain. The immediate result of the petition was an order, curtly revoking Steele's patent, and silencing the manager and actors at Drury Lane. The theatre was, accordingly, closed ; but Steele's former associates, Wilkes, Cibber, and Booth, submitted to the new order and received an ordinary licence to play at Drury Lane on the 27th January 1720.

But Dick Steele was by no means finished with. In 1721 his former ally, Walpole, became Chancellor of the Exchequer, and the Drury Lane patent was restored on 2nd May of that year. On the same day Cibber and his partners were ordered to account with Steele for his past and present share of the profits of the theatre, as if no change had ever been made. This order was signed by the Duke of Newcastle himself, and, in view of his previous tyrannies over Steele, we can guess that the task of signing it brought him no pleasure. In all the story of the court control of the theatre there is probably no more despicable and humiliating incident than this. It is unpleasant even to have to record an instance of power, vested in petty court officials, being abused in so tyrannous and mean a fashion. There was nothing in Steele's life or character to account for such an exhibition. His only fault was that he was too honest, too manly, and too unaffected for his time. He was, we may believe, a constant, genial reproof to many of the men with whom he came in contact. "He had," said Pope (not over-keen to praise men), "a love and reverence of virtue," a quality which has not always been regarded as indispensable in a courtier. His age owed him much. He had perhaps done more than any other author to brush aside that cynical coarseness which in his day ruled as wit. Women of all ages owe him homage for the classic compliment he paid to Lady Elizabeth Hastings when he said that to love her was a liberal education. Gay wrote of him :

> "It would have been a jest some time since for a man to have asserted that anything witty could be said in praise of a married state, or that Devotion and Virtue were anyway necessary to the character of a Fine Gentleman. . . . Instead of complying with the false sentiments or vicious tastes of the age,—either in morality, criticism or good breeding — he has boldly assured them, that they were altogether in the

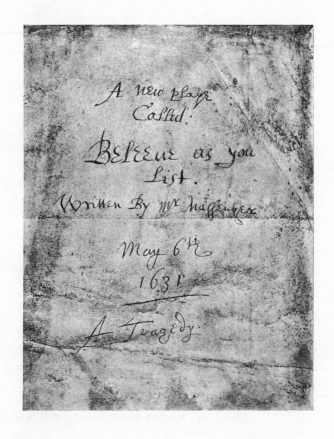

Reproduction of Title-page of manuscript play BELIEVE AS
YOU LIST, by Massinger, now in the British Museum. The
lettering, which is in parts almost illegible in the original, has been
lightly emphasised for reproduction purposes.

wrong; and commanded them, with an authority which perfectly well became him, to surrender themselves to his arguments for Virtue and Good Sense. It is incredible to conceive the effect his writings have had upon the Town, how many thousand follies they have either quite banished or given a very great check to ; how much countenance they have added to Virtue and Religion ; how many people they have rendered happy by showing them it was their own faults if they were not so."

A man of whom his contemporaries could speak in this key was a strange subject for the humiliating caprices of a court official, ostensibly acting in the public interest.

We have read of the stage reforming itself after Jeremy Collier's vitriolic outburst. Perhaps it was reformed too much. Weakness and silliness, those frequent companions of compulsory and unnatural virtue, began to characterise the theatre. Presently, further changes came. Dramatic authors—deterred by the moralists from trading on what Mr Gladstone once termed our " natural aversion to things divine," which had for so long filled the play-houses—began to seek in current political controversies a means of renewing the vitality of the stage. We come, then, to a period of moral but political plays, destined ultimately to provoke Walpole's drastic legislation of 1737.

On 29th January 1728 Rich produced at Lincoln's Inn Fields an opera by Gay, which was soon said to have made " Gay rich, and Rich gay." This play, THE BEGGAR'S OPERA, was an overt attack on the Government, and caricatured Sir Robert Walpole with some bitterness. Under the guise of thieves and highwaymen it satirised society and the corruption of the governing classes. It gave great offence because its allusions were so pointed, more particularly the song "Should you Censure the Age." There was in the opera a fight between Peachum and Locket, not many months after the fight between Lord Townshend and Sir Robert Walpole. The play achieved an extraordinary success. It was played in London for sixty-two or sixty-three nights ; Pope tells us that it spread into all the great towns of England and was played in many places to the thirtieth or fortieth performance. Ultimately it progressed as far as Wales, Scotland, and Ireland. Gay became a public favourite ; but a contemporary writer tells us that the fame of the play was not confined to the author only. The ladies carried about the favourite songs of it on fans, and houses were furnished with extracts from it on screens. Lavinia Fenton, who acted Polly, till then obscure, became all at once the favourite of the town. Her pictures were engraved and sold in great numbers ; her Life written, books of letters and verses to her published, and pamphlets made of her Sayings and Jests. After being the mother of several antenuptial children she obtained the rank and title of a duchess by marriage. The modern musical comedy star will recognise all the symptoms of popular infatuation, including the ancient substitute for the picture postcard.

By its thirty-sixth performance THE BEGGAR'S OPERA had brought Gay between £700 and £800, while his manager had made £4000. Encouraged by so much success, Gay set to work on a sequel, under the title POLLY. But when POLLY was ready for rehearsal the Duke of Grafton, then Lord Chamberlain, acting under express instruction of the King, who, in turn, was influenced by the caricatured Walpole, sent to forbid the representation. This censorship gave the play an interest not quite justified by its literary and dramatic merits. Its prohibition, as Mr Austin Dobson tells us, became a party question, and when the play was published in book form it achieved an extraordinary success, every opponent of the court taking an interest in its sale. The Duchess of Marlborough gave £100 for a single copy, and, for enlisting subscribers to the book within the palace itself, the Duchess of Queensberry was dismissed from court. The Duchess had flung herself heartily into the fight and had made Gay's quarrel her own. She pestered the King to cancel the order of the Lord Chamberlain, and even offered to read the play to him in his chamber that he might satisfy himself of its inoffensiveness.

The King gallantly replied that he would be delighted to receive the duchess in his closet at any time, but would hope to amuse her better than by any literary employment. However, her pleas were in vain, and for her persistence she was, as we have said, dismissed the court ; but she emerged triumphant from the incident by the spirited letter she sent to George II. :

    "The Duchess of Queensberry is surprised and well pleased that the king hath given her so agreeable a command as to stay from court, where she never came for diversion but to bestow a civility on the king and queen; she hopes by such an unprecedented order as this that the king will see as few as he wishes at his court, particularly such as dare to think or speak truth. I dare not do otherwise, and ought not, nor could have imagined that it would not have been the very highest compliment that I could possibly pay the king to endeavour to support truth and innocence in his house, particularly when the king and queen both told me that they had not read Mr Gay's play. I have certainly done right then to stand by my own words rather than his grace of Grafton's, who hath neither made use of truth, judgment, nor honour through this whole affair either for himself or his friends.   C. QUEENSBERRY."

The publication of POLLY brought Gay £1100 to £1200 (according to some writers, £2000), and he became not merely a political stalking-horse, but a popular martyr. On 19th March 1729 Arbuthnot wrote to Swift :

" The inoffensive John Gay is now become one of the obstructions to the peace of Europe, the terror of the ministers, the chief author of the *Craftsman*, and all the seditious pamphlets which have been published against the government. He has got several turned out their places ; the greatest ornament of the court (*i.e.* Lady Queensberry) banished from it for his sake ; another great lady (Mrs Howard, afterwards Countess

of Suffolk) in danger of being *chassée* likewise ;
but seven or eight duchesses pushing forward,
like the ancient *circumcelliones* in the church,
who shall suffer martyrdom on his account first.
He is the darling of the city. . . . I can assure
you this is the very identical John Gay whom
you formerly knew and lodged with in Whitehall two years ago."

It cannot be said that the incident was a brilliant
success from the censorial point of view. It merely
served to advertise the play,[1] and heated current
political controversies to an uncomfortable degree.
The only people who emerged with credit from the
business were Gay and his dramatic associates.

Walpole was not, however, the kind of man idly
to tolerate a succession of attacks by playwrights.
The futility of his attempted suppression of POLLY
had doubtless left him well inclined to seize any
favourable opportunity for muzzling these incon-
venient critics. Among those critics the name of
Henry Fielding stood prominent. Fielding had in
1736 opened the little theatre in the Haymarket with
his PASQUIN, A DRAMATICK SATIRE ON THE TIMES, in
which he attacked with wit and vigour the political
corruption of Walpole's surroundings. The piece,
which tilted against all the established conventions,
and in particular ridiculed the professions of divinity,
law, and medicine, had an enormous success and ran
for fifty nights, after which Fielding brought out his
HISTORICAL REGISTER FOR 1736, which contained

---

[1] POLLY was not produced till 1777, when it was brought out by
Colman the elder, with some alterations.

some good political and theatrical strokes and another stinging attack on Walpole as Quidam.

Long before this Walpole had found his position becoming intolerable and had made tentative efforts towards securing some relief. On 5th March 1735 Sir John Barnard had brought in a Bill "to restrain the number of houses for playing of interludes and for the better regulation of common players of interludes." At first the Bill was received with hilarious contempt and ridicule. Then Walpole made a passionate defence of it. Other ministers took it up and in the end the House, convinced of its necessity, gave leave to have it brought in. Surely one of the most interesting features of the incident is that the Master of Revels protested hotly against the proposed legislation! The Bill was read a first and second time, and then the wily Walpole, seeing the House fairly sympathetic, endeavoured to insert a clause ratifying and enlarging the powers of the Lord Chamberlain. At the same time he insinuated to the House that, unless this addition was made, the King would not pass the Bill.

But Sir John Barnard strongly objected to this clause. He declared that the power of the Lord Chamberlain was already too great and had been often wantonly exercised, particularly in the prohibition of POLLY. He announced his intention of withdrawing the Bill and awaiting another opportunity for introducing it, rather than establish by law a power in a single officer so much under the direction of the Crown—a power which might be exercised in an arbitrary manner, and consequently attended with mischievous effects.

Evidently Walpole had overreached himself, and the rebuff doubtless made him more vindictive toward his dramatic opponents. He waited quietly for a fresh opportunity to crush them, and the next time no mistake occurred. In fact, the incident we are about to relate ran so smoothly that Walpole has frequently been accused by historians of greasing its progress in a discreditable manner.

A particularly scurrilous piece entitled THE GOLDEN RUMP was submitted to Giffard, manager of the theatre at Goodman's Fields. Its attacks on the ruling powers seemed so extravagantly bitter that he carried it to Walpole. Walpole's biographer says that it is uncertain whether Giffard's intentions were to request the advice of the minister on the matter or to extort a sum of money from him to prevent its representation. Be that as it may, Walpole detained the copy and paid to Giffard the profits which might have accrued from its public performance. He then made copious extracts of the more scurrilous references, including some glancing hits at Royalty, and after submitting these to members on both sides of the House of Commons, read them in their entirety to the House.

It has frequently been suggested that Walpole was the instigator, if not the author, of THE GOLDEN RUMP. There is no evidence as to the truth of this assertion, which would not, if established, surprise any student of Walpole's career.[1] But with this scurrilous manu-

---

[1] A recent writer on the censorship has stated that "we may, in fact, *assume, in the absence of any documentary proof to the contrary*, that THE GOLDEN RUMP was written to save the face of the House of Commons." But the "absence of documentary proof to the contrary" is not a sound basis for any "assumption" whatever, otherwise we might accuse any man of having three wives.

script in his hand Walpole had a valid pretext for introducing at the close of the session of 1737 the famous Playhouse Bill,[1] conferring on the Lord Chamberlain a statutory power of licensing stage plays. The Statute constituted the Lord Chamberlain Licenser of Theatres within the City and liberties of Westminster, and wherever the Sovereign might reside. It required a copy of every new play to be sent to him not less than fourteen days before the proposed performance. It empowered him to prohibit, at any time and anywhere in Great Britain, the performance of any play, and it imposed heavy penalties on those who should perform any play in an unlicensed theatre, or any prohibited play or any new play without the sanction of the Lord Chamberlain or of letters patent from the Crown. We may surmise that a restrictive measure on dangerous outside criticism was not altogether unwelcome to Parliament in general, as much to the Opposition, already calculating on an immediate term of office, as to Walpole's Parliamentary supporters. The Bill became law with extraordinary expedition. It was brought in on 20th May, read twice, reported on, passed, sent to the Lords and read there on 1st, 2nd, and 6th June, returned to the Commons on the 8th, and received the royal assent on the 21st.

Naturally the Bill had opponents ; but there would seem to be little or nothing to justify the statement that the opposition offered to it was keen or persistent. Lord Chesterfield in a speech which has become famous took up the cause of freedom and wit and vigorously championed the threatened

[1] For terms of the Bill see Appendix.

liberty of the stage, but with little avail. The speech abounded in shrewd criticism and prophecy, and amply rewards perusal at the present time.[1] He also attacked the measure anonymously in a periodical called *Commonsense*, and asked pertinently, " Is then every Lord Chamberlain a wit and critic just as every Merry-Andrew is a physician, by his office ? " He also made the noteworthy suggestion that women should have a share in the administration of the Act, since its object was the preservation of wit and modesty, in which women were specially interested. A prophecy, which time has seen fulfilled, was that lovers of the stage would evade the Act by means of free performances.

The Act brought Fielding's work as a dramatist to a close, and, indeed, put an end to freedom of political reference on the stage. Modern critics of the Act have doubted whether the disadvantages of popularising political problems on the stage were not trifling when compared with the advantages. It is fairly certain that a little wholesome ridicule and advertisement on the stage would have prevented the passage of some measures and materially modified others. The stage, skilfully used, might easily become the most trenchant and dangerous critic of politicians.

In 1735–6, in addition to the companies playing at Drury Lane and Covent Garden, Giffard was playing at Goodman's Fields Theatre, and Fielding with his Great Mogul's Company of comedians occupied the Haymarket. The Act of 1737 closed the two irregular houses, leaving only Drury Lane and Covent

[1] The speech is given in its entirety in the Appendix.

Garden open. Giffard's position was rather interesting. He received £1000 for his "loyalty," which, however, destroyed the legal status of his own theatre. After the passing of the Act he took his company to Lincoln's Inn Fields, which breach of the law seems to have been winked at by the patentees, since he rented the house from Rich, the manager of Covent Garden. But the speculation did not prove a success, and in the following year he returned to Goodman's Fields. Giffard soon devised a way of evading the Act he had helped to pass. He conceived the idea of issuing tickets at 1s., 2s., and 3s. for a concert "at the late theatre in Ayliffe Street" and performing a play *gratis* between the two parts. The plays selected were those of the regular dramatic repertory, yet no one seems to have interfered with him. Some connection may easily be imagined between Giffard's profitable immunity from the workings of the Playhouse Act and his services to Walpole and the two patent theatres. Few Acts of Parliament have had their birth in such unsavoury circumstances.

In February 1738 William Chetwynd was sworn in Licenser of the Stage under the Lord Chamberlain, the Duke of Grafton, with a salary of £400 a year; but that he might not be too much fatigued with reading half a dozen or half a score plays in the course of a twelvemonth, a deputy was allowed him, with an additional salary of £200 per annum. This deputy, Genest tells us, was Odell, who had in 1729 opened the theatre in Goodman's Fields, but who, "having no theatrical experience," entrusted the management to Henry Giffard.

The new Bill was by no means so popular outside

the House of Commons as it was inside. The Abbé le Blanc has left some notes in his correspondence which go to show that the early working of the Act provoked extraordinary feeling. The Act, he tells us:

"occasioned a universal murmur in the nation, and was openly complained of in the public papers: in all the coffee-houses of London it was treated as an unjust law, and manifestly contrary to the liberties of the people of England. When winter came, and the play-houses were opened, that of Covent Garden began with three new pieces, which had been approved of by the Lord Chamberlain. There was a crowd of spectators at the first, and among the number myself. The best play in the world would not have succeeded the first-night. There was a resolution to damn whatever might appear, the word *hiss* not being sufficiently expressive for the English. They always say to *damn* a piece, to *damn* an author, &c., and, in reality, the word is not too strong to express the manner in which they receive a play that does not please them. The farce in question was damned indeed, without the least compassion, nor was that all, for the actors were driven off the stage, and happy was it for the author that he did not fall into the hands of this furious assembly."

The players were not dismayed, however, but, le Blanc tells us, "soon after stuck up bills for another new piece: there was the same crowding at Covent Garden, to which I again contributed. I was sure at least that if the piece advertised was not performed I should have the pleasure of beholding some very extraordinary scene acted in the pit. Half an hour before the play was to begin the spectators gave notice of their dispositions by frightful hisses and outcries, equal perhaps to what were ever heard at a Roman amphitheatre."

On 9th October 1738 there appeared at the Haymarket Theatre, "by Authority," a French company of comedians in L'EMBARRAS DE RICHESSES. There is an interesting reference to the performance in *Commonsense* for 21st October 1738—

"Soon after subjecting Plays and Players to the Power of a Chamberlain, it was resolved to bring a Foreign Company of Players from Abroad, and place them upon that Stage from whence our own had been just expelled. But when the Bill appeared for their playing, with the Word AUTHORITY placed at Top, the Publick was stung to the Quick, and thought themselves to exert that Liberty they enjoy, and to resent the Affront put upon them by the Chamberlain. They filled the House, and play'd off all the Artillery of Cat-calls, Bells, &c., against the Stage, and the miserable Comedians suffered for Sins not their own. . . . It is well known that the act for putting the Stage under a Regulation (as the Phrase was) went against the Grain of the Publick,—they declar'd against it, but had not Interest enough to hinder its passing; we look'd upon it as a Step towards restraining the Liberty of the Press; we think that everything which is the Product of our own Country, should be suffered to pass free, more particularly the Wit and Learning of our own Growth; for we can't help thinking that we shall see nothing but sad insipid stuff upon the Stage, while the Chamberlain and his Deputies, (who, for aught we know, may be his Footmen) have a Power over every Word to be spoke there. However, when the Act passed, we submitted, and tho' it was reported that a foreign Company of Actors would be sent for, we did not believe it; for we could not suppose that, while the Discontent occasioned by that Act was fresh in everyone's Memory, a Chamberlain would grow so wanton with his new Power, as to insult the Publick in this Manner."

The military were called in to secure the un-interrupted performance of the piece; but their appearance caused tremendous indignation, and a riot was only narrowly averted.

The report from which we have quoted continues:

" if the Fears of that little officious Fellow, who was going to read the Proclamation, had not made him steal off, what might have been the Consequence.—Perhaps a hundred Gentlemen of Fortune and Family, must have incurred the Penalty of Felony, for not dispersing, at the Word of Command, from a Place where they had paid their money."

In a dozen ingenious ways the new Act was continually evaded. A play would be performed under the name of a rehearsal, tickets being purchased at some private house near the theatre. Another method was to give a performance under the title of a "Concert" by a School of Actors. It was the intention of the Government, as we have said, to have no theatres, save Drury Lane and Covent Garden. The theatre in the Haymarket was not able to obtain a licence for twenty years, and was only opened intermittently by devices such as we have described. Five years after the Act was passed Garrick played RICHARD III. at the theatre in Goodman's Fields, which for some time escaped the operations of the Act by its remoteness from the West End. Garrick's success was "great and immediate," and ruined the theatre. Everyone talked of the performance—the Lord Chamberlain heard of it, and the theatre was promptly closed.

The Haymarket Theatre had originally been known as the New French Theatre at its opening in 1720. Ten years later, when occupied by an English Company, it began to be spoken of as the Little Theatre in Haymarket. In 1745, after several managers had opened with a provisional and temporary licence, Theo. Cibber opened it without a licence of any sort, evading the usual penalty by advertisements such as this :

> "At Cibber's Academy in the Haymarket will be a Concert after which will be exhibited gratis a rehearsal in the form of a play called ROMEO AND JULIET."

No doubt Cibber got a broad hint to stop this trick, however, for in the autumn of the same year he announced, " Mr Cibber's company being busily employed in reviving several pieces are obliged to defer playing until further notice."

In 1747 Samuel Foote succeeded Macklin as manager of the theatre, holding that post for thirty years. At that time the house was daily crowded by fashionable audiences to see Samuel Foote's humorous entertainments. The Westminster magistrates interfered, and then Foote hit on the device of summoning his friends for a specified date at noon to take with him " a dish of chocolate " or " tea "; tickets were obtained at George's Coffee-House, Temple Bar. On the invitation appeared " *N.B.* Sir Dilberry Diddle will be there and Lady Betty Frisk has absolutely promised." A large portion of the entertainment consisted of clever satirical imitations of the principal actors of the day. In November of the same year we find him giving " tea at six-thirty " at the Haymarket.

Every expedient to evade the law was resorted to. The *Strand* opened without a licence, but the patent theatres stirred up the Lord Chamberlain, who promptly closed the house. In 1834 it was opened again " admission gratis." At an adjoining confectioner's people paid four shillings for an ounce of lozenges and were presented with a box ticket ; while with half an ounce of peppermint drops, for which two shillings were given, was handed a ticket for the pit.

So, in various ways, were the traditions of the stage preserved, with the Chamberlain and his emissaries making sporadic descents with disastrous consequences to profits. In 1766 Foote was visiting at Lord Mexborough's, when a party of guests played a joke on him, mounting him on a high-mettled horse which threw him and fractured his leg in two places.   As compensation he was granted a patent to establish a new theatre, and purchasing his old premises at the Haymarket, he erected a new building which was opened in the next year.[1]

[1] Readers who desire to make a closer study of the fight between the proprietors of the patent theatres and their unlicensed rivals, may be referred to Mr Nicholson's admirable book, *The Struggle for a Free Stage*.   That phase of the subject, interesting though it is, does not come within our present scope.

CHAPTER VII

LARPENT AND COLMAN

But let us glance again at the course of the censorship after the passing of Walpole's Act. The new officials were quickly exercising their authority. The first play to be dealt with and officially " censored " was Henry Brooke's tragedy of Gustavus Vasa, in 1739. The play had already been rehearsed several times before it was stopped, the explanation being, according to Genest, that there was in it a good deal about liberty. Sir Robert Walpole was probably at the bottom of this prohibition. It was surmised that he was to be lampooned in the character of Trollis, Vice-Regent of Christiern, King of Denmark and Norway. Brooke, however, denied this in a prefatory note to the play in book form, and asserted that patriotism was the single lesson which he had in view throughout the play. Here again, the publication of the play proved immensely profitable. The public had been incensed at the Chamberlain's interference, and bought the book avidly at the subscription fee of five shillings a copy. The result was a profit to Brooke of over £1000. In dedicating his play to the subscribers, Brooke wrote :

" However singular and unprecedented this

treatment may appear, had I conceived it to be the intention of the legislature I should have submitted without complaining ; or had any among hundreds who have perused the manuscript observed but a single line which might inadvertantly tend to sedition or immorality, I would then have been the first to strike it out ; I would now be the last to publish it—the intention of the statute is to guard against such representations as may be conceived to be of pernicious influence in the Commonwealth ; this is the only point to which the prohibition of the Lord Chamberlain is understood to extend, and his prohibition lays me under the necessity of publishing this piece to convince the public that (though of no valuable consequence) I am at least inoffensive. Patriotism is the great and single moral which I had in view through this play. This is personated in the character of Gustavus."

It is curious to note that GUSTAVUS VASA was produced with great success in Ireland under the name of THE PATRIOT, where some of the sentiments expressed in it relative to Sweden, were construed as applicable to Ireland. In the words of the Scotch proverb, " A big nose is aye takin' tae it." We are always suspecting criticism of our pet deformities.

But, as any person of intelligence might have anticipated, suppression did not stifle criticism, but rather stimulated it. Writers who normally would have ignored the petty machinations of politicians took up this case with heat. Johnson published

anonymously a stinging and satiric pamphlet entitled
" A Compleat Vindication of the Licensers of the
Stage from the Malicious and Scandalous Aspersions
of Mr Brooke, author of GUSTAVUS VASA. With a
Proposal for making the office of Licenser more
extensive and effectual." Johnson's defence of the
Licenser covered all the points originally raised by
Brooke, and altogether it was a piece of champion-
ship with which the Licenser could very comfort-
ably have dispensed.

"The poet seems to think himself aggrieved
because the Licenser kept his Tragedy in his
hands one and twenty days, whereas the law
allows him to detain it only fourteen. Where
will the insolence of the malcontents end ? Or
how are such unreasonable expectations possibly
to be satisfied ? Was it ever known that a
man exalted into a high station dismissed a
Suppliant in the time limited by law ? Ought
not Mr Brooke to think himself happy that his
play was not detained longer. If he had been
kept a year in suspense what redress could he
have obtained ? Let the Poets remember when
they appear before the Licenser or his deputy
that they stand at the Tribunal from which
there is no appeal permitted, and where nothing
will so well become them as Reverence and
Submission. . . . Another grievance is that the
Licenser assigned no reason for his refusal.
This is a higher strain of Insolence than any
of the former. Is it for a Poet to demand a
Licenser's reason for his proceedings ? Is he

not rather to acquiesce in the decision of Authority and conclude that there are reasons he cannot comprehend. Unhappy would it be for men in power were they always obliged to publish the motives of their conduct. What is power but the liberty of acting without being accountable."

Johnson ironically urged the Government to extend the powers of the Licenser to the Press, and to edit and suppress all old plays dealing with such pernicious themes as liberty, virtue, and innocence, as being opposed to the causes of the existing Government! He suggested making it a felony to *read* without a licence from the Lord Chamberlain. "The Licenser having his authority thus extended will in time enjoy the title and the salary without the trouble of exercising his power, and the nation will rest at length in Ignorance and Peace."

James Thomson had been introduced in 1738 by his patron, George Lyttelton, to the Prince of Wales, and Johnson tells us that His Royal Highness, finding on inquiry that Thomson's affairs " were in a more poetical posture than formerly," granted him a pension of £100 a year. Thomson's connection with the prince indirectly involved the censorial rejection of his play, EDWARD AND ELEANORA, in 1739. The play was founded on a quite apocryphal episode in the history of Edward I., and was subsequently printed " as it was to have been acted." As a stage play, however, EDWARD AND ELEANORA was ruined.[1]

---

[1] The censorial objections were more than usually frivolous. Such phrases as "for the blood and soul of me" were apparently too vile to be spoken on an English stage.

The play roused Wesley to enthusiasm. In his journal for Wednesday, 14th October 1772, he notes :

> "A book was given me to write on, the works of Mr Thomson of whose poetical abilities I had always had a very low opinion : but looking into one of his tragedies EDWARD AND ELEANORA I was agreeably surprised. The sentiments are just and noble, the diction strong, smooth and elegant, and the plot conducted with the utmost art and wrought off in a most surprizing manner. It is quite his masterpiece, and I really think might vie with any modern performance of the kind."

Poor James Thomson was just the sort of deadly fish the censorial net has ever caught. A sensitive, broad-minded, fine-souled man ; generous ; without any mean faults ; a connoisseur of good wines, who used "to eat the sunny side off the peaches in his garden with his hands in his pocket, and cut his book with the snuffers" ; a man of culture and friends and epicurean tastes, whom fine poetry used to intoxicate so that he lost control of himself—this was just the sort of pernicious writer the dull-witted energy of officialdom would hurry to silence.

In Johnson's pamphlet, to which we have referred, was a curious statement destined to prove prophetic. Brooke had complained that the Licenser had kept the book of his play for a longer period than the law stipulated. "If," said Johnson, "it be the business of a good judge to enlarge his authority (*boni Judicis est ampliare suam auctoritatum*) was it not in the

Licenser the utmost clemency and forbearance to extend fourteen days only to twenty-one ? I suppose the great man's inclination to perform at least this duty of a good judge is not questioned by any, either of his friends or enemies. I may therefore venture to hope that he will extend his power by proper degrees, and that I shall live to see a malcontent writer earnestly soliciting for the copy of a play which he had delivered to the Licenser twenty years before."

Well, Charles Macklin's MAN OF THE WORLD was refused a licence by the Lord Chamberlain, and remained in the Licenser's office for ten years and was then only recovered with difficulty ! The play had already been produced in Dublin in 1766 as THE TRUE-BORN SCOTCHMAN, and Macklin had spent years in carefully polishing the dialogue. But the Licenser concluded that there was too much criticism of courtiers in the text to make it acceptable to the reigning powers, and in view of the unpopularity of the Ministry of the time he prohibited its performance. The whole incident was typical of the liberal and lofty conceptions of censorship at that time. The Censor was regarded merely as an instrument for stifling criticism of political corruption and tyranny. The piece was ultimately a great success, and criticising the incident, Charles Macklin wrote :

" The business of the stage is to correct vice and laugh at folly, and the Lord Chamberlain has a right to prohibit ; but such prohibition is not to arise from caprice, or enmity, or partiality. What he prohibits must be offensive to virtue, morality, decency, or the laws of the land. This piece is in support of virtue, morality, decency, and the laws of the land. It satirizes both public and private venality, and reprobates inordinate passions and tyrannical conduct in a parent.

"The Lord Chamberlain, when called upon, ought in justice to point out the passages that are offensive to Government, or to individuals, or to society at large. No man, in a public trust, should exercise his authority to the injury of another, or to the privation of any public right.

"To seek the truth, to separate right from wrong, to determine, according to sound judgment, equity and justice, is the duty of a Chamberlain, and the end of his trust.

"My copy being detained, I asked the Deputy, Why? or by what right he deprived me of my copy? For some time he would not assign any reason. I told him that I should resort to the laws of my country for redress, upon which he replied ' *that I should but expose myself, and that they kept the copy by the usage of the office.*'

"I told him that I knew the stage before that law existed, that it could not be by custom, that it was the first time I had ever heard of an author being deprived of his copy; and that I should not submit to it.

"I also informed the Lord Chamberlain that I had acted the comedy in Ireland; that they were as careful there as here about anything that affected Government; that the Lords

Lieutenants, who had seen it, laughed heartily at it, and deemed the satire generally pleasant and just.

" Some little creatures in office, to make their court to Lords Lieutenants, pronounced it offensive to Government ; but their masters saw it again and again, and all the emotions they showed were laughter and applause."

Macklin again was a kind of prey not over creditable to the censorial weapons.   There is something singularly amusing in the thought of this dear, conceited, precise gentleman being branded as a seditious or demoralising author.   The worst and most characteristic thing we can recollect of him at the moment, is that illuminating letter to his daughter, in which he begs her never to write "couldn't," "shan't," "wouldn't," nor any abbreviation whatever.   "It is vulgar, rude, ignorant, unlettered, and disrespectful. . . . It is the highest ill-breeding ever to abbreviate ANY word."   You may picture for yourself what sort of reckless, literary pirate such a man would make.

Foote's TRIP TO CALAIS was another play on which the censorial ban descended in 1775.   This was really a pretty little incident.   Foote, all of whose plays had been conceived with the idea of caricaturing some well-known individual, decided to honour Elizabeth Chudleigh, the self-styled Duchess of Kingston, with his literary attentions.   The fair Elizabeth's life had not been without incident likely to attract the attention of a dramatist.   We read that her first really serious love affair took place at the age of fifteen, and it seems to have inspired her with amorous tastes which the rest of her life failed to quench. We read of this and that personage " taking a strong interest " in her. We are told that as a maid of honour in the court of the Princess of Wales she was remarkable " even there " for the freedom and indelicacy of her conduct. On one occasion, in 1749, she appeared at a masked ball in the character of Iphigenia, " so naked," as Walpole wrote, " that you would have taken her for Andromeda."

George II. " pretended " to be in love with her and gave her a watch which cost " five-and-thirty guineas out of his own privy purse and not charged on the Civil List," and made her mother housekeeper at Windsor, a place of considerable profit. As mistress of Evelyn Pierrepoint, her parties were the best arranged and most fashionable in London, and were much frequented by foreign ambassadors. Frederick II. paid her some attention, alluded to her ability to consume a second bottle of wine, and sent her some little notes, discreet portions of which she used to show in after days.

In the midst of these many and useful activities came Foote's impudent attempt to ridicule her in the character of Kitty Crocodile. The shy duchess sought out Foote and offered him £1600 to suppress the play.[1] When he refused to accept such terms,

---

[1] Letter from Garrick to Colman the elder :—

"ADELPHI, 25 *June* 1775.

" MY DEAR FRIEND,—We wanted you much at the election to-day. Foote was in great spirits, but bitter against the Lord Chamberlain. The Duchess has had him in her closet and offered to bribe him, but Cato himself, though he had one more leg than our friend, was not more stoically virtuous than he has been. You shall know all when I see you."

her friend, Lord Mountstuart, prevailed with the Lord Chamberlain, Lord Hertford, to forbid its production. The friends of the duchess, and among them her chaplain—a very necessary and busy member of her staff, one would surmise—declared that Foote attempted to extort £2000 from her. Still fearing that Foote would somehow produce the play, Elizabeth wrote him an abusive letter, thereby delivering herself into her opponent's hands, for Foote replied in some brilliantly clever letters, which left him easily master of the situation. In 1776 the play appeared with many alterations as CAPUCHIN. The Lord Chamberlain, with his official powers, was evidently a handy man to have in court circles when one's mistresses were to be lampooned.

John Kelly's THE LEVEE was refused a licence after it had been accepted at Drury Lane 1741-4. The little play has but scant claims to dramatic merit, but cannot reasonably be regarded as offensive or subversive of morals. Its censorship cannot be justified on any known grounds, and the Rev. John Genest says of it that "this refusal to licence is one flagrant proof of the folly of subjecting the theatres to the caprice of an individual."

According to John Payne Collier, Reed's REGISTER OFFICE was sent to the Examiner's office on the 7th March 1761, by Garrick and Lacy, and returned marked "not thought fit to be acted." In the same season (the date of the month is not given), the manager "ventured to lay it again before the Lord Chamberlain" with some alterations, and it was licensed, though not without many marks and remarks by the Examiner.

Mr John Larpent was appointed Examiner of Plays by the Marquis of Hertford in 1778, holding the office until his death in 1824. In 1795 Lady Eglantine Wallace submitted THE WHIM for his approval. The play was to be given at Margate for the benefit of the poor of Thanet. The house was overflowing when it was announced that Mr Larpent had discovered that there were exceptional political sentiments in it, though, according to the authoress's own statement, he previously had "found no objections to it." Lady Wallace sent a long letter to the Lord Chamberlain (Lord Salisbury) who answered her very civilly, but refused to override his subordinate's judgment. What causes the Licenser's delay in these matters is a subject for speculation. Lady Wallace's play may be read through with ease in thirty minutes; but no doubt a professional reader of plays requires longer.

The Examiner found himself in a rather ludicrous quandary over this play. In Scene I. Act II. Fag says to Nell: "But, egad, I shall please myself. I shall ever prefer the symmetry of Venus and the rosy health of young Hebe to all the Fat Forties of Fashion." The passage was held to cast a reflection on the connection between Royalty and a certain lady who was commonly called "fat, fair, and forty." Apart from this one speech it is difficult to conceive a less objectionable play than THE WHIM. It is not brilliant from a dramatic standpoint, but coarse, suggestive, or indecent, it emphatically is not in a single line. It might be read in a convent without raising a blush, save by its stupidities, and we have frequently heard more indecency from ministers in pulpits.

Larpent's difficulty was how to deal with the offending passage.   To specify and censor this one passage
alone would be to admit its application, and he might
thereby lay himself open to a charge of insulting his
master.   On the other hand, to pass it was even more
dangerous, so he compromised by prohibiting the
whole piece on the ground of its "exceptionable
sentiments."   No wonder Genest says : "It would
not be easy to reprobate the conduct of the Licenser
on this and other occasions in stronger terms than it
deserves."

Perhaps the egregious Examiner had noticed these
lines which Lord Crotchett speaks :

> "I am sure I shall be a better master for
> having learned how painful it is for a British
> mind, however humble in fortune, to bend to
> any yoke but that of reason."

Or perhaps this caught his eye :

> "I have found how apt one is when in
> power to abuse authority, and amidst indulgences
> to forget the hardships we impose, and to look
> down with contempt on those who are our
> inferiors only in their fortunes."

The Examiner may have given these extracts
personal application and may have judged them to
contain, in the words of one of his predecessors, "too
much about liberty."   We have the option of regarding him, in that case, as a reactionary rather than
a fool.   Be that as it may, we have to note in the
incident another instance of "ladies of the Court"

being shielded from vulgar attention by an official claiming to protect public morals.

In 1809 Mr Larpent made another brilliant stroke with his blue pencil. Theodore Hook had submitted to him a farce, and Mr Larpent promptly censored it. Finally an arrangement was come to and the play adapted to the Licenser's views. In the second edition, entitled "KILLING NO MURDER, a farce in two acts as performed with great applause at the Theatre Royal, Haymarket, with the original preface and the scene suppressed by order of the Lord Chamberlain," Hook adds a new preface, in which he says that the refusals of the Lord Chamberlain and his deputy were as good as a dozen newspaper paragraphs to him.

Hook's aim in the farce was to ridicule the Methodist preachers "conceiving that the lash of ridicule might be well applied to their backs." It was against the "open and violent expressions of inspired tailors and illuminated cobblers" that he railed humorously, trying, "without touching indelicately on the subject," to raise a laugh against the absurd union of spiritual and secular avocations characteristic of the Methodists.

Once more Mr Larpent waited till the evening previous to the performance before announcing the refusal of a licence ; a thoughtful attention which authors and managers always appreciate. Hook was incensed at the suggestion of disloyalty or immorality, and set off in search of the gentleman who had so ruthlessly strangled his literary infant at birth.

"To find him I referred to the Red Book,

> where I discovered that John Larpent, Esq.,
> was *clerk* at the Privy Seal Office, that John
> Larpent, Esq., was *deputy* to John Larpent, Esq.,
> and that the deputy's *secretary* was John Larpent,
> Esq. This proved to me that a man could be
> in three places at once, but on inquiry I found
> he was even in a fourth and fifth, for it was by
> virtue of none of these offices he licensed plays,
> and his place, *i.e.*, his villa, was at Putney."

After a long delay Larpent appeared and told
Hook, with a chilling look, that the second act of his
play was a most "indecent and shameful attack on a
very religious and harmless set of people." "Government," went on Larpent, "did not wish the Methodists
to be ridiculed." Naturally, Hook was more than a
little surprised at a statement such as this coming
from a court official ; but the explanation was soon
forthcoming. Larpent was not only a rigid Methodist
himself, but had even built a little tabernacle of his
own. To all Hook's protests the great Licenser
shook his head, "as if there was something in it,"
but added, that if Lord Dartmouth concurred with
him, not a line should be performed. "I took my
leave," says Hook, "fully convinced how proper a
person Mr Larpent was to receive, in addition to his
other salaries, four hundred pounds per annum, besides
perquisites for reading plays, the bare and simple
performance of which by his creed is the acme of
sin and unrighteousness—his even looking at them is
contamination—but four hundred a year—a sop for
Cerberus—what will it not make a man do ? "

Hook, however, had his revenge, for he altered

the offending parts and in their place inserted speeches written purposely to ridicule Larpent himself, and as these speeches touched neither on politics nor religion, the Examiner was unable to expunge them, and, adds Hook, " I have had the gratification of hearing the audience every night apply it properly and not only laugh at his expense, but pointedly, by their applause, show their detestation of his arbitrary and strained prerogative."

Moreover, there was naturally a huge rush for printed copies of the play, with the expunged scenes as an appendix, and six editions were needed to satisfy the demand. The actual alterations were futile and absurd to the last degree. The two following extracts will give an idea of the alterations insisted on, and the ludicrous effect which the corrections had in the revised play :

> " BUSK : Leave that to me—he is a consummate coxcomb—a strange mixture of boor and beau—is in high practice as a cutter of capers at Swansea, and has been till lately a—what I must not mention,[1]—I'll settle all that."
> " BUSK : Why, she's as proud as a lioness, watchful as a lynx and for hypocrisy an over-match for—what must not be mentioned." [1]

The footnotes ran as follows : " (1) In the piece originally ' a Methodist Preacher ' but altered by order of the Licenser." It made the censorship appear a somewhat futile proceeding, nor were the other alterations calculated to remove that impression.

Reproduction from last page of a manuscript play entitled BELIEVE
AS YOU LIST, by Massinger, and now in the British Museum.
The first draft was refused a licence in 1631, the Censor noting:
"*I had my fee notwithstanding, which belongs to me for reading itt over,
and ought to be brought always with the booke.*" The play was
refused because it contained "dangerous matter" concerning Spain,
but a revised draft was duly passed and endorsed: "*This play
called BELIEVE AS YOU LIST may bee acted this* 6 *of May* 1631.
—*HENRY HERBERT.*"

The line "Bring my grey hairs in sorrow to the grave" was expunged by Larpent as profane. He seems, indeed, to have been a little sensitive on the matter of hair, for he crossed out "What! insult me in my grey hairs" for the same reason. The rather stupid part of Scene III. was forbidden, presumably because Apollo was mentioned some half a dozen times. Even the pagan divinities, it will be seen, were able to rest secure under Mr Larpent's fatherly protection.

The impressions created by Larpent's censorship varied very widely. Sir Martin Shee describes him as having been inoffensive; but then Sir Martin was not one of those who ever submitted a play to him, and, moreover, at the time, was needing a foil to emphasise the villainies of a later Censor. Strict and careful Larpent certainly was, and his strictness and carefulness might fairly be described in less kindly terms. No doubt he, in his official duties, lived quite up to his religious principles. The mistake was, of course, in ever appointing a strict and rather bigoted Methodist to any post dealing with the control of public amusements. Such an appointment was an astounding piece of administrative stupidity or worse. Hook reminds us that at Rowland Hill's Chapel the congregation were congratulated from the pulpit on the destruction of Covent Garden Theatre and the annihilation of a score firemen. This was regarded as a singular proof of the Wisdom of Providence, the pulpiteer exclaiming:

"Great news, my brethren, great news, a great triumph has taken place over the devil and the stage players—a fire in one of their houses—oh may there be one consumed every year !—it is my fervent prayer."

It was not fitting that the follower of so fanatic a leader should be chosen to supervise the amusements of the nation, or allowed to whittle a nation's drama uncontrolled.

There was one further instance of Mr Larpent's censorship mentioned before the Committee of 1832 which is worth repeating.   A witness, Mr T. Morton, who was decidedly friendly to Larpent, when asked by the Commission whether he remembered any flagrant erasures from his plays, replied : " No ; I cannot.   I remember Mr Larpent objecting to the word *gammon* being put into a play of mine.   He said there was a gentleman of that name in Hampshire who had been very much hurt by a play of O'Keefe's.   I think it is in WILD OATS—'What is your name ?' 'Gammon !'   'Then you are the Hampshire hog !' This rather hurt his feelings.   There was, of course, no harm in removing the word."

By the way, it is interesting to note that the same Commission brought out the fact that in addition to his salary of £400 per year Larpent's receipts during the last four years of his office were : 1820, £132, 8s. ; 1821, £165, 18s. ; 1822, £126 ; and 1823, £142, 16s.

On his death in 1824 Larpent was said to have left behind him official copies of all the dramas read for the purpose of recommending them for licensing, as well as copies of all those pieces which had undergone the inspection of his predecessors from 1737.

According to a contributor to *Notes and Queries*, the collection consisted of between two and three thousand manuscripts, many of which never appeared in print. In *The New Monthly* for 1832 there is an article signed "J. P. C." on John Kemble, in which the writer says, speaking of this collection of manuscripts, "These, in conjunction with a friend, I purchased two years ago, so that we are now owners of the manuscript of every tragedy, comedy, opera, farce or other dramatic representation, from the date of the appointment of the first Examiner until Mr Colman came into office. Each piece is accompanied by an original letter from the manager for the time being. . . . The copies of the productions are sometimes in the handwriting of the authors, not unfrequently corrected and altered by them, and generally, with the passages or scenes to which the Examiner objected, marked or erased." In this collection there was, we are told, three copies of Macklin's MAN OF THE WORLD, in three different states of moderation, in the latest the severity of the satire having been sufficiently softened to satisfy the scruples of Lord Hertford.

It is difficult to understand on what grounds this remnant sale of historic national manuscripts took place, and we are not aware that any explanation has ever been forthcoming. That it should be in the power of any private individual to sell as personal property State papers accumulated in an official department seems incredible. The initials "J. P. C." suggested that the purchaser of this unique collection was John Payne Collier, who acted as deputy-Examiner in Colman's absence during the summer of 1831, and further inquiry showed this to be the case. In his evidence before the Commission of 1832 he mentioned having acquired the manuscripts, though he gave no particulars as to the means. Collier was a man who did good service for dramatic literature. The Duke of Devonshire sponsored him for the Garrick Club and introduced him at Holland House. He would also have made him Licenser of Plays, but George Colman, who then filled the office, though guaranteed the income for life, refused to resign the position. Collier's reputation in literary matters was, however, very bad. He was notoriously dishonest, and in literary matters, at any rate, was devoid of conscience and any sense of moral responsibility. No book or manuscript which ever passed through his hands can be regarded without suspicion, and several notable literary forgeries were traced home to him. He was, at different times, on *The Morning Chronicle*, and *The Times* as law and parliamentary reporter, dramatic and literary critic, and leader-writer. While on the staff of *The Times* he got into trouble for misrepresenting a speech in the House of Commons, to the prejudice of Canning, and was committed to the custody of the Serjeant-at-Arms. In view of his reputation, none of his statements or quotations should be accepted unverified, but he would certainly appear to have become possessed of Larpent's manuscripts.

On 19th January 1824 George Colman was appointed to the position just rendered vacant by Larpent's death. Here, at last, was a gleam of hope for the unhappy authors whose wit and fancy had been so mercilessly castrated by the lean and holy

Censor. Colman at this time was sixty-two years of age. His life at Oxford had, by his own confession, been most irregular, and had ended in his being "removed." He was himself an author of frisky temperament, responsible for about a score of extremely witty plays and some poems which would nestle comfortably beside any literary infant of Rabelais. Early in 1797 he had prepared an entertainment to be presented at the Haymarket Theatre in Lent, which proved too strong meat for the Lord Chamberlain and was prohibited with some decision. He then published a portion of it under the title of MY NIGHTGOWN AND SLIPPERS, OR TALES IN VERSE, which in themselves show that the Lord Chamberlain was not actuated by needless prudery. In fact, much of Colman's writing was extravagantly coarse, though undeniably witty, and Genest says bluntly that his morality was disgusting. His biographer says of him that he was "disorderly, if not profligate in his writings and his life"; but he was a man of genial and attractive humour, an entertaining companion, flawed by an incurable tendency to puns. He was introduced by the Duke of York to the Prince Regent at Carlton House, and several stories were told about his behaviour there, which show that he was not inclined to over-much respect for the conventions of Royalty, though there is a curious servile undercurrent in the following anecdote :

"On his walking through the apartments Colman remarked : 'What excellent lodgings ! I have nothing like them in the King's Bench !' After dinner he exclaimed : 'Eh ! Why, this *is* wine ; pray do tell me who that fine-looking fellow is at the head of the table ? ' The good-natured Duke said : ' Hush, George, you'll get into a scrape.' ' No, no,' said Colman, in a louder voice, ' I am come out to enjoy myself ; I want to know who that fine, square-shouldered, magnificent-looking, agreeable fellow is at the head of the table ! ' ' Be quiet, George," interrupted the Duke. ' You know it is the Prince.' ' Why, then,' continued Colman, still louder, ' he is your elder brother. I declare he don't look half your age. Well ! I remember the time when he sung a good song ! and as I am come out for a lark, for only one day, if he is the same good fellow that he used to be, he would not refuse an old play-fellow.' The Prince laughed and sang. ' What a magnificent voice,' exclaimed Colman. ' I have heard nothing to be compared to it for years. Such expression too ! I'll be damned if I don't engage him for my theatre.' "

Here, then, was a most promising candidate for Censor, an ideal corrective to the lemon-hearted Methodist who had just died. Colman had himself incurred the censorial prohibition and might be expected to appreciate the resentment caused by its arbitrary exercise.[1] Moreover, he had shown a fond-

---

[1] Colman received very considerable sums for his plays. For THE POOR GENTLEMAN and WHO WANTS A GUINEA? he was paid £550 each, then the customary price for a five-act comedy, that is to say, £300 on the first nine nights, £100 on the twentieth night, and £150 for the copyright. For JOHN BULL (the most attractive comedy ever produced, having averaged £470 per night for forty-seven nights) Mr Harris paid £1000, and Colman afterwards received twice an additional

ness for witty indecency which should at any rate save his fellow-writers from the oppression of over-niceness. Authors breathed freely again, hunted out some of their censored plays, and began to test the full breadth of their wit.

Never was a greater mistake made. Of a truth, " the devil a monk would be." Colman took his appointment very seriously indeed, and even his biographer parts company with him in his new guise. About a month after his appointment, ALASCO, written by Sir Martin Shee, was submitted to his notice by Charles Kemble, who had accepted the tragedy for Covent Garden.

On the 29th of February 1824 Colman wrote the following precious epistle, which would seem to have been composed with a view to its being ultimately seen by his royal master :

" 5, Melina Place, Westminster Road.
" 29*th February*, 1824.

" Mr Colman presents his compliments to Sir William Knighton, and is much gratified by Sir William having expressed a wish to see his short remarks on ALASCO, a copy of which he has now the pleasure to enclose.

" Although the ferment of the times has greatly subsided, still plays which are built upon conspiracies, and attempts to revolutionize a state, stand upon ticklish ground ; and the

£100, making £1200. Mr Harris was accustomed to pay an author one or two hundred pounds above the £550 when the drama was very successful, which was the case with most of Colman's plays. To have a play censored must evidently have involved Colman in a heavy financial loss, and some sympathetic leniency in such cases might reasonably be expected from him.

proposed performance of such plays is to be contemplated with more jealousy when they portray the disaffected as gallant heroes, and hapless lovers. Thus drawn, *ad captandum vulgus*, their showy qualities and tender distresses of the heart throw a dazzle and an interest round their sedition, while they preach up the doctrine that Government is tyranny, that revolt is virtue, and that rebels are the righteous.

" ALASCO, in the tragedy of the same name, is a character of the above description, and Walsingham is set up against him as a contrast. Whenever these two gentlemen meet there is an effusion of clap-trap sentiments between them, in the alternate support of loyalty and radicalism ; and they *prone* in a *pro* and *con* dialogue, vying with each other, speech for speech, by turns, like a couple of contending swains in an eclogue. In respect to their good and evil influence over an audience they are the Messieurs Bane and Antidote of the tragedy ; and from a tragedy that needs so much counter-poison, for the chance only of neutralizing its arsenic, the deducement to be made as to its dangerous tendency is very obvious.

" It is my opinion that the objections against acting this play may be removed by the erasures which I have made ; in which should the managers think proper to acquiesce I will (on their altering the MS. and again placing it in my hands) submit the play to the Lord Chamberlain for his licence.

" GEORGE COLMAN, *Feb.* 1824."

"The foregoing summary remarks were written by me as Examiner of Plays ; and I communicated them to Mr Charles Kemble, one of the managers of Covent Garden, when the tragedy of ALASCO was under my official consideration."

As this was the first play on which Colman was called to exercise his new powers, it will be interesting to note his objections at some length, more especially as they were characteristic of the attitude he was to maintain during his period of office. The letter quoted above gives a hint of the sentiments he found offensive ; but the deleted passages themselves show that he pounced on anything like a liberal thought with feverish zeal. Let us take a dozen specimens. In the line

"Some district despot prompt to play the Tarquin"

the word "despot" was prohibited. When the virtuous Amantha cried out in terror,

"Oh, God ! he has rushed unarmed amidst his foes,"

the Censor objected to the expletive "Oh, God," the lady's scruples in the matter of language not, apparently, being sufficiently fine to meet with the approval of Colman, whose own language, by the way, was habitually of the kind which hallowed the old-fashioned cab rank.[1] The other lines which roused his expurgatory zeal were,

"Some slanderous tool of state
Some taunting, dull, unmanner'd deputy."

---

[1] Apparently Colman was desirous of reviving an old Statute, 3 Jac., s. 1, ch. xxi., which enacted "that if any person shall, in any stage-play, interlude, shew, may-game, or pageant, jestingly or profanely speak or use the holy name of God, Christ-Jesus, or of the Trinity, he shall forfeit for every such offence £10."

As a "tool of State" and "deputy" himself, Colman possibly felt himself called on to defend the official dignities, and possibly the same reason influenced him in expunging

> "To brook dishonour from a knave in place."

"Knaves in place" were now evidently to be protected against the attacks of "unplaced, unpensioned, and unprivileged bards."

Even the cause of religion was kindly sheltered by this knight of Censors—

> "No, no. Whate'er the colour of his creed
> The man of honour's orthodox"

could on no account be permitted, while so infamous and un-English a sentiment as

> "Our country's wrongs unite us"

was burnt out in a veritable flame of red ink. Every incitement to fight for liberty, or to protest against oppression and tyranny, such as

> "For your country
> Fight and be free,"

was ruthlessly deleted, and it must be remembered that the play was not cast in England, nor had reference to English conditions and problems. Colman's scrupulous delicacy shuddered before such a phrase as "Hell's hot blisters." Even Hell might not be called nasty names, apparently, and—to apply another of Colman's expurgations—

> "tingled in the startled ear of tyrants."

Pious invocations to the "God of Truth," or "God of Mercy," were literary contraband, and might not reach the ear of Heaven so long as Colman purged the stream of prayer. Heroic and patriotic sentiments were for the moment at a discount, such sentences as

> "The scaffold strikes no terrors to his soul
> Who mounts it as a martyr for his country"

were ruthlessly eliminated ; it may have been with a view to supporting the impressiveness and dignity of his brother official, the hangman.

Evidently the new Censor was going to be busier, if not better, than his predecessor. To quote a line from the play to which we have just referred, Colman evidently started off with the maxim that "All is mutiny that's not submission." His first acts were, we are told, those of petty tyranny, and his next those of grasping cupidity. One of the most licentious writers of the age, he out-Heroded Herod in his new authority. Larpent had put up a pretty high standard of authority to which authors had to conform, and Colman, eager to justify his position, had to go to greater extremities in order to demonstrate his authority at all. He started, then, on a series of extraordinary objections and prohibitions which, in the whole history of the office, had not been exceeded. If Larpent ruled the imagination of dramatic authors like a hectic nun, Colman rode it like a nightmare. He denied the right of a dramatic lover to call his mistress an "angel." An angel, he said, was a character in Scripture, and the term was not to be profaned on the stage by being applied to a woman.[1]   He was questioned on this point by the Commission of 1832.

> "The Commission have heard of your cutting out of a play the epithet "angel" as applied to a woman ?—Yes, because it is a woman, I grant; but it is a celestial woman.   It is an allusion to the scriptural angels, which are celestial bodies.   Every man who has read his Bible understands what they are, or if he has not, I will refer him to Milton.
>
> "Milton's angels are not ladies ?—No, but some scriptural angels are ladies, I believe.   If you will look at Johnson's Dictionary, he will tell you they are celestial persons, commanded by God to interfere in terrestrial business.
>
> "Must an allusion to Scripture have an immoral effect ?—I conceive all Scripture is much too sacred for the stage, except in very solemn scenes indeed, and that to bring things so sacred upon the stage becomes profane."

Colman would not licence any reference whatever to God.   The exclamation, "Oh, Providence!" was, he insisted, an address to the providence of God and ought not to be allowed.   How the Lord's Prayer would have emerged from Colman's office we dare not guess.   It would certainly have been stigmatised as seditious, and probably as profane. "Heaven" and "Hell" were words Colman could not bear to see in a play.   On one occasion he wrote, "The phrases 'Oh, Heaven,' and 'Ye Heavens,'

---

[1] When Douglas Jerrold submitted BLACK-EYED SUSAN, the sentence "He plays the fiddle like an angel" was prohibited and erased.

occur seven times in this piece—omit them !" He
expunged "Oh, lud !" because he said it meant
"Oh, Lord," which was inadmissible. "A Damn,"
says Arnold, "was a pill he could never swallow."
Yet few men were of coarser speech, or used the
grosser expletives more frequently and unmeaningly.
Once when a dandy had to say "Demme, my dear,"
Colman observed: "Demme means Damn me—
omit it." One might, apparently, call neither God
nor oneself names.

Colman was asked some questions on this subject
by the 1832 Commission.

> "What would be the result of using ordinary
> oaths, such as *Damme*, or anything of that sort ?
> —I think it is immoral and improper, to say
> nothing of the vulgarity of it in assemblies
> where high characters and females congregate ;
> I certainly think it is improper, and beyond
> that, I believe you will find there are Acts of
> Parliament where swearing is restrained under
> a penalty.
>
> "Do you speak from your experience as to
> the immoral effect, or is it your opinion merely ?
> —It is my opinion of the practice in general.
> I have seen a great deal of the stage, un-
> doubtedly, and so far I can speak from experi-
> ence, I think nobody has gone away from a
> theatre the better for hearing a great deal of
> cursing and swearing.
>
> "How do you reconcile the opinion you have
> just given with your making use of the terms,
> such as *Damme*, or any of the small oaths which

you say are immoral and improper, to say nothing
of their vulgarity, in some of your own composi-
tions which have met with great success on the
stage ?—If I had been the examiner I should
have scratched them out, and would do so now ;
I was in a different position at that time, I
was a careless, immoral author, I am now an
examiner of plays. I did my business as an
author at that time, and I do my business as an
examiner now."

Nothing that Colman could have said would have
illustrated the stability of his principles more than
that closing statement. His principles varied with
his official standing with a lightness that reminds us
of that American orator who said : "Them's my
sentiments, gentlemen. If you don't like them they
can be changed."

But to return to Colman's extraordinary dislike
of the milder oaths ; it is amusing to read his arguments against them. Coming from his predecessor,
Larpent, such arguments might have occasioned no
surprise ; but they seem singularly unfitting from a
man of Colman's licentiousness of speech and writing.
Asked whether some of the wittier oaths in his plays
did not contribute to their success, he answered,
primly :

"No, certainly not. It is from habit ; the
actors think it hammers the thing stronger if
they use a 'damme,' for which they are liable
to forty shillings penalty. I will give you an
instance in one of my own plays. Habit has
made it forcible and strong to say 'damme' ;

but if 'hang me' were generally adopted, it would be as strong; that is perfectly harmless to me, though not to the person hanged, and it would be quite as forcible to the audience. Sir Simon Rochdale, in JOHN BULL, says: 'Damn me! if it isn't the brazier!' Now, putting a gentleman in that position is wrong; in the first instance, morally so; if he happened to make a mistake and it wasn't the brazier, he would be damned. Now, if he said 'Hang me if it isn't the brazier!' would not that do as well?"

Colman's religious susceptibilities were equally fine. In one of his plays he made a very good joke about Eve. One of the characters has no more idea of something than Eve had of pin-money; but, when he took the censorial pen in his hand, strange waves of repentance came over him. He told the Commission that he thought his unregenerate reference to Eve was improper, and when reminded that the audience had always been struck with that particular joke, replied: "Yes, but I think all allusions to the Scriptures had better be avoided." Douglas Jerrold relates that in a piece called THE BRIDE OF LUDGATE, in which Charles II. figured as the hero and was disguised as a priest come to marry a young couple, Mr Colman insisted that in the present state of the bishops the character should not come on as a priest, but in some other guise, as, say, a proctor, to which ruling Jerrold was obliged to submit.

In a drama by John Banim, Colman objected to some lines to be chanted in a foreign cathedral by monks and nuns. The poetry of the piece was

beautiful, the passage was really essential to the
action of the piece, and none of the names of God
were mentioned at all. Nevertheless, Colman was
obdurate, and ruled that "No address to the Deity
should be permitted on the stage." He once said
that if the MERCHANT OF VENICE had been submitted
to him as Examiner, he would certainly have expunged such lines as

"It is an attribute of God Himself,"

though he did not know that he had the power to
do so now, as it "was licensed so long ago." Moreover, he admitted that however desirable such a
process might be, "a modern audience would not
allow of any further meddling with the text of
Shakespeare." If the picture pleases you, you may
imagine a man of Colman's senile coyness being
actually paid by the State to go through the works
of Shakespeare with a small-toothed comb. Our
imagination boggles at it. We feel grateful that
Shakespeare died before England developed her
modern nonconformist abhorrence of genius.

There was, however, one amiable trait in Colman's character. Having damned an author's play
he was not above suggesting to the ill-used playwright a quiet way of evading the censorial ruling.
In 1829 Frederic Yeates submitted a play to Colman,
and his excisions were so drastic that the author was
moved to a hot protest. That protest evoked the
following gem of official probity :

"BROMPTON, 27th *April*, 1829.

"MY DEAR YATES,—I hear that Beazley com-
plains I have reduced all his full-grown angels

into cherubims, *id est*, cut them in half and left them neither heaven or cloud to rest upon; that his comedy will sure to be d——d by the public, owing to the removal of some devilish good jokes by the Examiner, and further, that the Licenser's Deputy has taken most unlicensed liberties with the dramatist.

"Cannot you, my dear Fred, instruct him better? The play, you know, must be printed in strict accordance with my obliterations; but if the parts be previously given out, it will be difficult to induce the actors to preach from my text.—Truly yours,   G. COLMAN."

This easy morality must have been convenient when Colman found himself in hot passages with offended authors whose friendship was valuable to him. Arnold once asked him whether he ever troubled his head with what actually passed in the theatres, and if he ascertained whether his excisions were duly attended to or not. "Not in the least," replied Colman, "my duty is to object to everything immoral or politically dangerous. When I have marked my objections the play is licensed, subject to the omissions of the passages objected to; beyond this I have nothing to do, or an Examiner would become a spy as well as a Censor on the theatre." [1]

We have said that Colman's career was marked by cupidity. In time he became very sensitive to

[1] Mr Pigott had similar views. "I should be very sorry to pursue any manager with a sort of system of espionage. Indeed, it would be impracticable, and, I think, worse than arbitrary."

suggestions such as these. Arnold once remarked that, seeing the Examiner had a salary as payment for his labours, there could be no reason why a tax should also be levied on the proprietors for the same work. "Excuse *me*," retorted Colman, "but by God that remark is damned illiberal." The question of fees had become an acute one with him, and he seems to have studied the career of his predecessor, Herbert, to some advantage. He displayed a "restless and watchful anxiety to increase his fees" on occasions which former licensers had neglected. In this connection, at any rate, he was not above "making the Examiner a spy on the theatre." He would call on actors to know by what authority they advertised a new song or musical interpolation, many of them well known to the public, but not specifically licensed. He asserted that such songs, glees, etc., must be duly and separately licensed by him at a fee of two guineas a time. This new ruling was an intolerable one, but for a time there seemed no way of evading it. One actor, however, known as "little Knight," conceived the idea of stringing together all the songs, poems, imitations, etc., which he wished to make use of, connecting the various items with rubbishy and irrelevant dialogue. The whole innocuous conglomeration was then submitted to the Examiner and licensed as one play, after which the connecting dialogue was ignored and the songs and glees used as and when required. One has not much sympathy with Colman in the incident.

Colman went so far as to make a tentative claim to license oratorio, and on one occasion sued Mr Lawes as a sort of test case ; but ultimately the Lord

Chamberlain dropped the claim. What the Examiner would have done with an oratorio staggers the imagination. Since no address to divine persons was to be permitted on the stage, every reference to the Deity would have been expunged and prohibited as contrary to public morals, and what sort of limping absurdity would have emerged from Colman's rough surgery is not easily conceived. We may note here that on one occasion Arnold was mulcted in the stereotyped two guineas for a licence for a lecture by Mr Bartley at the Lyceum, the subject being the dangerous one of Astronomy !

When the French plays were produced in 1829 three or four light pieces were performed each evening, being seldom repeated. Colman put in a preposterous claim for two guineas for each of these trifling pieces, but his claim was peremptorily quashed by the then Lord Chamberlain, the broad-minded Duke of Devonshire. But when, later, the Duke of Montrose came into office, he was more sympathetic, and announced, through Colman, that his predecessor's ruling was now reversed, and the customary fees must be paid. The moral value of Colman's insistence was pretty clearly shown in the sequel, when Colman wrote offering to license all the plays which had already been produced, to the number of about one hundred and fifty, in *one* licence, a proposal which showed " a tolerable state of indifference as to what ribaldry, blasphemy, disloyalty, they might severally contain, in case of their being repeated."

We may mention one final incident of Colman's censorial career. In 1825 Miss Mitford, of all people in the world, fell under his ban. She had submitted the manuscript of Charles the First through Kemble; but Colman, alarmed at the "exceedingly delicate nature of the subject and incidents," sent the manuscript on to the Lord Chamberlain, the Duke of Montrose, at that time in Scotland. Then on 28th November 1825 came a letter marked "Private," from which we make the following precious extract:

"28th November 1825.

" My official opinion of her tragedy is certainly unfavourable to the author's interests. I was, however, so far from wishing it to prejudice the Lord Chamberlain that the play was submitted to his perusal at my suggestion. He therefore formed his own judgment upon it, and decidedly refused to license its performance.

" As to alterations, the fact is that the subject of this play and the incidents it embraces are fatal in themselves; they are an inherent and incurable disease; the morbid matter lies in the very bones and marrow of the historical facts, and defies eradication. Indeed, it would be a kind of practical bull to permit a detailed representation of Charles's unhappy story on a public stage, when his martyrdom is still observed in such solemn silence that the London theatres are actually closed and all dramatic exhibitions whatever suspended on its anniversary.

" I give Miss Mitford full credit for the harmlessness of her intentions, but mischief may

be unconsciously done, as a house may be set on
fire by a little innocent in the nursery.

"Believe me, my dear sir, most truly yours,
"G. COLMAN."

The contemptuous insult of the last paragraph
needs no emphasis. The play was subsequently
disposed of on very good terms, in 1834, but its
performance at the patent theatres was, of course,
impossible, and after a few surreptitious and unprofitable performances at the Coburg, it expired.

That the coarse-thumbed Colman, whose wit
stank of the cesspool, should have ever been in a
position to censor the delicate, reticent work of Miss
Mitford, was nothing short of an outrage. To have
won the reputation of offending the susceptibilities
of a man whose own literary productions were of
notorious indecency, must have been disgusting to the
mild, gentle-tempered authoress, the restraint of
whose pen was, as one writer has aptly said, "almost
a blemish."

Perhaps Miss Mitford *was*, as Colman suggested,
to blame in choosing her subject. What she ought
to have done was to write something in the style of
THE ELDER BROTHER—Colman's fragrant story of the
London doctor who ran an establishment near Hyde
Park for delivering reputed virgins,

". . . reducing ladies' shapes,
Who had secured themselves from leading apes,[1]
But kept the reputation of virginity."

and of Isaac, his neighbour, who, in a midnight

[1] Women who died virgins were said to be condemned to lead apes
in Hell.

adventure, discovered that his maiden aunt was in residence at the establishment.

> " ' Zounds ! ' bellows Shove, with rage and wonder wild,
> ' Why, then, my *maiden* Aunt is *big with child*.'
>
> Here was, at once, a sad discovery made !
> Lucretia's frolick, now, was past a joke ;—
> Shove trembled, for his fortune, Crow, his Trade,—
> Both, both saw ruin—by one fatal stroke.
>
> But, with his Aunt, when Isaac did discuss,
> She hush'd the matter up, by speaking thus :—
>
> ' Sweet Isaac ! ' said Lucretia, ' Spare my Fame !—
> Tho', for my babe, I feel as should a mother,
> Your fortune will continue much the same ;
> For, keep the Secret—you're his Elder Brother ! ' "

Or that other amiable story of the knight and the friar, where the knight, hearing that the friar was soliciting his wife, advised her to complaisance. When the friar came at midnight to her chamber, the knight thrashed him to death, afterwards disposing of the body, with numerous adventures, in a receptacle associated with corporation departments, but not otherwise to be specified.[1] Miss Mitford, however, for some inscrutable reason, preferred to write an historical romance, and for her pains saw her name added to the list of obscene and dangerous writers.

In speaking of Larpent's period of office, we had occasion to refer to Theodore Hook's witty account of his adventures with that gentleman. It was some-

---

[1] This was the man who, when THE BASHFUL MAN was submitted to him, would not permit mention of the word " thighs," because, he said, those were indecent !

what curious to find, then, in an early volume of
Bentley's Miscellany, a defence of Colman's rigour as
Censor from the same pen. "What," said Hook,
"had he to do as Licenser with what he had himself done as author? The *tu quoque* principle in this
case is even more than usually absurd; it is as if a
schoolmaster were to be prevented from flogging a
boy for breaking windows because, when a boy, he
had broken windows himself!" But Hook's shaft
was barb-less, and comes away at the first tug. What
was really the trouble was that, though Colman had
broken all the windows in his youth, he would not
later allow others even to use windows legitimately.
He had rankly abused certain elements in literature
himself and would not later allow their legitimate
and proper use to others. His chief sin was his
reformation. As Censor he would have been much
better if he had had the courage to be as bad as he
really was.

CHAPTER VIII

POLITICAL AND RELIGIOUS OBJECTIONS

WITH the death of Colman the individual Censors became less interesting. The office fell to less distinguished holders, the Lord Chamberlain becoming more and more clearly the actual official. To follow the individual careers of subsequent Censors would not only be difficult, but uninteresting and impertinent. We may briefly mention the names of Mr Colman's successors. Charles Kemble, the actor, took up Colman's pen on 17th October 1836. His biographer says of him that " he enjoyed the office of Examiner of Plays, which was for him a sort of sinecure, as he discharged it by deputy." He gave up the office in 1840, and Lord Melbourne then appointed his son, John Mitchell Kemble (24th February 1840), who held the office till his death in 1857. Kemble spent much of his time abroad, and for all practical purposes the duties of the office from 1849 devolved upon William Bodham Donne,[1] one-time librarian to the London Library, an office he resigned on 27th March 1857, when he officially succeeded

---

[1] It was once lyrically said of this gentleman that his influence was like that of a lady at a table! He earned the flattering reputation of a humorist by his statement before a Select Committee that *double entendres* were extinct.

to the post of Examiner of Plays. Donne held office till 1874, being succeeded by Mr E. F. S. Pigott.

Of these Examiners Mr Pigott, who held the office for twenty-one years, was the most notable. He was, however, not well suited for the post he held, as those who had intimate dealings with him could best testify. On his death, in 1895, a serious critic in the *Saturday Review*, protesting against some unwise panegyrics, wrote : "The late Mr Pigott is declared on all hands to have been the best reader of plays we have ever had ; and yet he was a walking compendium of vulgar insular prejudice, who, after wallowing all his life in the cheapest theatrical senti-ment (he was a confirmed playgoer), had at last brought himself to a pitch of incompetence which, outside the circle of those unfortunate persons who have had to try and reason with him personally, can only be measured by reading his evidence before the Commission of 1892, and the various letters of his which are just now finding their way into print. He had French immorality on the brain ; he had American indecency on the brain ; he had the womanly woman on the brain ; he had the divorce court on the brain ; he had 'not before a mixed audience' on the brain ; his official career in rela-tion to the higher drama was one long folly and panic, in which the only thing definitely discernible in a welter of intellectual confusion was his concep-tion of the English people rushing towards an abyss of national degradation in morals and manners, and only held back on the edge of the precipice by the grasp of his strong hand."

During his absences abroad Pigott frequently and,

it is to be feared, illegally, appointed a deputy to act for him, and that deputy was, for many years, George Alexander Redford, who in this way acquired a knowledge of the workings of the office sufficient to justify his appointment as Examiner in 1895. Mr Redford resigned in December 1911, Mr C. H. E. Brookfield taking up the duties of the post on 1st January 1912, after a nominal appointment as co-Examiner.

As we approach modern times it becomes desirable to dissociate the operations of the censorship from the personalities of individual examiners as much as possible. The responsibility for such decisions of the censorship as have become public must finally lie with the Lord Chamberlain. There has been a tendency for opponents of the censorship to associate their indignation too much with individual holders of the office. Nowadays little is to be gained by harping on the personal idiosyncrasies of individual examiners. They have no longer the autocratic power which Herbert, for instance, exercised, and more substantial allowance must be made for court influence and the authority of the Lord Chamberlain. Before the 1909 Commission, the Speaker commented on this, and laid great emphasis on the fact that the Lord Chamberlain was the person really responsible, the Examiner of Plays himself being nothing more than a clerk in his office who advised him. "The Lord Chamberlain," said the Speaker, "is the person to whom the public look ; he is the responsible official, a member of His Majesty's Government, in receipt of a considerable, though, I dare say, inadequate salary, and a man of affairs. He is the man who really ought to make himself responsible. I do not say he does so ; but he ought not to shelter himself in any way behind the Examiner." There is no reason for associating this very decided pronouncement with the fact that, for some reason, the Lord Chamberlain himself did not appear to give evidence before the Select Committee.

It is a noteworthy fact that the Lord Chamberlain is not responsible in any way to the House of Commons. When Sir Matthew Ridley was Home Secretary in 1900 and a question arose in regard to the censorship, he is reported to have said : "There is no discipline or check on the drama in the hands of any Government department." The reason for this appears to be that the Lord Chamberlain's salary is not on the Estimates ; it is drawn from the Civil List, and therefore his conduct cannot be challenged in the House of Commons, except by a definite special motion. The Lord Chamberlain, in fact, stands in the same position as one of His Majesty's Judges, the Lord Chancellor, the Irish Lieutenant, or the Speaker. Nevertheless, in the Memorandum of Appointment given by the Lord Chamberlain to the Examiner of Plays in 1895, it is stated that "the Examiner of Plays is an officer appointed to examine all theatrical entertainments on the part of the Lord Chamberlain, who is responsible to Parliament." Sir Douglas Dawson, the Comptroller of the Lord Chamberlain's department, has stated that "the Lord Chamberlain is a Minister of the Crown, a Member of the Government, and he acts under powers given him by Parliament. He is to be found

in his place in the House of Lords. The Lord
Chamberlain looks upon himself as perfectly capable
of answering questions where his action is called
into account." This accountability, however, is to
the House of Lords alone, and it is for this reason
that questions cannot properly be addressed to any
Minister of the Crown in the Commons on the
question of censorship.[1] When Mr Robert Harcourt (December 1911) raised the question of Mr
Brookfield's appointment in the House of Commons,
Mr M'Kenna, the Home Secretary, frankly replied
that he doubted whether it would be proper for him
to defend Mr Brookfield, for the simple reason that
he had no responsibility whatever for the appointment, and if he defended him he would be assuming
to himself a right which did not belong to him.

It need hardly be pointed out that however
satisfactory this state of affairs may have been in the
earlier days when the functions of the Lord Chamberlain were almost solely concerned with court
life, now that his duties have become very largely
administrative the old arrangement is no longer
acceptable. Administrative duties involving the
rights and incomes of a large body of respectable
individuals should certainly be subject to the same
public supervision and criticism as obtains in the

---

[1] It is worth noting that on one or two occasions questions have
actually been addressed to the Foreign Secretary or to the Home
Secretary, mainly relating to action taken as the result of representations to the Foreign Office in cases in which offence to some foreign
Power was in question. In 1901 a question was asked about the
SECRETS OF THE HAREM (see p. 207), and in 1908 one relating to the
suppressed MIKADO. These questions were probably permitted solely
for the sake of informing the foreign Powers in question of what had
occurred.

case of other ministerial appointments. The report of the 1909 Committee stated :

> " We would deprecate the detailed dis-
> cussion in Parliament, whether in debate or
> by way of question and answer, of particular
> decisions of the Lord Chamberlain in respect
> to the Licensing of plays ; but we consider
> that remaining accountable as now to the
> House of Lords his general administration of
> the functions entrusted to him by statute
> should be brought by whatever procedure is
> thought desirable within the same oppor-
> tunities for review by the House of Commons
> as the actions of other Ministers."

The jurisdiction of the Lord Chamberlain as Licenser of Theatres extends to the cities of London and Westminster ; to the areas which constituted in 1843 the boroughs of Finsbury, Marylebone, Tower Hamlets, Lambeth, and Southwark — the metropolitan boroughs at that time ; and to the town of Windsor and other places of royal residence. As regards provincial towns, with the exception of Margate, Bath, and Windsor, the Lord Chamberlain has no jurisdiction at all, so far as the licensing of the theatres themselves are concerned, though he has claimed and in one or two cases exercised jurisdiction as regards the stage plays performed.[1] The 1909

[1] In some of the provincial towns there have been patent theatres granted a licence by letters patent passed under the Great Seal; but the duration granted to these licences is limited, and they have in most cases died out. The Theatre Royal, Bath, and the Theatre Royal, Margate, are exceptions. The theatre at Windsor is still licensed by the Lord Chamberlain because Windsor is a royal residence. In the

Committee reported that it would be advisable for the licensing of the forty metropolitan theatres now in the jurisdiction of the Lord Chamberlain to be transferred to the London County Council, whose officers already visit them regularly in order to advise as to the safety of their structure and of their accommodation for the public.

By the courtesy of the Lord Chamberlain we are able to show what have been the actual numerical results of censorship in recent years,[1] but the measure of the Censor's activity is not to be arrived at in this way. It may freely be admitted that the percentage of plays actually prohibited has been small, though it would obviously be absurd to judge the *importance* of the censored plays merely by their numerical relation to the musical comedies and miscellaneous plays which have been passed. But the fact is that the actual percentage of plays prevented from appearing by the existence of the censorship is for two reasons much larger than that to be estimated from an inspection of the above figures. There is, in the first place, the impalpable check given to dramatists by the very existence of a Censor whose judgment and efficiency are challenged. As Mr Thomas Hardy says, " All I can say is that something or other—which probably is consciousness of the Censor—appears to deter men of letters who have

case of the Brighton theatre the house was licensed because Brighton, like Richmond, was formerly a royal residence, and even after it ceased to be a royal residence the Lord Chamberlain went on licensing it from usage. In 1865, however, the magistrates called attention to the fact that Brighton was no longer a royal residence, and the Lord Chamberlain relinquished his licensing rights.

[1] See Appendix.

other channels for communicating with the public, from writing for the stage." As the Lord Chamberlain stated before the 1866 Committee, "the authors know pretty well what will be allowed," a knowledge which undoubtedly tends to keep many serious and valuable writers from the English stage.[1]

In the second place it has been a frequent practice in the Lord Chamberlain's office to anticipate the presentation of a play by suggesting to the manager who is about to produce it that he had better not ask for a licence. The object of this practice would appear to be to give the author an opportunity of avoiding the stigma of having a play censored. This, however, is a deliberate though possibly well-meant, shirking of the censorial functions. A self-respecting author is certainly not grateful for the suggestion that he has done something which had better be hushed quietly out of existence, and it is not surprising that, in some cases, as, for instance, in the case of Mr Garnett's play, THE BREAKING-

[1] "I *do* consider that the situation made by the Englishman of letters, ambitious of writing for the stage, has less dignity—thanks to the Censor's arbitrary rights upon his work—than that of any other man of letters in Europe, and that this fact may well be, or rather MUST be, deterrent to men of any intellectual independence and self-respect."—HENRY JAMES.

"The censorship with its quite wanton power of suppression has always been *one* of the reasons why I haven't ventured into play-writing."—H. G. WELLS.

"Most decidedly the existence of the censorship makes it impossible for me even to think of writing plays on the same plane of realism and THOROUGHNESS as my novels. It is not a question of subject, it is a question of treatment. Immediately you begin to get NEAR the things that really matter in a play, you begin to think about the Censor, and it is all over with your play."—ARNOLD BENNETT.

"I am certain that a dramatic author may be shamefully hindered, and that such a situation is intolerable: a disgrace to the tone, to the character of this country's civilisation."—JOSEPH CONRAD.

Portrait by Hogarth of Lavinia Fenton, who took the leading part in Gay's Beggars' Opera, the public excitement concerning which was one of the chief causes of the passing of Walpole's famous Act of 1737.

POINT, the author and manager insisted on formally submitting the play and obtaining an equally formal refusal.[1]

This rather surreptitious method of controlling dramatic output brings us to the question of secrecy. Mr Pigott, the Censor who preceded Mr Redford, once went so far as to say that the secrecy of the office was essential and desirable. He said : " The essence of my office and its advantage to the art and profession of the stage is that it is preventive and above all secret." It has for long been the practice with succeeding Censors to mark their communications PRIVATE AND CONFIDENTIAL. Colman always insisted on any letters of his, in relation to censored plays, being regarded as private documents ; and Mr Redford before the 1909 Commission said that he certainly regarded his official communications as confidential, and that it was improper to make these communications public.

It need hardly be said that this secrecy has been

[1] The proceedings of the Censor have sometimes in other ways shown a regrettable lack of formality. In September 1907 the manager of the Midland Theatre, Manchester, submitted a copy of George Bernard Shaw's play, MRS WARREN'S PROFESSION, to the Examiner, with the usual two-guinea reading fee, and the intimation that he wished to produce the play. Three days later the play, the cheque, and the letter were all returned with the following censorial inscription *added to the returned letter* : " Surely you are aware that I have already refused to license this play.—G. A. R." ; a postscript which, in its autocratic brevity and economy, reminds one of Herbert's precedents. The humble manager mildly pointed out that the Examiner was a public official and that this footnote could hardly be accepted as an official refusal. He also pointed out that it was some years since the play in question had been refused, and that it was quite consonant with the custom of the Lord Chamberlain's office for an adverse decision to be revoked, mentioning particular instances. To this moderate letter he received no reply, nor did a further application for an answer ten days later receive any acknowledgment whatever !

one of the acutest grievances of dramatic authors. They have felt it to be an insult that a play over which they have perhaps spent many anxious months should be criticised and condemned without even the grounds of the condemnation being known and without the author being able to offer a word in self-defence. The Censor has always refused to recognise the existence of authors,[1] his dealings being solely with the producing managers. Secrecy in such a matter is very undesirable. Nothing is gained by it, and it gives rise to the strongest suspicions as to the fairness of the whole procedure. Why an aggrieved author or manager should be compelled to regard official communications from a State department as PRIVATE AND CONFIDENTIAL is hard to understand. Such an attitude inevitably suggests a disinclination on the part of the Censor to face the legitimate outcome of his considered decision. On this point it is interesting to note that Sir Douglas Dawson, Comptroller of the Chamberlain's department, stated that his own personal opinion was that such communications were not confidential, and that he " did not think there should be any secrecy in the matter at all. It would be wrong."

The fact that no code of rules has ever been drafted defining the principle of censorship has more than once led to some absurd situations. No one Chamberlain has considered himself bound by the acts of his predecessor, and the result has been that some plays have been licensed and withdrawn after

[1] "A play of mine called MAY AND DECEMBER was banned by the Censor. I wrote and asked him why. He replied that his office did not recognise authors and he could take no official notice of my existence."—SYDNEY GRUNDY.

eight or ten years, while others have been refused, and then, under a fresh Chamberlain, granted a licence. JACK SHEPPARD and OLIVER TWIST were stopped by Lord de la Warr after they had been acted for some years. In each case representations were made to him, in consequence of which his Examiner's ruling was overridden and the licences revoked.[1]

But although there is no code of rules in the Lord Chamberlain's office for the guidance of dramatists, it is possible to form an idea of the lines on which British censorship has in practice been conducted from the instances on record of the Censor's intervention. It will be interesting to consider some of these in an effort to crystallise the "use and wont" of the office into an intelligible code. When Mr Disraeli in 1845 brought out his novel of CONINGSBY, Shirley Brooks, who was very intimate with the manager of the Lyceum Theatre, came to the conclusion that it would be a good thing to dramatise the story. Everything was nearly ready for presentation when he suddenly received an intimation that the piece would not be allowed. In an interview the Lord Chamberlain courteously informed him that there were many reasons why it was undesirable to produce the piece, and as these reasons were unfolded Brooks's astonishment increased. The Lord Chamberlain said : "You see, you are writing a kind of quasi-political piece, and here you

---

[1] When Ainsworth's famous novel JACK SHEPPARD was staged at the Adelphi, it became a tremendous success. Baker says: "The Chadbands were again up in arms, advertising by their invectives the thing they condemned; the press took up a severely moral tone, and so much pressure was brought to bear upon the Lord Chamberlain that, by and by, *all* plays upon the subject were interdicted."

are exhibiting a sort of contrast between the manu-
facturing people and the lower classes. Don't you
think, now, that that would be a pity?" Then
Brooks continues : "This was not to be in, and that
was not to be in. Something might be construed
with an allusion to some family in Shropshire. Mr
Holloway's ointment was not to be in as Mr High-
gate's ointment, because really Mr Holloway was an
industrious tradesman and employed a good many
people," and so on. No wonder that Brooks, mildest
of critics, said that he thought the censorial functions
were exercised with a certain amount of caprice.

This question of politics on the stage had for
some time been an acute one. As we have seen, in
the earlier days, prior to the passing of the Act of
1737, politicians were satirised and criticised with
the utmost frankness, and we have yet to learn that
any serious disadvantage accompanied the practice.
But under Walpole's guidance politicians assumed a
shyer disposition, and from that date the Censor
has been peculiarly averse to anything approaching
political satire. And yet — there is always some
strange qualification in any statement of censorial
practice—in actual practice the political piece has
occasionally found its way through the net.

There was, for instance, the case of THE HAPPY
LAND, the famous burlesque written by Gilbert under
another name, and based on his own fairy play, THE
WICKED WORLD (1873). Never since the plays
which had provoked Walpole to retaliate had such
pungent satire been staged. Ayrtoun himself, Baker
tells us, went to see his counterfeit presentment going
about with a pot of slate-coloured paint, with which

he daubed all public buildings, statues, and monuments. " What is a ship ? " asks a competitive examiner. " I don't know," is the reply. " Then you shall be First Lord of the Admiralty," is the dictum. The trio and dance of Gladstone, Lowe, and Ayrtoun with the ensemble, " Here a save, there a save, everywhere a save," were frantically encored again and again. But the Prime Minister was wroth, and the Lord Chamberlain ordered the make-up of the actors, which was so marvellously like the originals, to be modified. Mr Gladstone does not appear to have been very sensitive on the matter of impersonations by comedians, and on one occasion, at any rate, he complimented a comedian on the correctness of his caricature.

Again, Mr J. M. Barrie's JOSEPHINE was passed, although it contained the most obvious political references. When Mr Shaw, however, essayed a political play, PRESS CUTTINGS, it was immediately censored. As is well known, the so-called rule prohibiting the representation of living persons on the stage has been on occasion broken with impunity. The difficulty has been that dramatic authors have never been able to foretell whether the rule will be broken in their case or not. To refer for one moment to Mr Shaw's position, it must be pointed out that JOHN BULL'S OTHER ISLAND, containing references to certain political personages, and in which a certain type of Liberal politician was gently ridiculed, was licensed without demur, and Mr Shaw had every reason for believing that another play of the same kind would be similarly received. In the case of PRESS CUTTINGS, however, the politicians ridiculed were on the other side in politics, and one can hardly wonder at Mr Shaw's bitter comment :

> "The objection is clearly to my politics, and not to my personalities. The fact is that I have to ascertain what the Censor's politics are before I know whether the play will pass. If he is a Liberal, apparently I have to ridicule Conservatives, if I ridicule politicians at all, and *vice versa*. It is exceedingly difficult to find out sometimes what the mind of the Censor is, or what his politics are."

There was also the case of THE ORCHID some years ago, in which a character made his appearance who was promptly accepted as representing Mr Joseph Chamberlain. Mr George Edwardes has asserted that there was really no resemblance to Mr Chamberlain at all, that he was only half the size of Mr Chamberlain to begin with ; but it is incontestable that theatre-goers as a whole recognised in this gentleman—who wore a monocle, was clean-shaven, was Minister of Commerce, wore an orchid in his buttonhole, was called Mr Chesterton, was an apostle of Empire, and sang a song about being "Pushful"—a presentment of Mr Chamberlain. We do not for an instant say that the rule prohibiting political caricatures is a defensible one ; but here was a case in which a licensed play transgressed what was asserted to be a rule of the Censor's office. The gist of the caricature lay, no doubt, in the make-up of the actor, and little or no caricature was to be discovered in the mere words of the play—further comment, if that were needed, on the futility of criticising a play on the strength of its written word alone.[1]

Arthur Roberts once produced a song at the Gaiety on Lord Randolph Churchill, who was referred to as Randy-Pandy. The song was objected to and was changed to Jack-a-Dandy, though the actor's make-up remained unchanged, and everybody recognised the impersonation. One line in the song, " A Churchill must be moral," was specially objected to by the Censor, and Roberts used to start singing, " A Ch . . . " ; then, pulling himself up nervously, would pointedly correct himself, " A *Noble* must be moral ! "

It is needless to point out that political and absolutely libellous personalities are still to be found on the legitimate stage of a nature independent of the make-up of the actor ; that is to say, of a kind which should have been detectable. Hardly a musical comedy makes its appearance without some more or less offensive reference to politicians, and these occasionally transgress any reasonable limit of good taste. Only a week or two ago we heard an actor in THE DOLLAR PRINCESS singing his wish to raise " Wales " of a different kind on Mr Lloyd George's back with a stick. We do not think songs such as this are really welcomed by theatre-goers, though they are apparently well received at the moment ; but the essential point is that representations of living

---

[1] It has very pertinently been pointed out that a play is to be defined as a story written and acted in dramatic scenes, with three collaborators —the author, the actor, and the audience. What a Censor reads and licenses is merely a piece of writing, and to assume that in examining such a scenario one is examining a play, is essentially foolish.

persons and offensive personalities do continually find their way on to the stage. It is probable that the very people who laugh heartily over the idea of thrashing Mr Lloyd George would be seriously offended if an actor of different political views were to introduce some song about " bashing Mr Balfour " or "lynching Bonar Law." It was very pleasant to hear Mr George Edwardes assure the 1909 Commission that, so far as his theatres were concerned, " on no account would a biassed political allusion be permitted." It need hardly be added that political allusions abound in songs and gags on the music-hall stage.

Where the satire relates solely to our own politicians it is difficult to see what pertinent defence of the rule can be made. It would be a big task to suppress ridicule by Act of Parliament. The cartoons of VANITY FAIR were for forty or fifty years atrocious satires of contemporary statesmen, and to-day practically every newspaper of note has its political caricature, in which considerable licence is taken with statesmen of the day. It is surely fairly obvious that so long as the political parties of this country are divided in anything like the present proportions, political references must, from the managers' and actors' point of view, involve questions of danger and delicacy. Nearly every political hit must be made at the expense of one half of the audience—and they, also, have paid. The political conditions which obtained in Walpole's time do not obtain to-day, and are not likely ever to recur. For this reason the rule is superfluous, and if it were not superfluous it would still savour too much of artificial protection of a class of men whose lives and actions are necessarily public, and are shaped largely by public criticism.

But even references to foreign politics have been permitted in circumstances where stringency might reasonably have been looked for. Proof of this is to be found in the following extract taken from a paper in 1896 relating to a performance of THE SHOP GIRL :

> "A remarkable demonstration showing the tendency of public opinion was witnessed at the Gaiety Theatre last night, at the performance of THE SHOP GIRL. One of the actors interpolated a remark, 'Why, you are as fond of interfering as the German Emperor.' Immediately from all parts of the house there was a burst of cheering, and it was several minutes before the demonstration sufficiently subsided to allow the play to proceed."

Some time later, in *The Daily Telegraph* of the same year, this appeared :

> "In the London theatres and music halls, as might be expected, opportunities are rather sought for references to the name of Dr Jameson, which everywhere evoke outbursts of enthusiasm with the utmost indifference to the international difficulties which his action has aroused. In a few cases allusions are made to the German Emperor, and then the popular response is of an altogether different character."

These political references to foreign affairs are in a category quite different from those solely concerned with domestic matters. It is reasonable to assume that a play introducing pointed political references might provoke outbursts of public approval capable of straining foreign relations during a critical period to breaking-point. Here, again, it may be remarked that a foreign nation would naturally attach greater significance to the incident from the fact that the play had been licensed by a court official, and to that extent stamped with court approval. The desirability of a stringent control[1] over such references is therefore obvious ; but in actual practice the sporadic operations of this rule have merely been provocative of farcical incidents.

The point we wish to make now is that no such control over the stage as a whole does in practice exist. We have already shown that these references have continually appeared on the legitimate stage, but the music-hall artist goes entirely uncensored. The writer of a sketch for a music hall might parody a foreign Power to his heart's content, unchecked, and the comedian, adding topical verses to his song night by night, has nothing to fear from the Censor.[2]

---

[1] This does not of necessity imply any control more formal than that of the ordinary management.

[2] The fact that the Lord Chamberlain has no jurisdiction over the music halls has repeatedly produced amusing incidents. Mr J. B. Mulholland mentioned a case before the 1909 Committee, in which Mr Redford wrote complaining that Mr Mulholland had produced an unlicensed play. Naturally the latter gentleman was concerned as to his licence, the theatre in question being his own. The play was a curtain-raiser, and the whole incident was unknown to Mr Mulholland personally ; but he made inquiries, from which he learned that the play in question had been performed for many weeks previously in different music halls, during which time it was allowed to work what harm it could unchecked. The fact of transferring it to a legitimate and serious theatre made its production a legal offence. Nothing could show more clearly how widely separated law and public policy have been in the control of the English stage.

At first glance the serious effect of a comic song on international politics would seem to be negligible ; but a song might be, and frequently is, much more potent in arousing feeling than a serious stage play. MacDermott's famous song,

" We don't want to fight, but, by Jingo, if we do,
We've got the ships, we've got the men, we've got the money too,"

aroused quite as much feeling as any political play has ever done, and if danger of an appeal to popular passion is in question, the risks would seem to be all on the side of the music hall.   Yet, in these houses, constituting the majority of the entire theatres in the country, the danger arising from international political references is, so far as the Censor is concerned, ignored.   There is, of course, a very practical check on the music halls, partly from public opinion and partly from fear of the disapproval of the local licensing authorities ; but the point to be made is that the actual protection afforded by the Stage Censor is negligible.

Foreign ambassadors have frequently intervened when popular plays seemed unduly scurrilous in their foreign references.   We have already referred to several such incidents ; but usually these matters can be remedied without any excessive formality. In June 1912 an article appeared in the Paris *Liberté* protesting against an Alhambra review and complaining that the permissible limit had been overstepped when President Fallières was shown on the stage wearing the ribbon of the Legion of Honour, while he was being made boisterous fun of and dancing the can-can with a girl. There does not appear to have been any deliberate intention to burlesque the French President in this case, and, as might have been expected, the Alhambra management promptly modified the actor's make-up.

We have said that this rule concerning political references has been productive of some farcical incidents.[1] Mr Tom Taylor has left on record an incident concerning a piece of his in which Mr Alfred Wigan represented a French naval officer, dressed, as it was

---

[1] Political censorship has had its humorous side in other countries also. After Orsini's attempt upon the life of Napoleon III. the Bourbonian censorship in the kingdom of Naples, which up to that time had already been rather too scrupulous and pedantic, became a real Argus, sniffing about everywhere and considering everything to be suspicious. It was, in 1858, in the San Carlo Theatre of Naples that THE MASKED BALL of Verdi was billed to be produced. In one of its scenes it presented the murder of a king. As a matter of course, after that Paris event the Censor suddenly and bluntly withdrew the permission for the performance, which had already been given, and in consequence the managers of the theatre asked the composer to adapt his music to a different libretto. As Verdi indignantly refused to submit to this strange demand, the management sued him for damages in the amount of 200,000 lire. Verdi, and with him the majority of the citizens, were highly excited at that. King Ferdinand's brother offered his services as a mediator; but this intercession would have necessitated Verdi's introduction at court, and as the composer was afraid the audience with the king might compel him to make material changes, and those to the worse, he flatly refused. For this refusal he was honoured in the city like a hero, and wherever he went in the streets people followed him with their "Viva Verdi!" A few months later this cry became the password of the populace, even in Rome. At every street corner the words were posted to the walls, and everybody knew their meaning. It was in Rome where finally the opera-manager, Jacovacci, succeeded in bringing Verdi's opera on the stage. The composer had, it is true, to rename every character of the play; Gustave III. of Sweden became a Count of Warwick; the Baron of Auckerstroem, a Count Renate; in addition some verses had to be changed; but the murder was there all right, as were the plot and the music. And the words, or rather the association of ideas, that had brought about the changed attitude? What really had been on the walls was: "Viva V. E. R. D. I."—Vittoria Emanuelo Re D'Italia.

said, as the Prince de Joinville. The Lord Chamberlain interfered, and the costume was changed ; but the only changes made were such as to make the costume more correct and to improve the portrait. Then there was the historic case of Gilbert and Sullivan's opera, THE MIKADO. After being performed for many years the Lord Chamberlain suddenly awoke to the unsuspected dangers in the piece, and forbade its further production, on the ground that it might give offence to our Japanese allies. Without any communication with the author at all, or any attempt to get him to modify the play in any way, it was simply prohibited, without anyone being able to raise a protest or claim a right. The stupidity of this incident lay in the assumption that a great foreign Power would attach any significance to a slight musical skit which had been running for twenty years. As a matter of fact, the music of THE MIKADO was being played by Japanese bands on the Japanese ships in the Medway during the prohibition of the play ! [1]

That the Japanese are not so frantically bigoted as our court officials feared was further proved by the reception of a later play, THE MOUSMÉ, in Tokyo in 1912. In spite of the fact that the play deals with the treachery of an officer of the Japanese Army and abounds in chaffing allusions to Japanese officialism

[1] " An amusing incident which would seem to heighten the absurdity of the entire affair occurred recently at Chatham, where the Japanese warship *Tsukuba* was lying. When Admiral Sir Gerard Noel, with the chief military and naval officers of the station, was entertained aboard the Japanese man-of-war, although these officers had issued imperative orders that their bands should not play any of the MIKADO music, it was with selections from this very opera that the band of the Japanese ship regaled them."—*Harper's Weekly*, 51-947.

generally, it was played in Japan with quite extraordinary success. The MOUSMÉ Company had the
distinction of being the first European theatrical
company to perform on the stage of the Imperial
Theatre at Tokyo, where it was received with great
enthusiasm. At Osäka, where the inhabitants are
almost entirely Japanese, the play was very warmly
received, the audience joining lustily in the " Banzai "
chorus, and calling for its repetition half a dozen
times.

We may mention here another incident supposed
to contain foreign political dangers. Count de Bornier
wrote a play on the subject of Mahomet ; it was a
poetic play, not an acting play, and Sir Henry Irving
was very much struck with it and wished to perform
it. He had long before wished to produce a play
on the subject of Mahomet, and the late Sir Richard
Burton was very anxious that he should. He accordingly bought the rights in the play, and had it prepared for the English stage by Mr Hall Caine. When
it was announced, a representation came, through the
Lord Chamberlain's office, pointing out that, inasmuch
as there were in Her Majesty's dominions so many
millions of Mahometans who would have been
" gravely offended " by any representation of the
Prophet put on the stage, the play could not be
performed. Now, if Sir Henry Irving had intended
touring this play among the Mahometan peoples of
the British Empire, we might have understood this
prohibition, but that a play should not be produced
in the West End of London because it might offend
Mahometan sensibilities on the other side of the
world, was a decision which illustrated English

officialdom at its brilliant best. We can only
wonder why pork was not prohibited to the English
Army for a similar reason, or Christianity suppressed
because a large number of British subjects were
Buddhists and Brahmins.

Then there was the case of a provincial melodrama called THE SECRETS OF THE HAREM. After
it had appeared for several years—not weeks or
months—the Lord Chamberlain suddenly withdrew
its licence. The reason given was that the play
was objected to by the representatives of a foreign
potentate in this country; it was understood that
somebody at the Turkish Embassy had seen the
play and objected to it. The sudden stopping of
the piece meant probably an all-round loss of several
thousand pounds to the proprietors; the whole of
the company was thrown out of employment at a
moment's notice, and the scenery, costumes, and a
number of heavy printing contracts thrown on the
manager's hands. Nevertheless, the Lord Chamberlain inflicted this loss on a holder of one of his
licences without, as Mr Raleigh put it, "turning a
hair or giving anyone a moment's notice." Neither
prayers nor protestations produced any satisfactory
response from him, and it was not until a number of
questions were asked in Parliament that the licence
was reissued on the understanding that the word
"Harem" should be omitted from the title. From
that time the play appeared under the title of
SECRETS —— —— ——. Everybody knew what
the three blanks meant and the incident became the
jest of the whole country; but the censorial dignity
and authority had apparently been vindicated in an

adequate manner. It need hardly be said that in its revised form the title was fifty times more suggestive and offensive than in the original, and the blank spaces of the poster became an attractive goal for the obscenities of passing schoolboys.

Another amusing case was that of THE ENGLISH-MAN'S HOME. When this piece of military propaganda was at the height of its fevered boom, the genial " Follies " proposed to skit it for one of their " Potted " series. The Censor of that time maintained that in his dealings with this skit he " obeyed instructions entirely," and that personally and individually he had nothing to do with the matter. However that may be, a telegram was despatched, " Am instructed to inform you that no skit will be permitted." The general impression which that telegram caused was that some influence had been brought to bear on the Chamberlain by those interested in fostering the military feeling which the play itself aroused ; it being perhaps felt that to permit any skit on the play would be to weaken the power of the original play as a dramatic tract. This, we say, was the current accepted explanation ; but the Comptroller of the Lord Chamberlain's department insisted that the skit was disallowed on the principle that the Censor was bound to take notice of plots or political allusions likely to cause international complications[1] or protest.

[1] This dread of " international complications " has made its appearance in other countries in connection with the stage. A masterpiece of censorship was once performed by the Turkish Censor, Nischan Effendi, on the occasion of the production of Shakespeare's OTHELLO at Constantinople. He " corrected " the drama so thoroughly as to leave hardly a trace of the original. Among other words, he expunged

The prohibition, he said, was imposed, not because the play in question was a patriotic one encouraging a desirable national object, but simply because of possible offence which the skit might give to a foreign Power. One would have thought that the original play was much more likely to give offence than any humorous skit on it; but the department evidently chose to reverse its customary rule of prohibiting serious treatment of a subject and passing a funny one. Most of the censorial bogeys have at some time or other been stood on their head in this manner. If the " Follies' " management had chosen to carry this part of their entertainment to a music hall each night, they could have done so without interference.[1]

Then again there was the case of Lola Montes, a piece written round one of the escapades of the notorious adventuress. The Lord Chamberlain passed and licensed this piece in the first instance, and it was played for two nights at the Haymarket Theatre. He then suppressed it; but a few days later it was sent in to him again with no alteration but a change of title to Pas de Fascination, in which form it made its continuous appearance. This was about

"Cyprus," giving ingenious reasons for this correction. "Cyprus," he said, "is a Turkish island; it would be politically unwise to send Othello to Cyprus, because the territorial integrity of Turkey is guaranteed by treaties. Why not put, instead of Cyprus, some Greek island, such as Corfu?" And thus it came to pass that, from respect to the Treaty of Paris, Othello had to go to Corfu!

[1] Such a case occurred in comparatively recent times. In 1905 a play, The Abode of Love, which was proposed to be acted at the King's Theatre, Walthamstow, was forbidden by the Censor. It dealt with the Agapemone business of Pigott. It was immediately afterwards presented at the Middlesex Music Hall, where the Lord Chamberlain ignored it entirely.

1848, and, curiously enough, this innocent trick appears actually to have been suggested by the Censor to the lessee. The only other alteration made was that whereas the King of Bavaria was supposed to have been alluded to in the first piece, on the second production he was simply made a Russian count.

A somewhat similar instance occurred in more recent times. In 1912 questions were asked in the House of Commons concerning the Lord Chamberlain's refusal to license a play, TRICKED, by Mr Laurence Cowen, although QUITS, another play by the same author, had been licensed ; the two plays being, it was said, almost identical in plot, except as regards the names of the characters and the localities. With this opinion, however, the Lord Chamberlain did not agree, though the similarity of the two plots may be gauged from the two synopses :

"TRICKED !	"QUITS !
" Refused a licence by the Lord Chamberlain, December 1911.	" Granted a licence by the Lord Chamberlain, February 1912.
"In this play, the scene of which is laid in a garrison town in Russia, the wife of a student sentenced to death for an assault on a military officer, in order to save her husband's life yields herself to the general in command of the troops, who has, in such event, guaranteed the condemned man's reprieve. Her sacrifice is in vain, for her husband is shot, and she strangles her betrayer the following morning."	"In this play, the scene of which is laid in London, an actress, the wife of a struggling actor, who is committed to prison for debt on the eve of his appearance in a new play which is to give him the chance of his life, yields herself to a dramatist-manager, from whom she obtains the money—some £37— to secure her husband's freedom in time to fulfil his engagement. She stabs her betrayer dead the following morning."

The essential understructure of the two plays is, it will be seen, almost identical. Indeed, so far as moral questions are concerned, the one actually licensed would seem to be less acceptable than the one banned, in so far as in the first play, TRICKED, the treachery of the betrayer is a workable justification for his subsequent murder.

Another rule that has continually caused ill-feeling among dramatists has been that prohibiting reference to Scriptural characters. There is nothing whatever in the Act of 1737, or the subsequent one of 1843, to justify the Censor in refusing to consider a play merely because it dealt with a Scriptural theme. Nevertheless, Mr Donne stated, " I never allow any association with Scripture or theology to be introduced into a play," and Mr Redford went so far as to state that plays founded on or adapted from the Scriptures were " ineligible for licence " in Great Britain.

The Censor's attitude in Mr Redford's time is fairly well illustrated by the following letter :

" DEAR SIR,—I have no power as Examiner of Plays to make any exception to the rule that Scriptural plays, or plays founded on or adapted from the Scriptures, are *ineligible for licence* in Great Britain. It would appear from your letter that your play would come under this rule, and I may say for myself that I am glad to be relieved of the difficult and delicate duty of deciding on the fitness of treatment in each particular case."

A precisely similar letter was sent in 1902, when

Mr Laurence Housman submitted his Nativity play, BETHLEHEM, for licence. The curious point is that in the previous year, EVERYMAN, a play in which the figure of God Himself appears and speaks upon the stage, had been publicly produced with great success without leading to any breach of good manners, decorum, or the public peace—the only terms of the Act of 1843 under which a play of religious character could legally be prohibited. Mr Laurence Housman's play was prohibited on other grounds than those of offensiveness or impropriety. As the Censor himself said, " It was not a question of propriety at all. It traversed the custom." Nevertheless, when asked to explain why BETHLEHEM was prohibited, and EAGERHEART, which introduced very much the same characters (Our Lady, St Joseph, and the Holy Child), was permitted, the Censor retraced his footsteps. " Every case must be judged on its merits, and every case is looked at from its merits."

SAMSON AND DELILAH, after being prohibited for a great many years, was suddenly licensed,[1] proving to be, in the Censor's own words, " the most popular opera of the season." Evidently, therefore, these positive statements of the Censor, that Scriptural plays were " not eligible," were not generally applicable, though up to the present date it has been impossible to obtain a statement of any reasonable principle on

[1] Common gossip (which is given for what it is worth) concerning this incident was to the effect that a certain highly placed personage had expressed a desire to see the piece performed, and that a licence was accordingly issued. We have no reason for believing that the inherent offensiveness of the piece was modified in any other way than by this influential approval.

which selection has been made. Custom and precedent have been the ruling deities of the Censor's office ; what one Censor described as " the unwritten law." But no statement of that law, and no justification of its fiats, has ever yet been attempted. Dramatists do not know what treatment of religious subjects will or will not be permitted. One moment they may be told that Scriptural plays are ineligible for licence in England, and a few moments later they may discover a very similar play going gaily on its way unchecked. The effect of these capricious actions has been to rule out the whole Biblical field from the playwright's scope.[1] It is impossible to write with any assurance, no matter how serious the treatment, that the play will escape the ludicrous ban of the Censor. It is surely time that the causes of religion should cease sheltering themselves behind so puerile a guard as that of the dramatic Censor. The Church has at all times been over eager to claim the protection of the law against irreverence and contempt ; but the theory of life or thought which cannot face frank discussion and even ridicule, must not hope to survive long in an age which questions every claim and challenges every opinion. It is not the function of the State to protect any code of thought or morals from the natural fluidity of public opinion.

---

[1] Mr Stephen Philips, the author of HEROD and PAOLO AND FRANCESCA, wished to write a play around King David, but was debarred because he knew the Censor would not pass that play. Many other modern dramatists find themselves in the same predicament. Nevertheless, there are many pieces dating from earlier times, such as George Peel's DAVID AND BATHSHEBA, which might be produced without licence as "old plays."

Mr Israel Zangwill's NEXT RELIGION was refused a licence in January 1912. The play tells of a Church of England clergyman who has doubt regarding individual existence after death, the personal dispensation of Providence, and so forth. He founds a new religion, based on a recognition of impersonal and universal law. His hope is that this new religion will need no building made with hands, no paid priesthood, and no mechanical ritual. Sure enough, however, no sooner is the new religion founded than up goes a new temple, dedicated to the now-canonised millionaire who had supplied the money, while the clergyman himself is led round in the robes of a High Priest, at the end of a procession. Meanwhile the lay friend suggests :

> "The next religion ! Before we've worked out the last ? What have you found more beautiful or uplifting than the words of Christ ? And this religion has the advantage of being already organised—it carries the inspiration and the consecration of centuries. . . . Then verify it, scour it, bring it back to the Founder. Perhaps Christ's own religion has never had a chance—perhaps that's the next religion."

According to Mr Zangwill, the Censor did not object to any character or the drift of any argument, or anything vital to the plot of the play. What he objected to were incidental phrases and opinions which the author was asked to alter. For instance, he objected to the phrase, " Christ comfort you," asking for the substitution of " Our Lord comfort you." This was really in the best style of Herbert, Buck, or Colman. Another phrase which was objected to was : " The real Good Friday would be that which brought the cure for cancer." Other passages which the author was asked to delete were : " The God who will send Tuberculosis even through the Communion chalice " ; " That shrine of superstition in Westminster " ; and " I've got my eye on a workmanlike little place in a commanding position with a ten-year lease—it was in the Baptist line before." In the last passage the Censor suggested the substitution of the word " Nonconformist " for Baptist.[1] Mr Zangwill admits that he allowed the actors to express beliefs—not necessarily his beliefs— which might shock an orthodox person of this or that denomination ; but the orthodox views are duly and sincerely represented, and there is nothing that treats of religious matters in a frivolous spirit. " No objection is raised," said Mr Zangwill, " when people treat for frankly spectacular purposes an old faith which the majority of the spectators do not hold to— as in THE MIRACLE—but when I write a play about genuine living beliefs and try to present some serious thoughts about them, the author of DEAR OLD CHARLIE must needs be allowed to exercise his blue pencil at my expense." It is worth adding that the play could not be objected to on the grounds of

---

[1] The isolation of censored passages, though occasionally necessary in a book such as this, is perhaps a little unfair to dramatists. Such passages without their context appear to bear an abnormal significance ; but no intelligent reader will need reminding that contrast is essential, and if no speeches are to be allowed in a play save orthodox and moral ones, the characters would assume a drab uniformity. True, the villain might carry a distinguishing label.

so-called morality, for it contains no sex interest of any kind.[1]

It will be seen that the modern practice of the Censor's office, which prohibits the discussion of Scriptural problems, is even more stringent and bigoted than obtained in 1559. The Queen then issued a proclamation, it is true, to the effect that no plays should be permitted " wherein either matters of religion or of the governance of the Estate of the Commō Weale shalbe handled or treated"; but she did at any rate qualify that prohibition, " but by menne of aucthoritie, learning and wisedome."

This continual ban upon criticism of what the Censor decides to be " orthodoxy " would have been by this time, one might have thought, intolerably insulting to intelligent professors of religion, for this nursery coddling merely suggests that orthodoxy cannot reply to such criticism by itself. The whole question of Scriptural plays has become extravagantly stupid. Mr Zangwill was careful to state that " the orthodox views are duly and sincerely represented." But suppose those orthodox views had not been re-presented at all ? Or suppose the play had been devoted solely to criticising them ? On what grounds can the State at this period attempt to stifle criticism of religious doctrines which are held by a minority ? The only reasons which have so far been given are that a great many people might find such criticisms or representations shocking to their sense of reverence,

---

[1] Mr Zangwill has not subsequently modified THE NEXT RELIGION so as to get a licence, but a well-known actress, who wishes to produce it, recently wrote to him : " If it were any use, I'd ask you on my knees to omit the few lines the Censor objects to and let it be played."

their religious susceptibilities might be offended, and so forth ; or, alternately, that such plays might lead to public disorder. We may retort that much is said in clubs and smoking-rooms every night which might shock people of narrow religious suscepti-bilities ; but there is no question of legally remodelling conversation in those public places to the level of what religious people would approve of. Such people, to the comfort of everyone, simply seek a congenial atmosphere. Further, it must be pointed out that no important advance has been made in any individual branch of human effort without shocking someone. It is only by shocking the theories and beliefs of yesterday that we shall clear the way for the better theories and beliefs of to-morrow. There are hundreds of thousands of books which are violently antagonistic to the orthodox beliefs in England to-day ; but it is not compulsory on any believer to read them ; he has full liberty to ignore other people's opinions or not, as he wishes. If Haeckel offends a devout but voluntary reader, it is the reader who is at fault for reading, and not Haeckel for venturing to differ.

The same liberty must apply to the theatre. If the Salvation Army should decide to write and stage a play dealing solely with their evangelistic methods, Catholics would have no right to demand the pro-hibition of the play because it offended their suscepti-bilities. They would, of course, have a right to stay away from the theatre ; and so long as citizens have that right, it is absurd to insist that nothing shall be done by one small body of writers likely to shock the susceptibilities of another small body of quite voluntary spectators. We are aware that the question of "orthodoxy" is involved here. But we cannot understand how the State ever expects artificially to support reverence in opposition to public taste. If there is not a public for irreverent plays, that fact will quickly become evident. If, on the other hand, there should prove to be a public for plays of that description, it is hard to see how the State has a right to intervene, or can, indeed, effectively intervene.

When Mr Shaw's MAJOR BARBARA was submitted, there was some discussion between the Censor and Mr Barker as to the advisability of passing that play. The Censor asked if Mr Barker thought that the feelings of the Salvation Army would be outraged by its being put upon the stage. This makes a very pretty little companion picture to Mr Larpent saying that "Government did not intend that Methodists should be ridiculed." Fortunately, however, Mr Barker was able to say that he had been in communication with the Salvation Army, and that, so far from their feelings being outraged, they regarded it as an excellent advertisement, using that word in its best sense. We mention the incident here, particularly, because of the solicitude shown by the Censor lest the Salvation Army should be outraged.

Now, again, we must draw a companion picture. This time the play in question was DEAR OLD CHARLIE. In that play a reference occurs to a prohibited play, by Mr Bleater, called SEWAGE ; Bleater, according to Mr Robert Harcourt, " being a colourable imitation of Barker, and connoting something mean, something ridiculous, and SEWAGE connoting filth and waste." Here was a case of something certainly calculated to outrage the feelings of Mr Barker ; but in this

case the Censor did not trouble to inquire as to Mr
Barker's feelings on the matter, or, what is more
probable, failed entirely to see the point of the
reference.

When Hauptmann's HANNELE was first performed
in German, at the German Theatre in London, the
Censor licensed it with the condition that the character of the Stranger who appears in the play should
not be made to represent the conventional pictures of
Christ. When it came to producing the same play
in English at the Afternoon Theatre, the Censor was
very loth to license it ; but in the end he agreed to
let the German licence be regarded as a licence for
the play, and nothing further was said about it. The
only practical result of the negotiations was that the
Stranger should be clean-shaven, and the play was
ultimately allowed and produced amidst a chorus of
approval from religious journals and the Salvation
Army. Mr Whelen, who tells the story, is of
opinion " that, for the Censor to have prevented for
some years the production in England of the play
HANNELE, was a very mischievous act indeed on his
part." In a letter on the subject the Censor wrote :
" Hauptmann's HANNELE was licensed with a caution
as to representing Christ on the stage, etc., for St
George's Hall (German plays) in 1901. I am inclined to think it was never produced ; but an
English version would have to be submitted : but it
does not follow that a play licensed in German
would be licensed in English. I should say that it
would be most difficult to translate and adapt for the
English stage and would only appeal to the highly
cultured." If the latter clause were assented to,

would that, we wonder, constitute a reason for censoring the play?

The quibble over the likeness to the Christ is equal to the rest of the censorial eccentricities. The stereotyped conception of Christ is a purely imaginary one. It has in all ages been open to any artist to paint a personage with that particular cast of face, and to any author to describe Him. Quite recently the manufacturers of cinematograph films have given popular representations of Christ on the conventional lines; but where the stage is concerned the Censor fatuously steps in with a prohibition of these imaginary features. The Stranger must use a razor, he says, lest religious susceptibilities be shocked. One wonders of what kind these religious susceptibilities are which can be disturbed by the absence or the presence of hair on an actor's chin, and something dangerously near contempt comes to us at the thought that a responsible official can have so grotesque a conception of what religious reverence implies. What would happen, we wonder, if one of the several men in England who strongly resemble the stereotyped features of the Christ, was to be a drunkard? Would anyone seriously suggest that he should be forced to shave to save religious susceptibilities? Religious reverence would really not be affected by any such trifle.

Mr Pigott, to some of whose eccentricities we have already referred, was harried by this same bogey of religious reverence. "Some scandals I have been obliged to prevent," he once said, and further investigation showed that the scandals he had in mind were such terrible things as a representation of the

Ober-Ammergau Passion Play in London and the placarding of the town with the title of a sensational drama which he thought would be offensive to the religious susceptibilities of the public. The irreverent title, which was not fitting for display in our public thoroughfares, was GOD AND THE MAN. "The play," said Pigott, "was good enough ; but the title was what was objected to. Exhibited all through London it would have given offence to many people, and it was quite unnecessary." If anything could be prohibited simply because it had "given offence to many people," we should have no Censor.

Mr Shaw wrote THE SHOWING UP OF BLANCO POSNET for His Majesty's Theatre, and it was accepted for production at the Afternoon Theatre. It was then submitted in the ordinary way to the Examiner of Plays, and he, following a frequent practice of his, returned it direct to Sir Herbert Tree with a private letter, the object being apparently to avoid having the play brought officially before him. On the matter being taken further, however, the Censor indicated a number of passages which he said were blasphemous. Many of these passages he waived after discussion ; but finally the position resolved itself into a statement that the play would only be licensed on the withdrawal of specific passages. Mr Shaw was willing to make some changes and emendations, but toward the end came to the conclusion that the alterations required were altogether too drastic, and refused to be a party to further mutilation of his work.

Mr Shaw has himself described BLANCO POSNET for us :

"It is a very simple and even crude melodrama, with absolutely no sexual interest whatever. It represents a little community of violent, cruel, sensual, ignorant, blasphemous, bloodthirsty backwoodsmen, whose conception of manliness is mere brute pugnacity, and whose favourite sport is lynching. Into this welter of crude newspaperised savagery there suddenly comes a force—not mentioned in THE MERRY WIDOW—to which they give the name of God, the slightest regard for which they make it a point of honour to despise as mere weakness of character. That force nevertheless, at the crisis which is the subject of the drama, makes them do its will and not their own in a manner very amazing to themselves, and, I should hope, not altogether unedifying to the spectators. I am given to understand that the introduction of this force into my play as a substitute for the simple cupidities and concupiscences of THE MERRY WIDOW is the feature that renders the play unfit for performance. It was precisely the feature which made the play worth writing to me."

The corrections which the Censor insisted on were puerile to a degree. Apparently he expected this crew of backwoodsmen to employ the polished periphrases of educated people. He condemned a number of phrases as blasphemous, and instructed that the following omissions be made in representation: "He hasn't finished with you yet. He always has a trick up his sleeve." "He's a sly one. He's a mean one. He lies low for you. He plays cat and mouse with you. He lets you run loose until you think you are shut of him, and then, when you least expect it, he's got you."

The interpretation of what is blasphemous has in England often been on a level which must make any broad-minded critic blush for shame. Even under the present state of our blasphemy laws a couple of ignorant policemen can, with a little equally ignorant help, succeed in getting a man branded by a police conviction merely for venturing to express in public his honest opinion on certain theological dogmas. In this respect our protection of the Christian tenets is on the same enlightened plane as the savage protection given to the rites of *ju-ju* worship. The explanation of these archaic remainders is not hard to discover. There is something in the English character inherently hostile to newness and change. We have sense enough to appreciate the value of new varieties and " sports " in horticulture or agriculture, but not in personal culture. In that realm England abhors change and quickly brings some punishment or other to bear on the offender. In England genius achieves its destiny in spite, and not by the aid, of public recognition. Mr Ford Madox Hueffer has told us something of those days—forty years ago—when there was a demand being made in this country for the prohibition of Wagner's new music. " Blasphemy was the charge alleged against some of the earliest upholders of Wagner's music in this country. This may seem incredible, but I have in my possession three different letters from three different members of the public to my father, who,

A reproduction of part of the last folio of a manuscript play, now in the British Museum, showing the Censor's licence to act. "*This SECOND MAYDENS TRAGEDY (for it has no name inscribed) may with ye reformacions bee acted publikely.* 31 *October* 1611.— G. BUC.*" Particulars of the "reformacions" referred to will be found in the text.

from the early seventies to his death, was the musical critic of *The Times*. The writers stated that unless Dr Hueffer abstained from upholding the blasphemous music of the future—and in each case the writer used the word blasphemy—he would be respectively stabbed, ducked in a horse-pond, and beaten to death by hired roughs."

The Censor's strange apprehension as to the evil effects which might follow from the production on the stage of some Scriptural or holy personage is, we are confident, exaggerated, and what few instances have occurred justify that belief. A few years ago Mr Hall Caine wrote a play in which he introduced the Pope. The play was, strange to say, licensed, though, to quote Mr Hall Caine, "how that fact was accomplished baffles my comprehension." Before the production of the play in London a provincial tour had been arranged ; but immediately after the first-night production of the play the manager of the Dublin Theatre wired saying that under no circumstances whatever could he allow the Pope to be represented on his stage. He said that if he allowed it there would be a riot and the theatre would be wrecked. In such a case, apprehensions as to the conduct of an Irish audience were perhaps not unreasonable ; but the producers were determined to carry out their programme, and the play was duly sent to Dublin. Everything went well with the performance down to the moment when the Pope entered. Then, instead of there being a riot and disturbance, the whole house rose and cheered the Pope for five solid minutes. "From which," adds Mr Hall Caine, "I judged that the fear of disturbance arising out of religious plays is generally a bogey."

Another interesting rule of the Censor's office has been that relating to the performance of old plays. It is interesting to see what the precise official attitude is in these matters, for Mr Redford's evidence before the 1909 Commission was confusing. We have already seen that it has been a fetish with some Censors, from Sir Henry Herbert's time on, to claim the right of editing plays already licensed by their predecessors. Herbert bluntly insisted on the right, partly because of the additional fees involved, and partly because, in his own quaint phrase, such authors were granted by previous Masters of Revels " greater licence than is allowed them by me." How far the fee question has influenced latter Censors is obscure ; but George Colman certainly objected to much that was to be found in Shakespeare's plays, and would willingly have undertaken the task of Bowdlerising them had he thought such a process would have been tolerated. There must be something strangely exhilarating in the functions of Examiner which can give any man courage or assurance to think himself capable of playing sub-editor to these old masterpieces. Just as the habit of speaking without contradiction produces a curious academic stupidity in some parsons and schoolmasters, so the exercise of unrestrained powers over the drama seems to produce feather-brained conceit in the Examiners of Plays. The fact that he occasionally has hardware transactions in connection with pictures does not usually inspire a picture-dealer with a fatuous belief that he could put improving touches to the work of Titian or Rembrandt.

When Mr Redford was asked how the Restoration drama stood in the matter of censorship, he said that it was " not legally necessary to send such plays to him, any more than it is with regard to Shakespeare's plays, which are not submitted. It is assumed that they are licensed." In the case of EVERYMAN, the Scriptural play which we have already alluded to, it transpired that the Censor actually recommended that the play should not be submitted ; that it should come under the heading of Shakespearean plays. " Take a play of Congreve," he was asked. " Can a manager produce at the present moment a play of Congreve's without submitting it ? " " It would come under the same head," said Mr Redford, " as Shakespeare's plays, I should say." Nevertheless, in answer to another question as to whether the Restoration plays of Wycherley, Congreve, and so on, would have to be submitted, Mr Redford said : " If they were performed they would have to be submitted."

All this is, as we say, decidedly confusing ; but, as a matter of fact, when Mr Philip Carr was producing old English plays at the Royalty Theatre under the organisation of the Mermaid Society, and wanted to produce Congreve's WAY OF THE WORLD, the play was returned to him by the Censor with a letter saying, " This being an old play is presumably already licensed for representation." The position, then, would seem to be this, that the Restoration drama, which, as it was the wittiest, was also the grossest of any period in our dramatic history, can to-day be performed without being previously submitted to the Censor. No sane author would waste his time writing a modern play half as suggestive and outspoken as these Restoration plays, and yet we are assured that the same audience would be irreparably injured if they saw these milder modern plays, before the Censor had officially disinfected them.

It was rather strange to see Mr Forbes Robertson ranging himself with those who would submit the masterpieces of our language to the meddling hands of some interfering Chamberlain's clerk ; but he stated before the 1909 Commission that the " acting edition of an old play should be submitted to the Reader before production." Those who have any respect for the history of English letters must regard such a process as similar to instructing a navvy to take his pickaxe and purify and castrate the Greek statuary in the British Museum. Frank Harris once said that if Shakespeare lived in our time, he would certainly be called an immoral dog, and his books would be lost, especially if he started off on his literary career, as he actually did, with the most sensual love-song in the world. Certainly there would have been a number of jealous parsons eager to suppress his work, or at any rate Bowdlerise it of that so-called coarseness, which Ruskin tells us is to be found in all the greatest English writers, is one of the marks of the true English spirit, and without which we never get the richest fruit of English literature. Even to-day there are a good many who feel themselves competent to polish and improve Shakespeare's works.[1] Like Ground Ivy, they think that " Shakespeare was a pretty fellow and said some things which only want a little of my licking to make them do well enough." But in politics we do not allow fools to govern, nor in questions of literature should they be permitted to exercise their vicarage quills on national treasures. We certainly should resent an Examiner of Plays putting his apprentice touches to Shakespeare's work ; but, as Medley says in THE HISTORICAL REGISTER, " As Shakespeare is already good enough for people of taste, he must be altered to the palates of those who have none ; and if you will grant that, who can be properer to alter him for the worse ? "

In any attempt to outline the rules which have guided the Censor in recent years mention must be made of his prohibiting a ragging scene in one of Mr Cecil Raleigh's plays. At that time, eight or nine years ago, there was a good deal of ragging going on, and it occurred to Mr Raleigh to deal with such a case on the stage. When the matter came to the Censor's ears, however, he objected, and said he could not have a ragging scene produced ; his instructions were not to allow ragging, and the word " ragging " must not be used. However, after some negotiations, a representative came from the Lord Chamberlain's department to inspect the rehearsal, and took exception to an incident in which an officer, while he was being ragged, drew his sword. The Lord Chamberlain insisted that under

---

[1] Nothing is sacred to the irreverent fingers of complacent fools. Tomkyns, the Censor of literature in 1667, pompously decided that he could not approve of certain tendencies in Milton's PARADISE LOST.

no circumstances, it did not matter where, would an officer who was being ragged use a weapon. While this controversy was actually in progress, a ragging case occurred on board one of His Majesty's ships. A young midshipman was ragged at mess, and was told on another occasion that he was to be ragged again. Being apparently of that vicious disposition which defends itself when attacked, he whipped out his revolver and fired. Here then was an actual case of an officer using a weapon while he was being ragged, so the objection to an officer being represented as drawing his sword was waived on one side and disappeared.

When in January 1912 the Pioneer Players proposed performing THE CORONATION, a new one-act play by Mr Christopher St John and Mr Charles Thursby, those engaged in its rehearsal were amazed to hear that the Lord Chamberlain had found in it something detrimental to the public interest. The play is an attack on the burden of armament and on the present social system. A king on the way to his Coronation realises that the cost of armament weighs heavily on the people. He remembers that before the crown is placed on his head he must swear to uphold his people and defend his poor from oppression, and, suddenly realising his opportunity, he refuses to allow the ceremony to proceed until an autocratic Cabinet consisting of the head of the army, the head of the navy, and the Prime Minister have made certain concessions. The whole play is strongly in favour of peace. The king and the nation in question were entirely imaginary, the king was an idealised and glorified one.   Nevertheless, without any reason being given, the play was prohibited, the communication stating that, "after taking the advice of his Advisory Board, he (the Lord Chamberlain) had been unable to grant a licence for THE CORONATION."

The Chamberlain's ban led to the usual farcical sequel.   Those who had purchased tickets for the performance were promptly nominated members of THE CORONATION Society, so that the performance became technically a private one.   A prompt protest appeared, signed, among others, by Ellen Terry and H. G. Wells, in the following terms :

"SIR,—May we, through the medium of your columns, call the attention of dramatists to the risk they run by introducing royal personages, even of the ZENDA variety, into their plays ?

"A one-act play, by Christopher St John and Charles Thursby, entitled THE CORONATION, and dealing with an entirely imaginary episode in the life of an entirely imaginary monarch of an entirely imaginary country, has been refused a licence by the Lord Chamberlain 'after taking the opinion of his Advisory Board.'   The grounds on which the Advisory Board came to their decision are not stated.

"The imaginary monarch in question happens to be an excellent person—so excellent, indeed, that, if by some impossible chance he could be mistaken for some existing ruler, the existing ruler would probably be flattered by the supposed resemblance.   The obvious conclusion, therefore—since Royalty is presented in so attractive a light—is that the offence consists in the mere presentation of a king.

"We submit that, if this rule had always held good, our dramatic literature would be considerably poorer than it is. We are aware that there is a precedent — the case of THE MIKADO—but it will be remembered that the prohibition in that case was speedily withdrawn.

"The action of the Lord Chamberlain does not, of course, prevent the private production of the piece ; neither does it prevent the public from contaminating their minds with the text of the play—which was published in book form some months ago.

" Yours faithfully,

H. G. WELLS.	E. F. SPENCE.
C. CHAPLIN.	CICELY HAMILTON.
ALIX EGERTON.	J. FRED. GREEN (Sec. Inter-
AUSTIN HARRISON.	national Arbitration and
ETHEL SMYTH	Peace Association).
(Mus. Doc.).	ELLEN TERRY."

The actual performance took place before an enthusiastic and distinguished audience, and at the conclusion, amidst some excitement, a resolution was passed, with only one dissentient, " That this house, after seeing the play called THE CORONATION, is of the opinion that the conduct of the Lord Chamberlain, in refusing to license the play, is wholly unjustifiable, and desires to put on record its protest against the refusal." Apparently the reason for the prohibition was that the Censor regarded it as an offence to introduce a king, even a magnificent and a brave king, on to the stage. Some disastrous gaps would be left in our dramatic literature if this rule were followed with approximate consistency. HAMLET and HENRY VIII. would only be two out of some hundreds of plays which would be relegated to a waste-heap which might prove big enough and potent enough to overwhelm the Chamberlain's office and all its works. Apparently English monarchy and English morals rest, in the Censor's judgment, on so slender a foundation that a little plain speaking would prove fatal to both institutions.

There had been a somewhat similar incident in the same theatre only a month or two before, when Mr Laurence Housman's PAINS AND PENALTIES was banned. The reason given by the Censor was that "it was inadvisable to put upon the stage so recent a royal personage," the play itself dealing with the trial of Queen Caroline. During an interval in the performance Mr Granville Barker and Miss Elizabeth Robins appeared before the curtain and addressed the house, which turned itself into a public meeting and passed with much enthusiasm a vote of censure on the Lord Chamberlain, there being only two dissentients out of some two thousand people. The occasion was also taken to criticise the appointment of Mr Charles Brookfield, the resolution being as follows :

"That the audience gathered to witness the production of Laurence Housman's forbidden play, PAINS AND PENALTIES, is of opinion that if the statement is true that Mr Charles Brookfield has been appointed Reader of Plays, then, in view of Mr Brookfield's recent published opinions on the modern drama, the action of the Lord Chamberlain is but further proof—if proof is needed—that he is hopelessly out of touch with the theatre, over which he exercises despotic control, and that a continuance of his legalised tyranny is inimical to the drama's welfare and good name."

In both the foregoing cases the position was all the more absurd in that the plays themselves had been published in book form some months before, and neither play contained anything in the least objectionable to any reasonably well-balanced mind. It ought not to be necessary to say at this time that we have long passed the period when kings were regarded as something superhuman and divine, and no courtly Chamberlain with discreet finger on lip can ever bring that period back. This excessive timidity on the subject of stage Royalties is as little flattering to the good sense and patriotism of the nation as it is to the ability of the monarchic régime to justify itself.[1]

[1] The prohibition of KING LEAR for thirteen years during the malady of George III. is in a different category, though whether that prohibition had any more practical value than an expression of respect and sympathy may at any rate be questioned.

CHAPTER IX

THE BAN ON SEX

But, of course, the bogey of the English Censor has not been the Scriptural play, has not been the political play : the battle of the censorship has been fought around the question of sexual drama in England. To anyone who attempts to take a philosophical view of the situation the average English attitude towards sexual questions is profoundly humiliating. Physically the most vigorously developed of the nations, England is also one of the most sensual. But the instinctive love of all that is beautiful and poetic, which redeems the sensuality of the Latin races, is fundamentally lacking in this country.[1] Ethnographically, the more southern races should have a larger share of hot-bloodedness ; but the frank recognition accorded to this phase of human nature by those races has produced a better balance and a saner outlook than we in this country can boast. For two centuries now

[1] Gladstone said that he had the strongest conviction "that all English industry has been defective in the matter of beauty and the quality which we generally hear that important element described as under the name of taste." In almost every English manufacture this defect can be traced ; it has been a formidable hindrance in competition with foreign goods. We make good solid articles, but they are ugly. Mr A. B. Walkley of *The Times* has, however, asserted " that the importance of all art in this country is very greatly exaggerated." Mr Walkley doesn't seem to have been conscious that he was actually illustrating the truth of Gladstone's criticism.

we have resolutely closed our eyes as a nation to certain phases of human instincts. We have called on Church and State to exorcise the demon of animality, and, failing in this—lamentably failing in this, as every student of his England must admit,—we have banded ourselves into associations for denying the thing that is. In no country has the satisfaction of the sensual instincts been degraded into the slimy, loathsome thing it has become in this England of ours. Generations of Puritanism have deprived it of its primal purifying fire, of its natural perfume, of its loveliness and lovableness. Instead, we have degraded it into a national obscenity, a thing of dark places, of shame and disease. The old pagan cleanliness and sincerity have left us entirely. England walks among the nations ridiculous and self-sufficient, waving as banner an inadequate fig-leaf and praising God that she is not as other nations.

This loathsome pruriency finds its outlet in scores of ways. The story of the Italian curator who runs to cover the museum statues with fig-leaves before he lets in the English tourists, is something more than a myth; it is a symbol. We laugh at the story and then promptly clamour for our own officials to do something equally obscene. Where else is a public to be found so eager in discussing the " immorality " of inoffensive things as in England ? We betray a lewd and hypocritical delight in scraping over our real or imaginary sores, which can only be attributed to the physiological inflammation due to suppression. We find the same influence working in scores of directions. Booksellers sit in judgment on our novels, prescribing what may or what may not be regarded as safe for us. Nowhere will a statue be scanned more eagerly for hints of our beloved "indecency" than in this country, and, when discovered, nowhere will it be more avidly investigated. We are as a nation sex-obsessed, and the most beautiful work of art may pass ignored, unless some prurient individual can find traces of obscenity in it.

Even innocence itself does not escape. We blush and correct the indiscretions of a happy child on the hearthrug. We have spent so long in deliberately ruling out sex from our national life that we are now only able to think in sex terms. The human body is no longer a God-like thing made in the image of its Creator, but a thing of shame and indecency, to be mutually concealed and suppressed. It was not in a comic opera, but in Great Britain, in the year of our Lord 1909, that a harmless poster representation of a baby's back was solemnly adjudicated on by a town council and ordered to be concealed. Anyone who believes that all this inflamed zeal runs in company with essential purity of thought or sanity of outlook need only bear in mind the obscene doggerels and drawings which face him at every turn where his fellow-men have found themselves secure in a few moments' seclusion.

It is under this befouling propriety that the modern stage has suffered most. The Censor, who must be assumed to be acting for "the slowest boy in the form," has had his eye most vigilantly on offences against propriety and morality.[1] It is, as

[1] "The most absorbing task of the censorship is that of barring the way against French immorality. Its vigilance is eluded, however, by a kind of conventional terminology. Where our authors have had the

we have repeatedly had occasion to point out, only in recent days that the censorship has seriously assumed the task of taking charge of the nation's morals, and it is questionable whether even now the legal constitution of the office justifies any such claim. The terms of the Act of 1843 provide that it shall be lawful for the Lord Chamberlain, whenever he shall be of opinion that it is fitting for the preservation of good manners, decorum, or of the public peace so to do, to forbid the acting or presenting of any stage-play. Lord Gorell has given it as his opinion that the Censor has only the powers which are specified by the Act, so that apparently the only grounds on which the Censor could justify any incursion into questions of pure morals would be under the term of "good manners." In the old Act of 1737 the matter was left entirely to the Lord Chamberlain's discretion, and it was in this respect mainly that the Act of 1843 modified the situation. Mr Redford, it is true, stated that "the words have become much more elastic in recent years"; but though this may apply to the Lord Chamberlain's reading of the Act, the legal position of the Act itself remains unchanged, and has been modified in no particular whatever. The actual form of licence granted by the Lord Chamberlain [1] certifies that the play "does not in its general tendency contain any-

effrontery to write the word 'cocotte' in black and white, they replace it by the word 'actress.' Where we have unblushingly written 'adultery' they have inserted 'flirtation.' The Censor gives his sanction and pockets his fees, and, on the performance of the piece, the byplay of the actors and actresses completes the translation, re-establishing, if not reinforcing, the original sense."—AUGUSTE FILON in *The English Stage*.

[1] See Appendix.

thing immoral or otherwise improper for the stage."
There does not seem to be any justification for the
use of these terms, and the power of discriminating
in this way does not appear to be granted by statute,
and to this extent the licence is not given pursuant
to the Act. Moreover, the licence, in a memorandum, states that "no profanity or impropriety
of language is to be permitted on the stage, no
indecency of dress, dance, or gesture, no offensive
personalities, representations of living persons, or
anything calculated to produce riot or breach of the
peace." It is at any rate doubtful whether these
so-called regulations could be upheld legally, and it
is worth noting that so high an authority as Lord
Gorell has stated that if the Censor refused to pass
a play, except on a ground that he could justify, the
author would have a legal right of appeal, though
a difficulty might arise over the interpretation of the
statute term, " good manners."

But however slender the right of the Chamberlain to exercise his discretion on questions of morality,
the fact remains that in practice plays have been
mainly censored on these grounds. Shelley's CENCI
has always been prohibited on the English stage,
though how such a play can by any stretch of
imagination be regarded as immoral passes our comprehension.[1] The objection was, presumably, in the

---

[1] "In those days to have a play censored was not considered the
honour it has since become; on the contrary, people were rather
ashamed of it. The fight really began in earnest with the well-known
case of THE CENCI, with which you are probably familiar. But few
people know the conclusion of that skirmish. It is amusing because
it shows the humiliation of pioneers when things get difficult. After
the play had been produced at the Grand, Islington, by the Shelley
Society, the Lord Chamberlain threatened to take the licence away of

words of the late Sir W. S. Gilbert, that the subject was " not a fitting and proper one for treatment on a public stage." THE CENCI is not a cheerful play, but a public wishing for salacious thrills would certainly find it a bad exchange for some of our lighter musical comedies.

When the management of Drury Lane submitted LA DAME AUX CAMELLIAS, the Censor concluded that it was of too inflammatory a nature to be released on the English public. But the Italian opera, LA TRAVIATA, practically the same play, was for some occult reason licensed. The refusal to license LA DAME AUX CAMELLIAS was intelligible, though not justifiable ; but the subsequent licensing of LA TRAVIATA reduced the whole situation to a farce.

Ibsen's plays for a long time lay under the

any theatre manager who produced it in future. At that time I had the Avenue Theatre (now the Playhouse). I had reopened it in '92 with THE DOLL'S HOUSE, but Nora (Miss Achurch) became in the first week terribly ill, and after nursing the play a couple of weeks with a substitute as Nora, the business was so poor we had to close. My lease of the theatre ran for some time longer, and having nothing to lose at the moment, upon the Society approaching me, I willingly offered to give them the use of the theatre. It appeared that in doing so I had unwittingly done an unexpected and even unkind thing. For the Shelley Society had exhausted their funds, which had never been very large, and had expected an apotheosis in a halo of glory consequent on every manager in London having refused them an opportunity of doing THE CENCI."—CHARLES CHARRINGTON.

[Among those who witnessed the play at the private performances at the Grand Theatre were Robert Browning, George Meredith, and James Russell Lowell. *The Academy* once defined those who were calling for the abolition of the censorship as " faddists, afflicted with the mania for the unclean," and probably the writer of that definition could really convince himself that such men as Browning, Meredith, and Lowell were merely desirous of wallowing in uncleanness when they patronised THE CENCI. This method of disposing of opponents has certain advantages which dwarfed intelligences always appreciate.]

censorial ban. Long after Ibsen's position in modern letters had been widely recognised in England, the Censor still opposed his shocked and obstinate personality between the British public and the great Norwegian author. Mr Pigott, indeed, seemed to find Ibsen merely contemptible, and volunteered before the Commission of 1892 the following piece of criticism :

> " All I can say is this. I have studied Ibsen's plays pretty carefully, and all the characters in Ibsen's plays appear to me morally deranged. All the heroines are dissatisfied spinsters who look on marriage as a monopoly, or dissatisfied married woman in a chronic state of rebellion against not only the conditions which nature has imposed on their sex, but against all the duties and obligations of mothers and wives ; and as for the men, they are all rascals or imbeciles."

Mr Redford, when dealing with a similar question, on one occasion wrote, " Ibsen's Ghosts was refused by Mr Pigott, and will never be licensed." [1] Mr Courtney, when asked by the Select Committee, " If Ibsen had been an Englishman and his plays had never been performed outside of England, and they had to be submitted to the test of the Censor here, he possibly would have been vetoed ? " replied, " I am perfectly certain that he would have been." No one who has followed the history of censorship could have any doubt on the subject. Without the leading example of other more

---

[1] Nor has it.

intelligent countries to influence official opinion here, Ibsen as a dramatist would have been smothered out. It is not necessary to be an ardent admirer of Ibsen to deplore such a conclusion. The mere fact that one of the few men with an international reputation as a dramatist would have been immediately snuffed out by an irresponsible court official is sufficiently damning in itself.

Maeterlinck's MONNA VANNA fell under the censorial ban on account of—according to Mr Redford—"the immorality of the play." The whole plot of this play, Mr Redford said, was not to his mind "proper for the stage." He added, "Our decision was almost universally upheld." The *Athenæum*, however, was of contrary opinion :

> "It will grieve the lovers of all arts, but astonish no one accustomed to the ineptitudes of the Censor, to learn that the MONNA VANNA of M. Maeterlinck has had to be confined to a private entertainment. . . . Once more the caprice of our Censor brings contempt upon us and makes us the laughing stock of Europe."

That that opinion was not unique was proved by the fact that immediately after the production of the play at the Victoria Hall, Bayswater, under impossibly bad stage conditions, a public protest was sent to *The Times*, headed "Maeterlinck and the Censor," signed by such names as Thomas Hardy, George Meredith, Charles Algernon Swinburne, etc. One well-known journal said, "Whatever may be the individual estimate upon the merits of MONNA VANNA as literature and drama, it requires the bat eyes of the Censor to be blind to its high-mindedness and the exquisite sense of feminine purity with which it is charged. . . . The interdict pronounced upon it is less of an affront to M. Maeterlinck than to English intelligence."

M. Maeterlinck himself has testified to the extraordinary reception which the' play has had on the Continent. Writing to Mr Zangwill in 1909, he said :

"It is impossible for me to recall the total number of performances of MONNA VANNA in Germany. They must exceed three thousand, seeing that the theatres of all the towns, from the tiniest to the capital, have maintained the piece in their repertory. It is almost the same thing in Austria-Hungary and in Russia, where I am told six different translations circulate. So far as I know, there has never been any question in Germany or Russia of the morality of the piece. On the contrary, it has been remarked that, when all was said, the piece exalted the sincerity and truth of love, which cannot well be open to censure. I remember, however, that a critic in Frankfort or Hamburg took offence at the fact that Monna Vanna is nude under her mantle. It was rather judiciously pointed out to him that we all, men and women, might be nude under our last garment without the modesty of anyone in the world ever taking alarm."

It was indeed this last scene which seems to have been too dangerous for English morals. It will be remembered that Monna Vanna, to save the inhabitants of the town, accepts the terms of the commander of the invading army and goes to him in his tent, naked under her cloak.[1] This situation even Mr Bram Stoker described as "in all ways thoroughly meritorious, I think." Monna Vanna not only leaves the camp unharmed, but unharmed because the hero is represented as being very much in love with her, and the whole idea of the play is that love is not only not identical with, but is the enemy of, lust.

The idea of a heroine appearing in a cloak, under which she was nude, was more than the inflammatory English imagination could bear. Such a spectacle would presumably send immorality raging through the nation like a pestilence. It is difficult to make adequate comment. As M. Maeterlinck has said, one would have thought that we all, men and women, might be nude under our last garment, without the modesty of anyone in the world ever taking alarm. There are, it must be supposed, even in this country, a small dissolute minority who have actually gazed on naked womanhood without suffering moral shipwreck thereby. We are supposed to view the exhibition of women in tights without national disorder, and we did not hear of any increase in the immorality statistics of Coventry when Lady Godiva recently revisited the town, nude, not under a shape-

---

[1] "Now, if the lady came on in an ordinary dress with a cloak, there cannot be any possible objection to it; but when it is described to the audience that she has nothing but the cloak on, *they naturally form the idea that the woman is nude* (!). That is a very harmless suggestion in itself, and yet a very important one when you consider what might be done."—BRAM STOKER.

less cloak, but under very confidential fleshings. Yet when an author incidentally brings a shapeless mass of drapery on the stage and the audience learns that somewhere in its obscure recesses a naked woman is supposed to be concealed, the scene becomes intolerably exacting on self-restraint. To what extent is an author expected to guard against the immorality of an audience's imagination ? Are Englishmen really incapable of passing, say, a bathing machine on the beach, or a hotel bathroom, without deriving harm from the thought that it perhaps contains a naked female ?

But the most ludicrous phase of the matter has to be mentioned. Another play, THE DEVIL, was duly licensed, containing almost an identical scene—" an extremely vulgar play," according to Mr Forbes Robertson. Questioned as to why MONNA VANNA was censored and THE DEVIL passed, Mr Redford said, " There was not the smallest analogy between the two plays. The one is a literary work, and the other is a flamboyant, lurid piece of stage business ! " No wonder that Mr Harcourt remarked, " The literary work is censored and the flamboyant piece of stage business is passed ? Is that your condition ? " Mr Redford contended that this was not the principle on which he acted ; but it is notorious that some such principle as that does seem consistently to have guided our Censors in their selections. The tendency has always been to censor the serious responsible treatment of a subject and license a frivolous comedy scraping thoughtlessly over the same ground. Providing an author was sufficiently funny he might transgress any or all of the supposed rules of the

Lord Chamberlain's office.   Before the Commission
of 1866, in dealing with the prohibition of caricatures of politicians on the stage, it was mentioned
that the elder Matthews once represented O'Connell,
the explanation given being that " it was allowed by
the Lord Chamberlain because it was so exceedingly
funny."   Sir Herbert Beerbohm Tree has told us of
a case in which he had a French play by a distinguished author to produce, and after taking the
theatre and engaging a company, was told that the
play would not be permitted.   " I went to see the
Lord Chamberlain on the subject, or the officials,
and I was told that it was rather terrible.   But I
said, 'The play is not immoral,' and they said, 'Yes,
it is.'   I said, 'A play is only immoral or moral in
so far as its tendency is moral or immoral'; and I
was told that it would be unacceptable—the subject
was adultery—but, *if it could be made more comic, it
would pass.*"   It is not possible to conceive a more
damning indictment.   One can imagine a Censor of
this calibre coolly handing back OTHELLO to Shakespeare with instructions to put in a funny man or
two and make it more comic.

This willingness of the Censor to pass any indecency so long as it was treated frivolously and
giggled over, has been one of the sorest points with
serious dramatists.[1]   In fact, it would not be too
much to say that the only plays which have emerged
in recent years likely to give offence to people of
sane moral outlook, are those which offer no shred of

[1] "It is only the serious dramatist who, in the present state of
public feeling, can be called to account for immoral teaching."
H. A. JONES.

justification for their existence other than that of causing amusement. Stated baldly the position thus becomes ludicrous. One may break all the censorial commandments carelessly and irresponsibly, and so long as it is done to the accompaniment of clownish gesture and music or wit, the Censor will license it as moral and proper for the stage. But a responsible author who attempts to interpret life dispassionately, with some serious purpose of advancing or broadening contemporary morality, is refused a hearing and branded as immoral. Prostitution? exclaims the Censor.—Never! Prostitution *and* Puns?—Why, certainly!

All this has had one result. The English stage at the present moment is being strangled with the soft ribbons and silks of frivolous musical comedy. We do not suggest for an instant that musical comedy is bad; in these modern days some form of brainless relaxation is a necessity. Nor do we say that the average musical comedy is indecent in any reasonable interpretation of that abused word. Far from restricting it, we would be inclined to give it as much licence and freedom as the public chose to permit. Our contention is, not that musical comedy is inherently bad, but that it is taking too large a share of our dramatic life. We may have no objection to chocolate éclairs, and yet despise the man who is willing to suppress every other dish in their favour. Musical comedy has brought to the English stage in recent years, in quite disproportionate numbers, a brainless, good-looking, superfluous sort of people who threaten to monopolise our evenings and belittle our dramatic traditions.

We are not anxious to see the actresses who can fill rôles entirely superseded by those who can fill tights. A lady with a pretty pair of legs has always had an enthusiastic reception from English theatre-goers, and we have no desire to quarrel with so popular a taste. But we may enter a plea against the extermination of the serious drama altogether. Some day we hope the English public will be less inflammable and content to regard the theatre as something more than an annex to a chemist's shop. When that day comes, it will be well to have kept alive the more serious branches of dramatic art. Meantime, the author who has only genius and a good play must not expect too much.

Authors of the more serious school have not hesitated to say that some of the musical comedies in recent years have been more flagrantly indecent and immoral than anything they themselves would have dreamed of staging. They complain that immorality *has* been tolerated, providing it was fluffy-headed and brainless ; and the Censor's vagaries in this direction have been bitterly criticised. It may be that what the Censor passes is not in itself immoral or indecent. Here, again, we have to refer to the fact that what the Examiner reads is in no sense a play, but merely a book of words. In the case of a serious drama the Censor finds in that book of words all its inherent " improprieties " set down plainly, and in most cases the further acting of the play does nothing to accentuate their effect. But in the case of the musical comedy there may, in the book of words, be nothing which could be stigma-tised as indecent or improper ; while the actual staging

and acting of the play may evoke a thousand unsuspected suggestions. There may be improper
songs or gags, improper gestures, dresses, dances, or
emphasis, none of which are likely to operate in
the case of the serious play, but which, in themselves, are capable of producing an ensemble of
genuine impropriety. Here, obviously, the serious
author is at a disadvantage. His play may be, by
any fair standard, less "improper" than the musical
comedy, but all his "improprieties" are submitted
to the Censor. It was once said of Henry James
Byron that he never offended the most delicate ear ;
but that he nevertheless did more than anyone else
to lower the standard of stage morality.

For obvious reasons it is not desirable to mention
plays specifically which have been regarded as improper, and, indeed, we should be slow to apply that
term in any narrow sense to musical comedy ; but
cases have occurred where the Censor has licensed
a play which has subsequently been condemned by
high authorities. There was, for instance, the case
of THE GIDDY GOAT, over which a libel suit was
fought. The defendant was a dramatic critic who
had expressed " disgust for such stuff," and described
it as an " enormity." The author brought an action
for libel, and the court awarded him a farthing
damages, thereby virtually endorsing the view of the
critic. Mr Justice Ridley, in charging the jury,
said : " The jury were not bound by what the
Licensing Authority did. It was not for them to
criticise him ; but neither could he complain if a
play he had passed was found on representation to
be improper. . . . They must, however, remember

that the play which was criticised was not the play as it passed the Licenser ; it then contained passages which were worse than any left in." And Mr Justice Ridley added : "I am still more surprised at the Lord Chamberlain. I say so without hesitation."[1] There have been numberless musical comedies which have—let us be moderate—contravened the code of morals which the Censor has imposed on serious playwrights ; but it is neither necessary nor desirable to specify these by name. We repeat that in this fact playwrights find a serious grievance.

But let us return to the censorial interventions on the ground of sex. Mr Charles Charrington has told a very amusing story, which is worth repeating :

"Long, long ago, before stage societies or independent theatres saw the light, my wife (Janet Achurch) and I used to give matinées of plays not popular enough to meet the demands of the audiences who went to the theatre in the evening. In the 'eighties the English stage lived almost entirely on adaptations from the French, and we were so far in the fashion that on more than one occasion we chose a French play to produce.

"Among them was Octave Feuillet's JULIE.

---

[1] In June 1912 Mr Moul of the Alhambra was sued for refusing to allow a certain sketch to be staged at the Alhambra. He described the sketch as "most objectionable, and a farrago of coarse rubbish." The judge, in giving judgment for Mr Moul, said he should be strongly inclined to agree with Mr Moul's description of the sketch. "I desire to say," he added, "that I am not sorry the court has been able to support a music-hall management in raising the character of its performance. I am surprised that the Lord Chamberlain's department should have passed some of the stuff contained in the manuscript."

Having a particularly severe moral tone, it was, of course, too much for the Censor. However, we were young and ardent in those days and not easily beaten. So we made, after great efforts to understand each other on both sides, a working compromise.

" Between the first and second acts of the play the heroine " falls," as the Censor *would* put it, and the whole of the last two acts depends on the remorse she feels for an act of unfaithfulness which at the end of the play she confesses—the excitement bringing on a heart attack that kills her. Husband and lover meet over her dead body.

" The compromise took this shape : Julie was to say somewhere—never mind where— ' Thank God, I have only sinned in intention.' As it made complete nonsense of the whole play, perhaps Miss Achurch may be excused for not saying it very loud. But she *did* whisper it, and no doubt it is still in the copy which reposes upon the shelves in the Censor's office."

Mr Shaw's plays have, as might have been ex-expected, fluttered the censorial heart. Mrs Warren's Profession was promptly and completely banned, a course which can only be justified by people who have not seen the play. It was taken to America, trailing its censorial slur behind it, and before it was produced, created in the United States an impression that it must be hideously indecent. Americans are naturally aware that a good many plays passed by the English Censor are not moral and are not decent, and the inevitable conclusion was that Mr Shaw's play must be a horrid example of vice. In consequence, the worst elements of New York attended its performance in crowds. There were almost riots outside the theatre, and fabulous prices were paid for seats. Mr Hall Caine, who was staying outside the Garrick Theatre in New York at the time, has described the crowd which assembled, and the arrest of the entire company, actors, actresses, and the manager, who were marched off to the police court. Of the chief of police of the district, who was to sit as arbiter over the fate of this drama by one of the most distinguished of living literary men, Mr Hall Caine says: "I made inquiry about this gentleman, the chief of police, and I found that he had risen to his present rank by his skill in catching thieves and rogues and vagabonds; but it did not appear that he knew anything about the drama, or that he had any knowledge of the Ten Commandments outside their interpretation in the criminal code. But there he was, doing this work."

The magistrate decided to adjourn the case, because, he said, he would have to read the play, and he publicly expressed his extreme loathing of the unpleasant task before him. At the next hearing he, in Mr Shaw's words, "exhibited a certain amount of temper which, one would almost think, suggested disappointment. He said that he had read the play, and there was not in it what he had expected it to contain." The final result was that the defendants were acquitted by the decision of the court, in which it was stated that there is nothing in the words themselves or in any particular phrase or expression which can be said to be indecent, and that the court was compelled to resort to the theme and motive of the play to find the indecency complained of. " It must be said for the playwright," proceeds the decision, " that he has in this instance made vice less attractive than many other dramatists whose plays have escaped the censorious attention of the police. His attack on social evils is one which may result in effecting some reform." Since then the play has been permitted all over America ; in this country, however, the original stigma which the Censor cast has remained, and Mr Shaw is very commonly regarded as a writer of indecent and improper plays. At the risk of being tedious we must repeat that the Censor has repeatedly lacked the intelligence to discriminate between the beggar who exposes loathsome sores from cupidity and the physician who uncovers the same sores for the purpose of healing them. When he has been in doubt, it has been the mere flaunter of disease who has had the benefit of it.

Fortunately, however, as is well known, there are means of securing, in spite of the Censor's refusal, a certain amount of publicity for serious plays. By these means MRS WARREN'S PROFESSION has been produced in this country, and these performances have at any rate convinced spectators of the injustice of the Censor's ban. The play is far from being a masterpiece, and a literary agent would probably say that it was not " quite nice," but how it could be regarded as in any way provocative of immorality only a Censor could explain. As a reviewer has said, there is not a leer or a nasty laugh in it. In its present form we must assume that it is " not sufficiently comic." The trouble is that Mr Shaw's property in the play has been wrecked,[1] and his reputation soiled, while any profit which might legitimately accrue from the work seems destined for his executors. Mr Shaw cannot even imitate the author of THE GIDDY GOAT and bring an action for libel against his traducer. It may be assumed that Mr Shaw is as sensitive as the average man in the matter of his reputation. A good reputation is at least as necessary to him as to a minister or a bank clerk. It is as

[1] " The prosecution in America was so far successful that it ruined the management. When a manager has spent a considerable sum in hiring a theatre and producing a play, and he is stopped by the police after the first night, it is no consolation to him that the courts declare after a long interval that the police were in the wrong and he in the right : he is ruined all the same. I myself, in addition to the loss of author's fees, had to forego fees on other plays to the amount of £1000 to alleviate the situation. Later on the play was taken up by Miss Mary Shaw, who, not very long ago, published an account of the whole business in one of the American magazines—I forget which. She took the play on tour in the United States, playing the part of Mrs Warren herself. There was also a tour in which Miss Rose Coghlan played the title part ; and this Company was on one occasion arrested under a local by-law, and warned to leave the town. Except for this incident the play was not interfered with. It was also played to some extent in the stock houses ; but as I have had no applications for licence to perform for some years past, I conclude that it made no special mark. In short, as far as England and America are concerned, the play has been effactually killed by the censorship.

" On the Continent it was very successful in Berlin. I am told that it is also played a good deal in Holland ; but as there was no international copyright with Holland until very lately, I have nothing but hearsay to go upon. The same remark applies to Russia. It has been produced in the Imperial Theatre in St Petersburg. Some of the St Petersburg critics ridiculed it as a goody-goody sample of English Puritanism. At the recent technically private performance by the society called the Pioneers, it seemed to me already old-fashioned in its stagecraft, and left the audience wondering why on earth it had been banned."—G. BERNARD SHAW.

important to him that the quality of his work should not be impugned recklessly as it is to the maker of bridges or bread. The fatuity of the position is that all the other artisans have a legal redress for libel.

This phase of the matter has always been regarded officially as a very simple thing. Before the 1892 Commission Mr Pigott said : " The essence of my office and its advantage to the art and professors of the stage is that it is preventive, and, above all, secret ; if authors, whose plays are rejected, choose to advertise themselves and their rejected plays in the hope of getting other orders for similar pieces, that is their affair, not mine." This was a delightfully simple way of disposing of the matter ! Presumably no one would write a play offensive to Mr Pigott except from the basest motives, and no author would protest against his decency and morality being impugned unless it was "in the hope of getting other orders for similar pieces." One is inclined to get a little hot at reading such intolerable impudence ; but it is, after all, the logical result of giving a commonplace individual autocratic and unrestrained powers.

Before the 1909 Commission Colonel Sir Douglas Dawson, Comptroller of the Lord Chamberlain's department, seemed to find the matter almost as simple. " Let the author submit his play through the manager within a reasonable time ; if any alterations appear necessary to the Censor, the manager can, if he and the author choose, smooth over the difficulties privately with the Examiner beforehand ; or, failing this, it may be arranged when submitted to the Lord

Chamberlain and Comptroller, in which case the play is assured production ; or, if the negotiations are futile, it is refused and no one need be any the wiser."[1] Of course no one need be any the wiser, if the troublesome author will only behave like a good boy and acquiesce in the destruction of property on which he has perhaps spent months of hard work. It can be carried into a back-office and simply burned, and even the office-boy need know nothing of the incident. That is, of course, assuming that the troublesome author does not feel aggrieved and impelled to ventilate that grievance. Normally, a mere author will accept quite eagerly the assurances of a real live Lord Chamberlain and a Comptroller that his work is all wrong and unfit for publication. Two such gentlemen must be better judges than he on the matter, so a well-dispositioned author will bow respectfully and thank them for hiding his obscenities from the public gaze. We like the picture !

Mr Edward Garnett's THE BREAKING-POINT was another play which the Censor refused to frank. It is not necessary now to outline Mr Garnett's tragic and moral story, with which most playgoers are familiar, either through private performances or the book. Mr Garnett naturally felt incensed that an

[1] This amiable summary spirit has had more vigorous, but not less logical, exponents in other countries. We are reminded of a Scandinavian author, the writer of a political book, who was compelled to choose between being beheaded or eating his manuscript boiled in broth. Isaac Volmar, who wrote some spicy satires against Bernard, Duke of Saxony, was not allowed the courtesy of the kitchen, but was forced to swallow them uncooked. Still worse was the fate of Philip Oldenburger, a jurist of great renown, who was condemned not only to eat a pamphlet, but also to be flogged during his repast, with orders that the flogging should not cease until he had swallowed the last crumb.

Scene by Hogarth from Gay's Beggar's Opera.

Examiner who could pass so many musical comedy
indecencies should profess himself unable to tolerate
a serious tragedy like THE BREAKING-POINT. He
wrote inquiring the reason for the veto. In reply
he received the following highly informative letter,
which was marked *Private* :

"*5th July* 1907.

> "DEAR SIR,—I trust you will absolve me
> from any discourtesy if I point out that my
> official relations are only concerned with the
> managers of theatres. It is always painful to
> me to decline to recommend a licence, and in
> this case I hoped to avoid any possible appear-
> ance of censure on anyone by suggesting
> privately to Mr Harrison the desirability of
> withdrawing this piece. I cannot suppose that
> he has any doubt as to the reason.—I am, dear
> sir, yours faithfully,   G. A. R."

Now, the faults of this epistle are not confined to its
English. The insulting refusal to acknowledge the
existence of a mere play-writer was consistent with
censorial traditions ; but it was surely unnecessary,
having deigned to acknowledge the author's existence,
to make the suggestion that after all Mr Harrison's
and Mr Garnett's consciences ought to tell them why
the licence was refused. Again, why should a public
Censor try to avoid "any possible appearance of
censure on anyone," since that is his sole *raison
d'être* ? Authors as a class certainly do not wish
this false kindness, which merely suggests that they
have done something shameful. Mr Garnett wisely
refused to recognise the privacy of an official com-

munication from a State department, and pointedly asked the Examiner, " Is it possible you really imagine that any intelligent person feels the slightest stigma in your disapproval, or would be at the smallest pains to conceal from the world the fact of his having incurred it ? "

It is not necessary to heap comment on an incident which carried its own damnation so clearly ; but we would refer once more to that last sentence in the above-quoted letter, with its quiet suggestion that Mr Frederic Harrison, who wished to produce the play at the Haymarket Theatre, was trying to sidle something past the Lord Chamberlain, knowing it to be moral contraband. The point is hardly worth discussing, to those who know anything of Mr Harrison ; but what he actually thought of the play may be gathered from his letter to the author :

> " There is no money in THE BREAKING-POINT for a run, because the general public sets its face stubbornly against sad plays. And yours is more than sad. It is tragic. . . . I should be proud to introduce your dramatic work to the public or to that section of the public *which is alive to what the theatre might be.*"

When Tolstoi's THE POWER OF DARKNESS was first introduced to the Censor, some difficulty was raised over licensing it. According to Mr Whelen, Mr Redford for a long time resisted giving a licence. " I saw him and had a long talk with him, and the upshot of the talk was that he did pass the play. He said that he thought the play was very sordid in its realism." It was ultimately produced without any alteration. Tolstoi, we may assume, would have been another dramatist who, had he had the fortune to be born in this free land of ours, would have been waved back from the stage.

Mr Granville Barker's WASTE was another play which the Censor put his official foot on. He first of all wrote to Mr Barker and demanded general alterations. On being asked to specify these, he replied in a letter that it was not necessary to indicate particular lines, but Mr Barker must be prepared to modify the extremely outspoken references to sexual relations. Mr Barker replied that he considered, in such a play, sober plain speaking to be the only course ; that innuendo would be indecent, and that while he naturally could not admit that he had written anything unfitting to be spoken in the theatre, and it was difficult to delegate his responsibility in such a delicate matter to the Censor, still, if the objectionable phrases would be specified, he would consider their alteration. To that, says Mr Barker, " he paid no attention whatever. You see that it was clearly impossible for me to reply to a vague accusation, because it would have been admitting that I had written something of which I was ashamed, which I considered was indecent—and that an author cannot do. I pointed out to him that it was difficult to delegate my responsibility to him, in case the play was produced, by cutting out certain lines or certain things which he disapproved of."

The Censor further demanded that Mr Barker should eliminate entirely all reference to a criminal operation. The stupid part of this prohibition was that only a few months before, at the Court Theatre, Mr Barker had produced, under the Lord Chamberlain's licence, a play, the plot of which apparently turned upon a criminal operation which was quite openly referred to on the stage. In writing WASTE, therefore, it was quite impossible for him to know that any reference to this subject would be made a definite reason for refusing to license the play. That play does not require praise or justification from us. By means of the unpleasant subterfuge which has to be resorted to in such cases, the play was shown to a select and critical audience, and so conservative a critic as Mr A. B. Walkley of *The Times* wrote of it :

> " It is a work of extraordinary power dealing with some of the most fundamental facts of human life with an unflinching truthfulness, and, at the same time, blending those facts with certainly the most vivid and probably the most authentic presentation we have yet had on the English stage, of great social and political questions that come home to all Englishmen's business and bosoms."

What Mr Barker could have done to enlist the benevolent approval of the Censor was to have written WASTE in such a way that Mr Edmund Payne, Mr Harry Tate, or the White-Eyed Kaffir might have taken a leading rôle. The English Censor's appreciation of serious moral drama has always been stimulated by a liberal helping of bladder and peas.

When Sudermann's MIDSUMMER FIRES was submitted to the Censor in 1906 it was duly licensed ; but on the licence, which was addressed to the manager of the Scala Theatre, was endorsed, " Omit in representation Act III., page 28 : *Marikke*—If you follow a girl such as I am into the cellar, then surely she knows, or at least thinks she knows, what your intentions are." That passage was duly cut out ; otherwise the play was performed according to the author's original draft. One cannot avoid speculating as to what object was served by cutting out this solitary passage. Usually censored passages taken without their context appear fifty times as offensive as they normally are (even a tooth from one's own mouth seems offensive when removed from its proper surroundings) ; but how Marikke's naïve statement could be regarded as dangerous to the morals of the community passes our comprehension.

Niggling prohibitions such as this are about equivalent to the art critics prohibiting the use of blue to the more serious-minded artists. In a parallel circumstance they might say, " We know such a colour exists, directly or indirectly it forms the topic of half the conversations in the world ; but some of us have agreed to deny the existence of such a colour, and you must paint without it, and secure your contrasts and effects as best you can. We know that half the artists in England are allowed to use that colour almost as freely as they wish, but then, you see, they are not in our power." Imagine the directors of a hospital telling students of physiology, " We simply won't have you touch the lower large intestine. We know a large proportion of human troubles commence there ; but we don't think it is a fitting subject for study or discussion." The inevitable result would be that in time this censored spot would become the chief seat of disease, and would ultimately result in unbalanced specialisation and over-emphasis. There is an obvious moral.

One of the plays which succeeded in earning the official benediction of the Censor, but which subsequently came in for a great deal of discussion, was Mr Brookfield's DEAR OLD CHARLIE. Mr W. L. Courtney has described it as " a play which brought a blush to several cheeks, even of hardened ruffians like dramatic critics." And another critic, Mr William Archer, gave it as his opinion before the 1909 Committee, that it was a play which, if censorship existed at all, decidedly should have been stopped. The original French story was purchased by Mr Hawtrey, who engaged Mr Brookfield to adapt it for presentation in the English theatre. On its appearance at the Vaudeville Theatre in 1908 it was somewhat severely criticised. It is, we think, undeniable that much of the vigour of that criticism was due less to the inherent features of DEAR OLD CHARLIE than to the absurdity of it being licensed, while such plays as WASTE or MONNA VANNA were censored. The *Morning Post* frankly said : " We do not for a moment say that it should not have been licensed ; we do say that it makes it more than ever difficult to imagine why such a play as MONNA VANNA should have been prohibited." In general its reception ranged from lukewarm approbation to unmitigated abuse. One journal described it as " a Palais Royal piece of the rankest type."

The incident was brought to a more acute stage by the appointment of Mr Brookfield in November 1911 as Joint-Examiner of Plays with Mr Redford. Instantly a storm of protest was raised. It was contended that Mr Brookfield's sympathies were in favour of just the kind of play which was causing the deterioration of the English stage. He had, it was asserted, failed to show any sympathy with the more serious and advanced dramatists, and had further assisted toward the production of a number of plays, many of which were indisputably frivolous, and, in the judgment of others, immoral and indecent. The appointment was considered all the more offensive because of an article, written by Mr Brookfield, which appeared the same month in the *National Review*, in which, writing of the theatre, he said :

> " I think the influence of the theatre, either for good or for evil, is much exaggerated ; but if a young person could be harmed by seeing a play, I think it would more probably be by a sombre dissertation on the right of a wife to desert a degenerate husband—or one of the many kindred topics so dear to the new dramatists [1]

---

[1] Mr Brookfield once satirised the "new drama" in the following lines :—

My lords and ladies in the stalls, good people in the pit,
I want to give a short address, that is, if you permit.
I am sure that you will, all of you, support me when I say,
How very much we've purified the drama of to-day.
In olden times the melodramas bristled thick with crime,

—than by a frivolous burlesque of ill-sorted marriages such as one finds in the old French vaudevilles "; and he added, " particularly of those which have been adapted and played over here with the licence of the Lord Chamberlain. I cannot for the life of me see how they can be deemed demoralising."

The whole article was read as revealing an attitude decidedly hostile to the most vital forces at present influencing British drama.

The matter advanced still further when it was announced in the height of the controversy that the play in question, DEAR OLD CHARLIE, would be revived by Mr Frank Curzon at the Prince of Wales's Theatre to afford the public a fresh opportunity for judgment. Opinions differ as to the reception the play received. The audience showed both approbation and dislike, and it was suggested that the calls for the Censor and the epithets which were showered on the play were not altogether spontaneous. *The Times* wrote of it : " There really cannot be two opinions about the cynical, shameless immorality that underlies the play—none the less cynical and shameless because it is conveyed by innuendo, by double mean-

---

With murder, drink, and forgery, and people doing time.
But the history of ladies who go morally astray
Is the motive of the elevating drama of to-day.

Refrain.

There's nothing in the plays to-day a maiden mustn't see,
    The commandment that they turn on's not the seventh,
But that excellent and very philosophical decree
    Which is popularly known as the Eleventh.

ings, by nods and winks." The main trend of news-paper criticism was unfavourable to the play.

In our judgment the whole incident was given an undue importance. We are not of opinion that marital infidelity, on which the play turns, is so phenomenal a thing in England that its presentation on the stage is likely to produce a national scandal. What is intolerably offensive is that a play which deals with such a situation frivolously and irrespon-sibly should be selected for the stage, while others which take a graver view of the moral questions involved should be suppressed. It was once again the question of these themes being treated funnily ; Mr Brookfield and the author he translated had succeeded in being sufficiently comic.

As for Mr Brookfield's appointment as Joint-Examiner, we may usefully remember the example which Colman set. Colman was, as we have seen, " a careless, immoral author " in his youth, but immediately he took up the Censor's pen he became a very rigid and scrupulous Puritan. Perhaps no Censor made more frantic efforts to keep the drama in full dress and on its best behaviour than Colman did, and it may have been with a brilliant appreci-ation of this fact that the Lord Chamberlain recommended the appointment of Mr Brookfield. And, of course, it may not.

In February 1912 Mr Eden Phillpotts's THE SECRET WOMAN, billed for performance at the Kings-way Theatre, was banned. The play had had a successful reception as a novel ; had, in fact, run into three editions without raising a breath of protest, and the Censor's action in attempting to suppress so sincere and fine a piece of craftsmanship roused another storm of protest. The following letter appeared in *The Times*, signed by twenty-four distinguished authors :—

"We, Mr Phillpotts's fellow-writers, have read this play, and find it to be the conscientious work of an artist doing his best in his own way. . . . To our mind the play is worthy work, such as a stage of high aims should ever be ready to welcome, and we feel a warm indignation over the stigma cast by the Lord Chamberlain upon an author whom his fellow-writers and the English-speaking world generally have for many years held in admiration and esteem. Never in all these years of novel-writing has a word been breathed by any responsible person or paper against his fair fame ; but the moment he has the ambition to write a play in the same spirit that inspired his novels he is at the mercy of an official who knows no better than to serve him thus.

"Mr Phillpotts is the victim to-day, but of course it may be any of us to-morrow. Many of us have never written plays, though most of us would like to do so. There is not perhaps another field so fine in the England of to-day for a man or woman of letters, but all the other literary fields are free. This one alone has a blind bull in it.

"We who sign this letter may be otherwise engaged ; some of us may be old and done, and no longer matter. Our chance has gone by.

But there are men and women who are coming —are they also to be warned off? Can we strike no blow for the young?

WILLIAM ARCHER.	HENRY JAMES.
J. M. BARRIE.	JEROME K. JEROME.
R. C. CARTON.	GEORGE MOORE.
JOSEPH CONRAD.	GILBERT MURRAY.
ARTHUR QUILLER-COUCH.	JOHN MASEFIELD.
W. L. COURTNEY.	ALFRED NOYES.
ARTHUR CONAN DOYLE.	ARTHUR WING PINERO.
JOHN GALSWORTHY.	ELIZABETH ROBINS.
FREDERIC HARRISON.	G. BERNARD SHAW.
ANTHONY HOPE HAWKINS.	ALFRED SUTRO.
MAURICE HEWLETT.	H. G. WELLS.
W. H. HUDSON.	I. ZANGWILL."

Mr Phillpotts was just the kind of author whose assistance the stage was urgently needing, and this insolent rap over the knuckles was very different from the reception which people who had the genuine welfare of the stage at heart would have liked to have shown. For years Mr Phillpotts had been depicting the life and glories of Dartmoor in novels which received the seal of public approval. As soon as he attempted to use the stage for the same purpose, he found his way obstructed. "In that sphere, and only in that sphere, he finds himself thwarted by a crude, autocratic officialism which brands him as a purveyor of indecent wares." The whole incident was a scalding insult to Mr Phillpotts.

When the play was actually produced at a private performance in February 1912, it met with a good reception, and the critics were unable to discover what the objectionable lines might have been.[1] *The Times* wrote : " No one who obtains an invitation in the hope of finding prurience or blasphemy will be paid for his trouble "; and another journal stated, with absolute truth, " that the average playgoer, after hearing the piece, would admit that he failed to guess which were the passages in question, or to recollect any one of them." There are in the play passages of healthy passion and of broad farmyard humour, without which the characters could not possibly have been true to life, and the Censor probably took offence at these passages because they were not couched in drawing-room periphrases. After all, to expect an author to put the *double-entendres* of Mayfair into the mouths of Dartmoor farmers is no more absurd than forbidding him to use the word " thighs," as Colman did, on the ground of indecency.

Mr Cosmo Hamilton's THE BLINDNESS OF VIRTUE was another play not sufficiently soothing to the bloodshot imagination of the Censor. No one who knows Mr Cosmo Hamilton's work will question its delicacy, its inherent sanity, and artistic candour ; but these qualities are as mere dust upon the scales on which the English drama is officially weighed. Here again the play had been published in book form and had met with substantial public approval ; but the Censor for some time boggled over passing it as a stage play. It was ultimately produced with some

[1] This play had the distinction of converting Lord Ribblesdale, a member of the 1909 Select Committee, to the ranks of those who challenge the censorship. He stated that the censoring of such a play made it necessary for him to reconsider his position. See p. 309.

success, though the latter item is, of course, one of unimportance so far as the question of censorship is concerned. If anything, the play tended to over-morality, and it was pointed out that at parts there was " an air of propagandism about it that spoiled the delicate structure of what is otherwise a delightful work of art, one that every father and mother should see, and one that should do no harm to the young people themselves." It ought not to be necessary for a dramatic author to turn his play into a tract to ensure its passing the Censor. We ought by this time to accept the truism that a work of art ought not to be looked on as necessarily a work of morality also. A simple statement of human passion or complexity may be artistically complete and interesting in itself, even if the " moral " is not heavily and primly underlined. Even the latter process, which has many disadvantages,[1] is not enough, as may be seen in the case of M. Brieux' plays.

The delay in connection with THE BLINDNESS OF VIRTUE seemed to be caused largely by the newly appointed Advisory Board. It had been gravely announced that in order to assist the Censor in his deliberations it had been thought advisable to constitute an Advisory Board. This Board consisted of

---

[1] A problem may be intelligible to an entire audience, but its solution may be applicable only to a small minority, and, in some cases, indeed, only to the imaginary characters presented on the stage. It is for this reason that a simple problem may be received with greater sympathy than any suggested solution, the appreciation of which must depend on the capacity of the audience to dissociate their own personalities from the consideration of the imaginary problem before them. That capacity is, with average and untrained audiences, not very considerable ; but its importance only becomes acute in proportion as the personalities in the play are distinctive and unique.

half a dozen gentlemen[1] whose services were honorary and who were otherwise engaged professionally in different parts of the kingdom. The difficulty of assembling these overworked and scattered gentlemen to discuss the advisability of blue-pencilling this or that phrase in a play is sufficiently obvious, and might have been humorous, had the results been less serious to the stage at large. It cannot be said that the constitution of the Advisory Board was particularly happy, and in practice the scheme has proved slow and far from satisfactory.

These defects came into prominence over M. Henri Bataille's famous and successful play LA VIERGE FOLLE, which was to have opened the French season at the Coronet Theatre in 1911. The play had been extremely successful in Paris, and was hailed everywhere as an extraordinarily fine and serious effort. *The Times'* correspondent described it as one of the richest products of the French intelligence, confirming M. Bataille's arrival among the little group of great playwrights. Possibly before submitting it to an average English audience some slight adaptations might be necessary ; but it was absurd in the extreme to suppose that its production in French for the amusement of the French colony in London could possibly have deleterious effects on our national morals. Nevertheless, after the play had been submitted for some days to the Censor a telephone message was received to the effect that he had " just glanced at

---

[1] The Lord Chamberlain.   Mr S. O. Buckmaster, K.C.
Sir Edward Carson.   Sir John Hare.
Sir Squire Bancroft.   Sir Douglas Dawson.
Professor Sir Walter Raleigh.
It is understood that Sir John Hare has now left the Board.

the play," but would not like to take the responsibility upon himself, though he personally would like to see it produced. The matter was therefore to be referred to the Advisory Board. A visit to the Comptroller, however, evoked the fact that the Advisory Board could not possibly meet, as one member was in Egypt and another accompanying the King to the Durbar. In the interval a company of eleven had been specially brought over from Paris at very great expense, and the absurd and unnecessary delay resulted in substantial loss to the unfortunate producers.

Another case of irritating delay occurred in connection with INTO THE DARKNESS, which Miss Marie Tempest desired to produce at the Coronet Theatre in January 1912. The playlet only consisted of twelve typed pages, interspersed with stage directions. But after the Censor had had the manuscript in hand for the statutory seven days, he wrote on the Friday evening, two days prior to the performance of the play, that he would require further time to consider the matter. " I am desired by the Lord Chamberlain to inform you that the play is one which calls for special consideration, and while every effort will be made to suit the convenience of the producers, a decision may not be arrived at for some days." As usual, the letter was not sent to the person most directly interested, which caused further delay ; but on receipt of the letter Miss Tempest sent her business manager down to try and negotiate matters. The business manager was unable to see the Lord Chamberlain, and was unable to see the Examiner of Plays ; but ultimately he saw an official who informed him that there was no real objection to the play or to the characters in it. It was not the scheme of the play that was objected to, but something in the dialogue.

The official was immediately given carte blanche to cut out anything in the dialogue that was deemed objectionable ; but that offer was declined. The manager then complained that Miss Tempest was pressed for time, that she must open on Monday night, and that she had nothing to take the place of this play. Further inquiry as to when the decision would be made known evoked the reply, " About Wednesday, I think." This amiable indifference to any loss caused to producers who have complied with all the legal requirements on their side has been one of the most irritating features of the censorship. No amount of personal courtesy can compensate for the wanton dislocation of carefully planned business arrangements. As Miss Tempest herself said, she did not wish to go into the question of the ethics of censorship. " What I am concerned about, and what I object to, is this interference with what I may call the commercial side of a production. It is unfair to interfere with one's business arrangements with so little consideration." It was certainly absurd that seven days was not adequate time in which to come to a decision on a play which could be read by a person of average intelligence in ten minutes. Even if the play had been ten times as long, it would not have been unreasonable under the circumstances to expect the Chamberlain's department to make some special effort to come to a decision within the legal time. The views of the Censor's department on this question of time may be judged from the Comptroller's statement before the Select Committee that he thought the department ought to be allowed " a good month " in which to deal with every play ! It need hardly be said that such a period would be utterly impracticable from the producer's point of view.

The objections which the Censor took to this little play show the censorial mind at its best. " INTO THE DARKNESS emerged from the ban of the Censor after the alteration of the term of imprisonment, which stood at two years in the text, and seemed to the Censor to convey the fact that the nameless crime for which the man suffered could only be one of ' degeneracy ' ; a view which had never occurred to the author or anyone connected with the management. However, the quarrel with him on this occasion was not with his point of view, which may have been justifiable, and removed a possible misapprehension, but with the fact that he ignored the inconvenience to the management and refused to state the grounds for his objection. The phrase was altered to ' a term of imprisonment ' in a moment, and the delay was quite inexcusable." The Censor must indeed have been badly gravelled for something to complain of, when he had to read some immoral significance into the length of a term of imprisonment. This brilliant piece of divination opens up a new field of horrors : it raises the question as to how far a dramatic author must be expected to guard himself from the unpleasant misinterpretations of an obsessed imagination.

We have mentioned M. Brieux' plays as failing to pass the Censor, in spite of the fact that in his

own country M. Brieux is regarded as being too fond
of sermonising and accentuating the moral lessons of
his plays. MATERNITÉ, THE THREE DAUGHTERS OF
M. DUPONT, and LES HANNETONS were refused
licences by the Censor; but a new translation of
the latter was subsequently permitted, and has been
played in this country and America on many occasions as THE INCUBUS. Before granting the licence,
however, the Censor insisted on the alteration of
certain passages. He referred to "bald and outspoken indecencies," and added: "Unless you care to
make the thing fairly decent, such as could be performed at any theatre in Great Britain, I cannot
possibly recommend the licence." The alterations
which were made do not appear to have been very
important, for Mr Frederic Whelen stated that when
he saw THE INCUBUS he was "totally unconscious of
any difference in the play, although there must have
been a phrase altered here and there." We have the
authority of Mr Laurence Irving for saying that the
two words the Censor objected to were the words
"lover" and "damn." The actual line he would
not pass was: "The first time we met, I told you
I'd had a lover; that was a lie." He, however,
consented to pass the line as follows: "The first time
we met, I told you I'd not been straight; that was a
lie." These were the only alterations made before
the piece appeared as THE INCUBUS. Nothing
could illustrate more clearly the sex-obsession of the
Censor, for he here took an innocent sentence and
pruriently changed it into a suggestive one! M.
Brieux was evidently another of the distinguished
foreign dramatists who, had he been an Englishman,

would have been branded as immoral, and silenced by our stage dictator. It would be interesting to know whether English officials abhor genius, fear it, or merely cannot recognise it.

ŒDIPUS REX was for many years regarded as impossible for the English stage. Even when so responsible an actor as Sir Herbert Tree desired to produce it at His Majesty's Theatre, he was prevented. No specific version of the ŒDIPUS was in question. Sir Herbert had seen a famous French actor playing in the tragedy in Paris, but when on his instructions the Censor was again asked about the play he was told that it could not be licensed. He gave no specific reason, but stated that the licence had been refused before, and that it was no use submitting the play again. This was another piece of stupidity, for the ŒDIPUS is of course read by schoolboys, and its performance by undergraduates has not been known to produce objectionable or disastrous effects on the audience.[1] In time the Censor slowly followed public opinion, and the ŒDIPUS was performed at Covent Garden in 1912 for twenty-six performances, with the most unstinted public approval.

Mr William Heinemann has, on two occasions, failed to secure the Censor's approval of plays he has written. THE FIRST STEP was a little play dealing with one phase of modern life in a perfectly sane and

---

[1] "Now, of course, if any considerable body of Englishmen are arranging to marry their mothers, whether by accident or design, it must be stopped at once. But it is not a frequent occurrence in any class of English society. Throughout the course of my life I have not met more than six men who were anxious to do it."—HENRY ARTHUR JONES.

inoffensive manner. Its morality was of an austere type ; but Mr Heinemann had made the fatal mistake of not preaching, and, as the new Professor of Literature at Cambridge University has already pointed out, to be popular in this country you must preach. Mr Heinemann's play was assuredly a sermon ; but since it had not been clearly labelled so, the Censor did not recognise it, and promptly earmarked it as immoral. In his *History of the English Stage*, M. Filon says : " The censorship would not sanction THE FIRST STEP. The piece might have made it known to Londoners that there are couples in their great city whom the registrar has not united, and whom the clergyman has not blessed ; men of good position who get drunk and beat their mistresses ; young girls who leave home in the morning and don't return at night. The censorship thought it better to spare them this revelation." Another Continental authority, Dr Edward Engel, in his *History of English Literature*, says : " THE FIRST STEP is, on account of its terribly moving fidelity to life, the most valuable drama of the modern English theatre. It stands on a par with good German and French plays, and suffers less than other modern English plays from their customary crudities of construction. There is nothing in it that could be objectionable to grown up people, and if a ' purpose ' can be found in it—otherwise than that of its art— it is assuredly a profoundly moral one. Nevertheless, its production was prohibited by the English Censor of Theatres. It goes without saying that the English Censor is guilty of injustices and stupidities equal to those committed by Censors in other countries, and the prohibition of the best modern English play is certainly one of them." Perhaps we should be less enthusiastic than Dr Engel in discussing the literary value of THE FIRST STEP, but there is certainly nothing whatever in the play to justify censorship. Mr Heinemann's fault was that he was ahead of his time, for his play would certainly be passed to-day without comment. The men " on the forehead of the coming time " are, of course, the only men the Censor can distinguish clearly enough to aim his pot-shots at.

The other play of Mr Heinemann's which had the compliment of censorship was SUMMER MOTHS (1898). This play was sent before publication to one or two whose opinion the author could rely upon, and their criticism especially emphasised the "relentless morality" of the play : " The British Licenser of Plays, equally sensitive if less discriminating, did not hesitate to remove the 'relentless morality' for 'acting purposes.' Requiring with ladylike niceness a good character for the frail heroine, he not only deprived the play of its purpose, but rendered it, if not positively *im*moral, *un*moral to say the least. It was played in its thus de-moralised state for copyright purposes only, on the morning of 26th January 1898, at the Court Theatre, Liverpool, but cannot, naturally, in that condition, be repeated."

Professor Max Reinhardt, whose production of THE MIRACLE, SUMURUN, and ŒDIPUS REX had fascinated all London, and whose work for the salvation of the drama has been fully recognised all over the Continent, made arrangements to pro-

duce a fourth piece in this country at the Palace
Theatre, in November 1912. It can safely be said
that there was not a theatre-goer in London who
was not aware of the coming production, and eagerly
looking forward to it. Long and elaborate prepara-
tions had been made ; a huge revolving stage had been
erected in the theatre, and forty German and English
artists engaged. Everything was ready for production for the evening of 4th November, but in the
afternoon a letter was received from the Lord
Chamberlain's department, officially vetoing A
Venetian Night. A special rehearsal took place
on Sunday evening, 3rd November, at which a
representative from the Lord Chamberlain's office
attended, and it was announced that the objections
taken were so serious that the alteration of an
incident or scene would not suffice : the whole
theme was objected to, and it looked as though the
man who has done more than anyone in England
at present to revolutionise and reform stage methods
would be ignominiously refused the right to offer
his work to the English people.

This new exploit caused something like con-
sternation. Fortunately, the distinguished Germans
responsible for the production refused to take the
decision meekly. They appealed to the German
Embassy, and telegrams were sent to Berlin. Personal friends of high standing in this country were
roused to action, and came to plead for the suppressed
play. The producers insisted that in view of the
magnitude of the production the Lord Chamberlain
ought himself to inspect a rehearsal, but it was stated
that the Lord Chamberlain was shooting in the

country, and his decision was delayed. Finally, as a result of the agitation, the Lord Chamberlain intervened, inspected a rehearsal, and, with some small modification, passed the play. It may confidently be assumed, however, that in the hands of less important producers the censorial ban would have been maintained. As finally produced, the theme was found to be rather involved, and not excitingly interesting, but less objectionable than many licensed plays. Only in England, where we look at life through half-closed fingers, could the theme have been objected to. We cannot blink the fact, however, that there is a noisy, if trifling, minority in this country, who will before long be complaining of the " immorality " of keeping two canaries in one cage, and it was probably in deference to the obsessions of this minority that the Lord Chamberlain's assistants hesitated over A VENETIAN NIGHT.

The manager of the theatre issued the following statement :

> " When the Lord Chamberlain saw a dress rehearsal of A VENETIAN NIGHT, he stated that he had no fault to find with the manner in which the performance was presented to him, and subsequently wrote Mr Butt to that effect. His Lordship's objection was to the ' theme ' and plot of the play. The plot of the play is that a bride, married to a man she does not care for, gives, on her wedding night, a rendezvous to her lover in her bedroom. Originally, the bride and lover were shown in the second episode to enter the bride's bedroom, and the

fourth episode showed what the young stranger *dreamed* took place, viz. : The bride and the lover embraced each other, but were interrupted almost immediately by the hurried entrance of the bridegroom, and during the time the husband was in the room the lover was killed. The subsequent episode showed how the young stranger, in his dream, endeavoured to get rid of the body of the lover for the bride ; and the twelfth episode showed the lover coming down into the hall of the hotel from the bride's room ; subsequently the bride coming out of her room and meeting the bridegroom, who came out of the adjoining room.

" The whole question is whether the ' theme ' of a man and woman going into the room, and the audience, by suggestion alone, being led to assume that they had been there throughout the night, is fit and proper for treatment on the stage. The ' theme ' of husband, wife, and lover is one that has been used to a very large extent by authors and dramatists of all ages, and at the present time serves as the plot for several plays being presented in the West End. Seeing, therefore, that no exception could be taken to the manner in which this ' theme ' was presented, the question arises whether it is not invidious to permit the ' theme ' elsewhere, and prohibit it in A Venetian Night ? "

The incident was especially interesting in so far as the production was being staged at a music hall. The progress the music-hall stage has made in recent years without the interference of the Censor has been admitted by everyone, and we shall have occasion to point out the extraordinarily small number of instances in which the London County Council has found it necessary to take action in recent years. Here the censorship of the public and of the managers themselves has been found extremely satisfactory; but apparently the Examiners of Plays were eager to exercise their new powers over the music hall and were not satisfied to let well enough alone. The whole incident called forth a good deal of criticism in the press, the *Pall Mall Gazette* saying, that apart from the particular question of A VENETIAN NIGHT, the Lord Chamberlain had no moral or artistic rights to his powers of veto.

> "We have protested against their use in the case of the theatre; we are no less against them in the case of the music hall. We claim that the press and the public are quite able to take care of the propriety of the stage. The Palace Theatre itself has lately provided an illustration of this. The sketch in which Mlle. Gaby Deslys lately appeared there was found, at its first public performance, to call for rather severe criticisms; the management of the theatre took note of these, and the character of the piece was duly modified. Such is the only form of censorship a self-respecting people can be expected to tolerate."

In this the *Pall Mall Gazette* was, it cannot be doubted, voicing the growing feeling of the community.

Dr Karl Vollmoeller, the author of A VENETIAN NIGHT, mentioned that an objection was raised in regard to the costume of one of the dancers ; a matter which could, of course, be rectified without any trouble.   Theatre-goers will remember with shame and horror the black " football knickers " which the dainty dancers and actresses in SUMURUN wore in deference to our English prejudices.   About forty years ago the Lord Chamberlain stopped the performance of a piece called BARBE BLEU because, he said, the skirts were too short ; and the dresses had to be lengthened before the piece was resumed. Other Censors have, however, been sensible enough to see that indecency and suggestiveness are not things to be gauged by the length of clothes, measured when the wearer is in an upright position.   The most cursory examination of some recent fashions should convince a sane observer that a woman wearing long skirts may be much more improper and suggestive than one who frankly wears short skirts.   But this is a little matter of common sense, and ought hardly, therefore, to be associated with censorship.

But perhaps the most colossal stupidity which the censorship has perpetrated in recent years came to light in connection with KISMET.   In that altogether delightful Oriental play there was a scene in which a young girl, clothed in pink fleshings, slipped off her white draperies and plunged instantly into a bathing-pool.   The girl did not come to the front of the stage or indulge in New-Art dances before the footlights.   The whole incident took place in dull diffused moonlight.   The girl was carefully wrapped from head to foot in fleshings and was in the water the instant she was out of her drapery. It was a pretty and perfectly innocent little picture, occupying only a few seconds, which could not have given offence save to the most rabid and prurient bigot. For seven months—245 performances to be exact—the incident passed without a word of protest. All London, led by the King and Queen, went to see the play, and during that time there was no person filthy-minded enough to dare raise his voice and say he had found the dainty little picture smeared with sex-indecency. Then one day came an order from the Lord Chamberlain to the effect that the scene must be modified—the girl must wear more clothing when she jumped into the harem bathing-pool.

London figuratively sat back after this exploit and gasped. It could to some extent understand—with pitying compassion perhaps—the delicacy of mind and morals which banned, let us say, Mrs Warren's Profession; but to interfere with a performance which had been licensed and gone unchecked for seven months without evoking a word of protest in the press, was so unmitigated a piece of asininity that only two solutions seemed open. One was that the Censor was deliberately trying to kill his office by smothering it under ridicule, and the other was that he was not acting as a free agent. It was, perhaps, the latter hypothesis which was most generally accepted, and that theory served to emphasise the need for ending the autocratic and unchallenged powers of the censorship. A tasteless official was a sufficient evil; but an official open to the suggestions and influence of tasteless and bigoted individuals who remained in the background would be an intolerable anachronism. It need hardly be enunciated that there is not one person in the State whose judgment and opinion are sufficiently sure in matters of morals to be imposed on the rest of the nation by methods, such as this, which cannot be publicly challenged.

An ideal Censor of national drama should aim at granting the stage the utmost possible liberty consistent with good manners, without bending in the least to individual prejudice or caprice, whether for or against Puritanism. Save in a strictly official manner, he should not be subject to outside influence. It is because these qualifications are frankly impossible that so many people wish the abolition of the censorship, nor would the appointment of any individual Censor—no matter how good—affect the principle at stake. But it is doubly undesirable that such an official, if appointed, should belong to the court, where patronage and favour rather than public service are of importance. Moreover, it must be remembered that in this country, at any rate, the morality of the court has in general been lower rather than higher than the average morality of the nation.

Just about the time of the KISMET incident one or two ministers had been busily concerning themselves with the morals of London playgoers, and had been searching eagerly for tea-cup scandals in different parts of the city. Some officials had shown themselves unwarrantably influenced by this blatant minority of egotistical bigots, and the KISMET incident suggested disagreeable possibilities. An anæmic parson's excitement on making his first acquaintance with a London pantomime ought not to be a sufficient excuse for forbidding pantomimes to the rest of the city. A number of performances at different music halls were protested against, and in one or two cases action was taken. Instantly a number of people appeared anxious to carry the process to further lengths. Again there was a characteristic outcry against any public recognition on the stage of the fact that the female of the species is a biped. When the matter came up for discussion in November 1911 in the London County Council, Mr Reynolds pungently summarised the position when he said : " The point was where a line should be drawn if they were going to see the human form divine [1] at all. If they went on in this way, they would soon have to stop all modern forms of dancing on the stage, all representations of negroes, all human savages, all Oriental scenes, and so on. They would have to abolish swimming contests in public baths, where both sexes mixed freely in a state of practical nakedness. Also they would have to abolish statuary in the public parks and museums."

There are a few people who visit the theatre with apparently no higher aim than to discover and denounce it as a sink of iniquity. It is not always uncongenial work. When the Commission was sitting in 1866, Mr Buckstone, then lessee and manager of the Haymarket Theatre, told an amusing story apropos of this subject. After saying that during his

---

[1] Mr Reynolds's use of this phrase was probably sarcastic. Judged by any *practical* standard, the vast majority of people, especially of the more religious kind, regard the human form as essentially obscene.

predecessor's sixteen years' management and his own fourteen years' management they had never had a stranger, and, indeed, hardly a friend behind the scenes, he went on to tell of a clergyman who asked him to break the rule, and begged to be allowed to go behind the scenes. Mr Buckstone said, " There is nothing particular to be seen," but the clergyman was persistent, and pleaded to be allowed "just a peep." At last Mr Buckstone impatiently took him behind, where the clergyman found nothing going on in the way he expected. " You see there is nothing to be seen," said Mr Buckstone, and the clergyman replied, disappointedly, " I shall go now ; I expected to see a sort of saturnalia here."

There have been other clergymen who, failing permission to go behind the scenes, have made it their smug and pleasant duty to search for indecencies on the stage. Of course they have found them, just as they would find them in the corolla of a flower or in their own Bible if they approached them in the same spirit. Unfortunately, officials in this country sometimes seem to be unduly susceptible to clerical opinion. It is difficult to understand why a costume indicating acquiescence in certain theological opinions should entitle its wearer to speak with special authority on secular questions. Excessive other-worldliness usually results in a narrow and ill-balanced knowledge of human activity ; not always compensated for by those dogmatic habits of thought which result from habitually speaking without fear of contradiction.

CHAPTER X

THE GENERAL POSITION

IT may be worth while summarising briefly the legal changes which have occurred in the dramatic censorship since Sir Robert Walpole's Bill of 1737.[1] That Bill—which was entitled " An Act to explain and amend so much of an Act, made in the twelfth year of the reign of Queen Anne, intituled an Act for reducing the laws relating to rogues, vagabonds, sturdy beggars and vagrants, into one Act of Parliament ; and for the more effectual punishing such rogues, vagabonds, sturdy beggars, and vagrants, and sending them whither they ought to be sent, as relates to common players of Interludes "—constituted the Lord Chamberlain Licenser of Theatres within the City and liberties of Westminster, and wherever the Sovereign might reside. It required a copy of every new play to be sent to him not less than fourteen days before the proposed performance. It empowered him to prohibit at any time and anywhere in Great Britain the performance of any play, and it imposed heavy penalties on those who should perform any play in an unlicensed theatre, or any prohibited play or any new play, without the sanction

[1] See Act in Appendix.

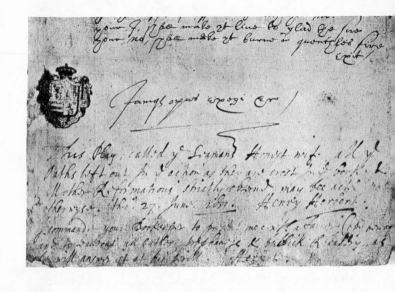

Reproduction from last folio of manuscript play entitled THE
SEAMAN'S HONEST WIFE, which was examined by the Censor in
1633. The licence ran as follows : " *This play, called YE SEAMAN'S
HONEST WIFE, all ye Oaths left out in ye action as they are crost in ye
booke & all other Reformations strictly observed may bee acted, not otherwyse. this 27. June. 1633.—HENRY HERBERT.*"

To this licence the Censor added the following note : " *I
commande your Bookeeper to present mee with a faire Copy hereafter and
to leave out all oathes, prophaness & publick Ribaldry, as he will answer
it at his perill.—H. HERBERT.*" In spite of this curious footnote it
must be observed that what is to-day regarded as indecency was
quite ignored by the Censor of those days.

of the Lord Chamberlain or of letters patent from
the Crown. On the passing of this Act, and
although not required by it to do so, the Lord
Chamberlain appointed and swore in a Licenser or
Examiner of Plays, with a salary of £400 a year
to act under him, and also appointed a deputy.[1]
This was the official creation of the office of
Examiner of Plays. The 1832 Commission elicited
the notable statement that " it should be clearly
understood that the office of Censor is held at the
discretion of the Lord Chamberlain, whose duty
would be to remove him should there be any just
ground for dissatisfaction as to the exercise of his
functions." Thereafter few changes of importance
occurred, with the exception of an Act in 1788
which empowered Quarter Sessions to grant licences
for occasional theatrical performances in the provinces.

We have already briefly referred to some of the
devices which were employed to evade the drastic
terms of the 1737 Act. According to Ward, the
Lord Chamberlain licensed the Haymarket for the
" legitimate," the Lyceum and St James's for musical
performances, and the Olympic and Adelphi for
" burlettas," defined—by anyone rash enough to
attempt a definition—as plays containing " not less
than five pieces of vocal music in each act." All
other metropolitan theatres were actually illegal.
The power of the local magistrates was confined to
granting licences for music and dancing, which might
cover ballets, pantomimes, and equestrian performances, but could not possibly extend to dramatic

---

[1] For copy of oath taken by the Examiner of Plays and a specimen
form of appointment see Appendix.

representation. Accordingly Astley's, the Surrey, the Victoria in Tottenham Street, and the City of London, the Pavilion, and the Garrick Theatres in the West End all existed on sufferance, and adopted some of the absurd subterfuges we have already hinted at. Perhaps the commonest of all was to have a piano tinkling continually, in a transparent attempt to give the performance a legal standing. The Strand Theatre—to which we have elsewhere referred—went on its way in flat defiance of the Lord Chamberlain's authority. During the ten years 1830–40 the injustice of this chaotic state of matters was rapidly becoming unbearable. The patent theatres played the dog in the manger, making no effort themselves to preserve the legitimate drama from extinction, but clamouring loudly of their privileges whenever the smaller houses attempted to trespass on the "legitimate" domain. The class of entertainment at the patent theatres was rapidly lowered, and soon the patentees came to rely mainly on cheap melodrama, "tame wild beasts," and so forth.

In 1832, on the motion and under the chairmanship of Mr Lytton Bulwer, afterwards Lord Lytton, a Select Committee of the House of Commons sat to review the operations of the Act of 1737. This Committee reported in favour of some unimportant changes in the authorities which should license, and in the principles upon which they should proceed ; but recommended the retention of the Lord Chamberlain's censorship over plays themselves. Following on the general lines of this report, Parliament, in 1843, passed a fresh statute for the regulation of

theatres.[1] This measure, THE THEATRES ACT, repealed previous statutes, including Walpole's Act.
It substituted new provisions, and, with some alterations of machinery effected by Local Government
Acts, is now the operative law. Under this 1843
Act the performance of stage-plays is prohibited
except in authorised places. Places may be authorised by letters patent, as are Covent Garden and
Drury Lane, which hold patents dating from the
time of Charles II., and the Theatre Royal, Bath,
and the Theatre Royal, Margate. Places may also
obtain a licence from the Lord Chamberlain or from
the Justices of the Peace in special sessions. The
jurisdiction of the Lord Chamberlain as Licenser of
Theatres extends to the cities of London and Westminster, to the areas which constituted in 1843 the
boroughs of Finsbury, Marylebone, Tower Hamlets,
Lambeth, and Southwark—the metropolitan boroughs
at that time—and to the town of Windsor, and other
places of royal residence. Among these Brighton is
no longer included (p. 189 f.). The power of the
justices to license theatres in other localities was
delegated to the County Councils in England and
Wales by the Local Government Act of 1888.[2] The
County Councils in turn may, if they wish, delegate
their powers to the justices in Petty Sessions, or, in
the case of non-county boroughs within their area,
to the Borough Councils. The Lord Chamberlain
may order any theatres licensed by him, or any patent
theatres, to be closed on account of riot or mis-
behaviour, or on such public occasions as " to the

[1] 6 & 7 Vic. c. 68. The relevant clauses will be found in Appendix.
[2] 51 & 52 Vic. c. 41.

Lord Chamberlain shall seem fit." The justices may order any theatre licensed by the local authority to be closed on account of riot or breach of any regulations made by the authority.

So far as the actual licensing of the plays themselves as apart from the theatres is concerned, the entire authority is in the hands of the Lord Chamberlain ; the local authorities have no functions in the matter. A copy of every new stage-play and every addition to an old play must be sent to the Lord Chamberlain by the manager who proposes to produce it, at least seven days before it is intended to be performed, accompanied by a fee, to be fixed by the Lord Chamberlain, not being more than two guineas. The Lord Chamberlain may prohibit the acting of any play, or any part of any play licensed, "anywhere in Great Britain or in such theatres as he shall specify, either absolutely or for such time as he shall think fit." The Statute of 1737 conferred upon the Lord Chamberlain an unfettered power of veto, with no indication of the grounds upon which he was to act. When the Bill of 1843 was passing through the House of Lords, words were inserted, on the suggestion of Lord Campbell,[1] restricting

[1] Lord Campbell begged to move an amendment upon the 15th Clause. That clause empowered the Lord Chamberlain to prohibit, at his pleasure, the representation of any play whatever, in any theatre within his jurisdiction. He (Lord Campbell) was quite ready to invest the Lord Chamberlain with full powers to prevent any performances which were calculated to offend public decency or to peril the public peace ; but beyond this he did not think that officer ought to interfere with a manager's arrangements. He did not propose to omit any of the words of the clause, but merely to guide the Lord Chamberlain in his exercise of this power by proposing these words before the existing clause :—"Be it enacted that for the preservation of good manners, decorum, and of the public peace, it shall be lawful for the Lord

vaguely his powers of prohibition to cases in which " he shall be of opinion that it is fitting for the preservation of good manners, decorum, or of the public peace so to do." It is upon these words alone that the Lord Chamberlain bases his statutory powers in the operation of the censorship. The Act of 1843 defined a stage-play as being " taken to include every tragedy, comedy, farce, opera, burletta, interlude, melodrama, pantomime, or other entertainment of the stage, or any part thereof," with a partial exemption for performances at fairs. The Act applies to Scotland, but not to Ireland.

Since 1843 there have been three occasions on which the House of Commons have considered some different aspects of the matter. In 1853 a Select Committee of the House of Commons on Public-Houses and Places of Entertainment reported that on the whole the censorship had worked well, and should be maintained. In 1866 a Second Committee considered the question of Theatrical Licences and Regulations. The Committee took an enormous amount of evidence, including that of the Examiner of Plays and the Lord Chamberlain himself. The instructions of the Committee were to inquire into the working of the Acts of Parliament for licensing

Chamberlain, for the time being,"—the rest of the clause remaining as at present.

Lord Wharncliffe objected to the amendment because it would restrict the powers of the Lord Chamberlain within narrower limits than they had at present, whereas the object of the Bill was not to restrict his powers but to extend his jurisdiction. The Lord Chamberlain was a great officer of State, a member of their Lordships' House, and always ready to defend any proceedings which might be deemed an abuse of his powers.—*Parliamentary Debates*, 3 S., vol. lxxi.

On the suggestion of the Lord Chancellor the clause took its final form.

and regulating theatres and places of public entertainment in Great Britain, and to report any alterations which might appear desirable. The report stated that the system of double jurisdiction by the Lord Chamberlain and the magistrates, as regards theatres and music halls respectively, was unsatisfactory, and recommended that the entire regulation of such places should be in the hands of one authority.

It also recommended, "for ensuring the safety and accommodation of the public," the compulsory inspection of these places of entertainment, as regards stability, security against fire, etc., and stated that it was desirable to continue the existing restrictions which prevented music halls from giving theatrical entertainments. It further recommended that the Lord Chamberlain's control should be extended to all places of entertainment in the metropolis, for which licences were required; and after stating that the censorship of plays had worked satisfactorily, recommended its extension, " as far as practicable," to the performances in music halls. As far as the country in general was concerned, it was recommended that the licensing of new theatres should be done by the Lord Chamberlain instead of the local magistrates, but that the powers now exercised by the magistrates, both as regards the renewal of licences and as regards regulations, should continue in force. In 1892 a Third Committee of the House of Commons repeated and endorsed the opinions of their predecessors, only one witness, Mr William Archer, appearing to condemn the Censor.[1]

---

[1] Mr Archer's evidence was, however, contemptuously brushed aside by Mr Pigott, the Examiner at that time, in this way: " I make

In 1909 a fresh Select Committee was appointed to inquire into the workings of the 1843 Act.[1] This Committee, which consisted of five members from the House of Commons and five from the House of Lords, under the very able chairmanship of Mr Herbert Samuel, made what was by far the most thorough investigation into the whole subject. Forty-nine witnesses, including the Speaker of the House of Commons, were examined. The Comptroller of the Lord Chamberlain's department and the Examiner of Plays both appeared as witnesses; but the Lord Chamberlain himself, who is, of course, the real Licenser of Plays, did not appear, though questions were asked by members of the Committee as to what powers, if any, the Committee had to enforce his appearance. It was unfortunate that no official statement of the Lord Chamberlain's attitude in particular instances was forthcoming; more especially as the Lord Chamberlain is not answerable in the ordinary way to the House of Commons. The Comptroller stated that he was authorised to state the views of the Lord Chamberlain on the question of the censorship as it then stood; but this arrangement was by no means so satisfactory as the attendance of the Lord Chamberlain himself would have been, and it was frequently necessary to ask the Comptroller whether specific answers were

allowance for Mr Archer because he has some interest in these plays; he is a translator of Ibsen's plays, and therefore, I suppose, has a certain interest in their being produced."

[1] One of the most noteworthy things about the 1909 Commission was the indifferent printing of the Blue-book containing the evidence of witnesses. In the official report some of the evidence appeared the exact contrary of what was said. It was regrettable also that an index to the evidence was not included.

personal expressions of opinion or official statements of the Lord Chamberlain's views. It was regarded as strange that a Parliamentary inquiry into the working of a State department should not have been honoured with the presence and evidence of the head of that department in person.

In 1909 the Committee did not find themselves able to arrive at the simple and sweeping conclusions of their predecessors. With few exceptions, all the dramatists asked for the abolition or modification of the censorship ; but, on the other hand, the managers of theatres, with equally few exceptions, asked for the retention of some control over plays, prior to their production. In explanation, some of them stated that abolition of the censorship might possibly result in the production of a class of play tending to cast discredit on the theatre as a whole ; others were unwilling to assume the responsibility of deciding as to the innocence of proposed plays ; while a majority insisted that if the control by Censor was replaced by a control exercised by the local licensing authorities, or by means of police prosecution—and one or other of these they regarded as inevitable alternatives,—their position would be rendered intolerable, by reason of the uncertainty that would result. The actors, as a whole, seemed to share this fear of insecurity, and the Speaker of the House of Commons, expressing himself as an ordinary theatre-goer, stated that there was, no doubt, a large number of people who would regard the sudden abolition of the censorship as preparing the way for the gradual demoralisation of the stage.

The Committee came to the conclusion that the ordinary law, which prevents or punishes indecency, blasphemy, and libel in printed publications, would not be adequate in the case of theatrical representations. The personalities of the actors gave the ideas and situations presented a more powerful effect than mere descriptive writing could do. Moreover, a great deal that was offensive might nevertheless not fall within the strictly legal definitions of vice, indecency, or blasphemy; while offence might be given to foreign Powers without coming within the purview of any law whatsoever. They also pointed out that the security of the whole touring system rested on censorship and allowance, prior to production. The representations of this large body of witnesses, who stated that the abolition of the office would seriously injure their commercial interests, could not, the Committee concluded, be put aside as of no importance. The uncertainty which would result if the manager could never tell whether or not a piece would be accepted at the various towns in his touring arrangements, would tend to restrict enterprise, and discourage the people who undertook the financial risk of theatrical management.

On the other hand, the evidence had made it abundantly clear that a censorship on the lines of the existing one was open to grave objections. " Secret in its operation, subject to no effective control by public opinion, its effect can hardly fail to be to coerce into conformity with the conventional standards of the day, dramatists who may be seeking to amend them. Those standards are not absolute. It is an axiom underlying all our legislation, that only through the toleration of that which one age thinks to be error can the next age progress further in the pursuit of truth.   More and more the theatre is attracting writers of intellect who desire to present through its agency sincere and serious dramas, critical of existing conventions."

The plays actually censored were, it was admitted, comparatively few ; but, on the other hand, it had been brought out that almost every week, plays were modified in a greater or less degree to meet the objections of the Censor ; and playwrights asserted that their fear and dislike of this intervention seriously hampered their work.   The Committee pointed out that the actual prohibitions of the Censor were not a fair measure of his activities.   " A censorship," they reported, " of the press might not touch one newspaper article in a thousand submitted to it ; but its effect might be immense."   They wisely decided that the fact of a play being painful or disturbing was not sufficient to justify its suppression.   In that case, " it would be necessary to avoid tragedy and melodrama and license comedy alone."   It was not the function of the State, the Report proceeded, to insist that there should be no presentation on the stage of anything unsuitable for youth to see.   " This is not so under the existing censorship, and ought not to be so, for that standard is not one to which the community should be required universally to conform."   It was recognised that the suggestion to provide an arbitrator to whom appeal could be made, in the event of hopeless differences between an author and the Censor, was in no way a solution of the question.   " The question at issue is not to be regarded in the light of a dispute between two individuals, to be decided by the opinion of a third party acceptable to both. It is the question by what means the State, on behalf of the community, is to prevent the public performance of plays which are improper for stage performance."

With reference to the Advisory Committee which the Lord Chamberlain was appointing, it was suggested that while such a committee would perform useful functions its formation would not be adequate for the solution of the question. In course of years the same objections that attach to an individual Censor would attach to it also.

In conclusion, the Committee recommended that legislation should be enacted to the following effect :

> " The Lord Chamberlain should remain the Licenser of Plays.
>
> " It should be his duty to license any play submitted to him unless he considers that it may reasonably be held—
>
> " (*a*) To be indecent ;
>
> " (*b*) To contain offensive personalities ;
>
> " (*c*) To represent on the stage in an invidious manner a living person, or any person recently dead.
>
> " (*d*) To do violence to the sentiment of religious reverence ;
>
> " (*e*) To be calculated to[1] conduce to crime or vice ;

---

[1] This use of the phrase " to be calculated to " forms a blemish in an otherwise carefully phrased document. " Calculate " means to compute and to reckon, to work out by figures ; the essential thought being the careful adjustment of means to end. To speak, therefore, of a play being " calculated " to conduce to vice, is an unhappy and vulgar colloquialism which would provide endless opportunity for legal quibbling. Shakespeare used the word correctly : " A cunning man did *calculate*

" (*f*) To be calculated to impair friendly relations with any Foreign Power ; or
" (*g*) To be calculated to cause a breach of
the peace.

" It should be optional to submit a play for
licence, and legal to perform an unlicensed play,
whether it has been submitted or not.

" If the Director of Public Prosecutions is
of opinion that any unlicensed play which has
been performed is open to objection on the
ground of indecency, he should prefer an indictment against the manager of the theatre where
the play has been produced, and against the
author of the play. When notice has been
given to the manager of the theatre by the
Director of Public Prosecutions of his intention
to take proceedings, it should be illegal for any
further performances of the play to take place
until the case has been heard and decided.

" The Court before which an indictment is
preferred should be empowered to make one or
more of the following orders according to the
merits of the case :

" (*a*) Prohibiting the performance of the play
for such period as they may think
fit, but for not more than ten years.
" (*b*) Imposing penalties on the manager of
the theatre.
" (*c*) Imposing penalties on the author of the
play.

---

my birth." To use it as expressing a tendency is to take a greater
licence with the word than some Americans do when they say they
"calculate" to go a journey.

" (*d*) Endorsing a conviction on the licence of the theatre.

" A play which has been prohibited by an Order of Court from being performed for a period of ten years, should not be eligible for performance after that period unless it has been licensed by the Licenser of Plays.

" The licence of a theatre which has been endorsed three times within a period of five years should be liable to forfeiture by the Court which directed the last endorsement, and be incapable of renewal, for a period of five years following, to or for the benefit of the same licensee.

" If the Attorney-General considers that an unlicensed play which has been performed is improper for performance on any of the seven grounds specified above, he should be empowered to apply to a Committee of the Privy Council for an Order prohibiting the performance of the play for a period of not more than ten years, and, if he thinks fit, for an endorsement on the licence of the theatre. Pending the decision of the Committee, the performance of the play should be suspended as in the case of pending prosecutions. Similar consequences should follow a prohibition of a play and an endorsement of a theatre licence by order of the Committee of Privy Council as would follow where the order was made by a Court. The Committee of the Privy Council could not be empowered to impose penalties on the manager or author, and penalties beyond such prohibition and endorsement would in such cases be unnecessary. The Committee would have an inherent power of hearing cases, if it wished, *in camera*.

" It should be lawful, for reasons which we shall specify, to take proceedings against the producers of a licensed play ; but in those cases the performance should not be liable to suspension pending the decision of the proceedings, the manager and author should not in any case be liable to penalties, nor the theatre licence be liable to endorsement.

" The measure of immunity conferred by the licensing of a play should attach only to the text as passed by the Licenser.

" The powers of the authorities which license theatres should remain as they now are ; that is to say, that they should be empowered to withdraw a theatre licence provided that they are acting ' according to the rules of reason and justice.' But it should not be regarded as a valid reason for withdrawing the licence of a theatre that a licensed play to which objection is taken has been performed there ; or that an unlicensed play has been performed there, if proceedings have been taken and the Court or the Committee of the Privy Council, as the case may be, have not ordered the theatre licence to be endorsed."

The Commission further pointed out that the officer who performed the censorial duties should not be exempt from Parliamentary responsibility. When the Theatres Bill of 1843 was passing through the

House of Commons, Sir James Graham, then Home Secretary, urged that the control should be retained in the hands of the Lord Chamberlain in order that it should be wielded by an officer accountable to Parliament. The Commissioners stated that they could not consider it to be in accordance with constitutional principles for an officer of State, in a matter such as this, to be accountable to one House of Parliament and not to the other, and they recommended that while "remaining accountable, as now, to the House of Lords, his general administration of the functions entrusted to him by statute should be brought, by whatever procedure is thought desirable, within the same opportunities for review by the House of Commons, as the actions of other ministers."

In connection with the formation of a Consultative Committee to act with the Censor, it should especially be noticed that the Report stated that it was a matter of importance to the interests concerned that no undue delay should be involved by the additional examination of the plays submitted. It was also recommended that the present period of seven days allowed for the examination of plays should be extended to fourteen days. The departmental rule of the office — already only partially observed—that plays are ineligible for licence if they contain characters drawn from the Scriptures should, the Report continued, no longer be maintained. "Plays which touch upon religious subjects should not be licensed if they contravene the principle that they must not do violence to the sentiment of reverence." The Lord Chamberlain is now authorised to receive plays for examination only from the managers who propose to produce them, and for various reasons it was recommended that this practice should continue, unless it should appear that the authors as a body would prefer that this right should be given to them.[1]

Two other clauses in the 1909 Report are worth repeating :

> " In course of time the Licenser of Plays will receive guidance in his action from the attitude of public opinion towards the unlicensed plays which have been performed, and from the decisions of the Courts and of the Committee of the Privy Council on the cases which have been brought before them.
>
> " It may be anticipated that the more elastic system we propose will develop, as our institutions usually do, along the lines that experience indicates. To seek a licence for a play will remain the rule, or it will become the exception, according as licences are found in the future to be necessary, or to be superfluous, in the public interest, and for the protection of producers."

---

[1] In this connection it may be recalled that Mr Redford as dramatic author submitted a play for licence to himself as Examiner of Plays. The play, which was a comedietta entitled A SNUG RETREAT, written many years before, was, in Mr Redford's own words, "of no consequence whatever. I had anticipated the possibility of my successor having to license the manuscript when I copyrighted it a year ago, *so I merely submitted it to the Lord Chamberlain's department, and, in the ordinary way, passed it myself.* Of course there is nothing to which anyone could take exception. It is the most ordinary straightforward piece that ever was."

Sir Henry Herbert, Master of Revels from 1623 to 1663.

To face page 304.

The war between the music halls and the theatres over the " dramatic sketch " has little or no interest for us here. The whole subject has nothing to do with censorship, except in so far as it was incongruous that unlicensed plays should be performed at one public theatre, but necessarily licensed before they could be presented to a similar audience in another theatre. The Select Committee of 1892 recommended—though no legislation resulted—that the performance of dramatic sketches should be licensed in music halls without the possession of a licence for stage plays, provided that " the duration of each such performance shall not exceed forty minutes, and no more than six performers take part therein, and that there shall be an interval of at least thirty minutes between any two such sketches, and no two sketches performed on the same evening at such place of public entertainment shall have a connected plot."

In the absence of legislation a voluntary arrangement was made in 1896 between the music halls and the chief theatres to the effect that the former should limit sketches which they performed to the abovementioned conditions, with substitution of thirty for forty minutes, in which case the latter would abstain from further prosecutions. As is well known, this agreement has not proved satisfactory. Both sides have complained of its terms, and continual friction has resulted. For dealing with this position, the Report continued, three courses were open :—

" (*a*) To enforce the letter of the existing law and restrict the performance of

dramatic sketches to places licensed
to perform stage plays ;

" (*b*)   To legalise the performance of sketches
in places licensed for music and
dancing under restrictions approxi-
mating more or less closely to those
proposed by the Select Committee
of 1892 ; or

" (*c*)   To abolish the present legal differentiation between the theatre and the
music hall, and to allow each to
present whatever form of entertainment it desires."

" The first of these alternatives we regard as
neither practicable nor desirable.   The performance of sketches in music halls is a practice too
firmly established to be uprooted.   Nor is there
any reason why the public which frequents
music halls should be deprived by force of law
of the pleasure of witnessing whatever form of
entertainment those who cater for their amusement are able to provide.   We believe—and
we are supported in this belief by the evidence
given before us by many of those best qualified
to speak in the interest of the serious drama—
that the competition of the variety stage is
not likely appreciably to affect the well-being
of those forms of British drama which are
entitled to solicitude.

" The second alternative we regard as unjust
to the proprietors of theatres.   They ask that,
if the existing law which ostensibly protects

their interests is not to be enforced, they shall at least be allowed to meet their competitors on equal terms, and, if they so desire, during a part of the year or, it may be, as a portion of their entertainment, to present performances other than stage-plays. This cannot but be regarded as a reasonable demand.

"We recommend, therefore, the third alternative—a single licence for both classes of houses, giving them freedom to produce whatever entertainment may best conform to the tastes of the public which they serve."

Finally, the Report recommended that the same provisions for licensing, for the punishment or prohibition of unlicensed productions which are found to be improper, and for control through the licence of the building, which it was proposed to apply to plays, should apply also to all words sung or spoken in any licensed place of entertainment. It also recommended that the licensing of the forty theatres which were now in the jurisdiction of the Lord Chamberlain, should be transferred to the London County Council, whose officers already visit them regularly in order to advise as to the safety of their structure and of their accommodation for the public.

The recommendations of this Report have not yet been embodied in a statute. On several occasions the question has been raised in the House of Commons, and also in the House of Lords. In December 1911, Mr Harcourt suggested that Mr Brookfield's appointment as Joint-Examiner of Plays should be cancelled, and in his reply the Home

Secretary, Mr M'Kenna, while agreeing that it would be desirable to have a short Bill embodying the recommendations of the Committee, was unable to hold out the smallest hope of dealing with the matter immediately, unless some non-controversial measure could be devised which could be carried by consent.

In the House of Lords, on 20th March 1912, Lord Newton contended that the whole matter had been treated with too much solemnity, and its importance greatly exaggerated. He did not recognise that any author had any special mission to elevate him or anybody else, and he saw no reason for change in the present procedure. Lord Ribblesdale, who also had been a member of the 1909 Committee, said he believed the evidence of the censorship encouraged people to turn out good plays, and in his opinion the public generally approved of some safeguard. The Earl of Lytton, whose grandfather was in 1832 prominent in condemnation of the Censor, strongly objected to that official as an institution, but Lord Sandhurst, the Lord Chamberlain,[1] asserted that the present procedure was prompt and inexpensive, and had the approval and support of the great mass of managers. He assured the House that great care and thought were bestowed before the

[1] Earl Spencer, who had held the post of Lord Chamberlain since 1905, resigned in February 1912 because of ill-health, and a day or two later the appointment of the Right Hon. Lord Sandhurst to be Lord Chamberlain was announced. The last act of Earl Spencer, in his capacity as Lord Chamberlain, was the appointment of Mr Ernest Alfred Bendall, a gentleman in his sixty-sixth year, who had been dramatic critic of the *Observer* since 1874, and had written the dramatic notices for the *Daily Mail*, 1910–12, "to be Joint-Examiner of Plays with Mr Charles Brookfield, in the room of Mr G. A. Redford, resigned."

decision was come to, and gave it as his personal opinion that there must be some control in these matters.

It is interesting to note, however, that Lord Ribblesdale's opinion has undergone change since he sat on the Commission. "On the balance," he said, "and after hearing most of the evidence as a member of the Stage Censorship Parliamentary Committee, I came with some misgiving to the half-hearted conclusion that no sufficiently strong case had been made out for the abolition of the censorship." But after THE SECRET WOMAN had been banned, Lord Ribblesdale took an opportunity of personally examining the nature of a censored play, and he wrote : "We must look out. . . . I have just returned to this club (Brooks's) from seeing THE SECRET WOMAN at the Kingsway Theatre—in the original text, as I am assured—and I feel most uneasy about the notions I then entertained.

"We all know that the old censorship moved in a mysterious way—it is the nature and the essence of that kind of engine to do so—but what is going to happen now that it has been reconstructed ?

"I confess that I do not like the look of things, by the light of its most recent performance : the refusal of a licence to Mr Eden Phillpotts's play. We must look out."

Apparently Lord Gorell was also convinced, though rather late in the proceedings, of the inherent impracticability and unwisdom of any system of prior censorship. The very last amendment to the Report stands in his name, and is in the following significant words : "*We consider that an optional censorship is not logical*, although it might work, if the powers of licence and of prohibition subsequent to performance were in the same authority with adequate competent advice. Rather than separate these powers, as was suggested by some witnesses, it would be advisable to abolish prior licence altogether. We consider that the choice, therefore, lies between control prior to, or subsequent to, performance, and that, *having regard to all the difficulties of the matter, the system of licence before production should be abolished, and that reliance should be placed on subsequent effective control*." It is futile to speculate as to how Lord Gorell's influence would have modified the findings of the Committee had he arrived earlier in the proceedings at the attitude phrased above. Nevertheless, the change of attitude is noteworthy.

On 11th June 1912, an anti-Censor petition, with an unusually impressive array of signatures, was addressed to the King.[1] On 18th June the Home Secretary stated in the House of Commons that this petition, together with other representations, would be laid before the King. On 7th August a letter was received from the Home Office stating that it had been laid before the King. The preparation of this petition was left in the able hands of Mr Frederick Whelen, and the list of signatories made it a document which could not be ignored without casting a slur on the whole body of contemporary dramatists in England.

Although not directly germane to the question of dramatic censorship, we must mention a deputation

[1] See Appendix.

which in January 1912 waited on Mr R. M'Kenna, the then Home Secretary, to impress upon him the need of more stringent legislation in regard to pernicious and demoralising literature—a phrase obviously intended to be made applicable to a large proportion of modern novels. The deputation, which was headed by Mr St Loe Strachey, and consisted mainly of editors and publishers, aimed at emphasising and stimulating police action. The deputation asked the Home Secretary to introduce a Bill, and also to require the Home Office and the police to be more vigilant and active in the matter of prosecutions. The composition of the deputation called forth a good deal of comment, for not a single author was represented, though it was the liberty of authors as a body which was mainly threatened. We cannot here go into the suggestions of the deputation in detail, which showed a rather curious ignorance as to what can and what cannot be enforced by legislation and repressive police measures. Literary London was amazed to hear some of the names associated with the deputation, and to find men, normally considered broad-minded and tolerant, associating themselves with proposals so bigoted and narrow.

But the most significant thing was the reception accorded the deputation by the Home Secretary. In a singularly indiscreet and unstatesmanlike speech he assured the deputation that immediately the Commissioner of Police returned from India he would consult with him and see what could be done towards securing a more vigilant enforcement of the law, and finally assured the deputation that they

would find the Home Office only too anxious to
carry out the wishes that had been expressed. Mr
M'Kenna's speech was too youthful and futile to
be given at length ; exactly how youthful it was
may be gauged from his remark that " Every man
of common sense knows when he sees a book or a
picture of a particular kind whether the intention
was artistic or whether it was mere obscenity."
That one sentence showed a distressing innocence
of the perilous quicksands on which he was so
eagerly planting his feet. Dicta such as this
naturally provoked indignation among more thoughtful and experienced students of the question, and
though the very exuberance of the Home Secretary's statement discounted any value it might have
had, it was interesting as showing with how very
small and dubious a bait a public official might be
lured from the paths of sanity. With the recollec-
tion fresh in his mind of the difficulties in which
the dramatic censorship had become involved, a more
thoughtful and intelligent approach to the problem
might have been expected.[1]

[1] " The judge or magistrate is to be invested with vague, general,
ill-defined powers over the second class of book, for which reason a
vague, general word like 'indecent' is used. What value, then, can
we attach to the opinion of the deputation that such books should be
left to voluntary action ? Do not let us be duped by words. Let us
ask ourselves how far this Act will apply to books which may be considered works of art. Such books obviously come within the scope of
the proposed Act, for, to quote Mr Strachey, 'if *bona-fide* witnesses
can be brought to declare that, in their opinion, a particular book is a
real work of literature, and that the intention of the author was not to
make money out of indecency, but to carry out his particular view of
art or to further some genuine opinion, such evidence should be given
due weight to by the magistrate.' The deputation, to put it bluntly,
asked that an artist in literature should first be humiliated in the dock
and then dismissed on a quibble. It is a monstrous suggestion. Upon

It was obvious that the enormous popularity of the cinematograph would before long be attracting the attention of those peculiar people who believe themselves specially fitted, by intellect or morality, to " reform " their fellows. England has probably never seen quite so clean or wholesome a form of entertainment introduced as the cinematograph, but to these " reformers " its mere popularity was an offence. It was obvious that there must be something terribly evil in an entertainment which at once attracted the sympathetic support of the majority of the citizens, and which, worst of all, threatened to diminish still further the dwindling Sunday congregations. A number of ministers, whose discourses were too flatulent and insipid to hold the attention of intelligent listeners, made vehement attacks on the new amusement. Those attacks were not always too scrupulous. Not only was the principle of Sunday recreation denounced, but it was broadly hinted that

another ground I object to the same proposal. The law may take cognisance of the intention of a man to commit murder, but I can imagine nothing more mischievous than the present fashion, that seeks to extend this principle, and speaks of the 'political' motive which induces a suffragette to burn His Majesty's mails. All crimes are political. The laws that govern a society should take cognisance not of motives but of effects. We know the prejudice which a charge of indecency provokes, and we know how questionable expert opinion invariably seems to magistrates and to juries, who should only be called upon to decide questions of fact. To me, after a careful consideration of Mr Strachey's speech and the course suggested to the Home Secretary, Mr Strachey's further statement that he does not wish to establish a censorship has an irony about it which is almost Sophoclean. I regret his attitude and that of the gentlemen with whom he was associated, because with the best intentions and with a conspicuous sincerity they are advocating a course which if persisted in will make literature subject to administrative torpor, and liable at any moment to be sacrificed to the clamour of a narrow and intolerant faction."—*Spectator*, 3rd February 1912. Correspondence columns.

the new theatres were, by the mere fact of their darkness, encouraging sexual immorality. The extravagance of this charge stultified it. Every regular frequenter of the theatres merely ridiculed it, and asked at what houses immoralities occurred. These details were naturally not forthcoming, nor was any explanation offered as to how these objectors, who did not visit the theatres, could know more regarding the management of the houses than those who frequented them twice and sometimes three times weekly.

This charge finally died away, as, indeed, it was bound to. The "Sunday desecration" idea, however, lasted longer. It was a striking fact that from one end of the country to the other the police testified that the opening of Sunday picture-theatres had lessened Sunday drunkenness and made an enormous improvement in the condition of the streets. The dreadful English habit of walking the main street for four or five hours, which is the only innocent relaxation our churches for a long time permitted us on Sunday, was at last threatened with extinction. The police who, other things being equal, have been inclined to side with the religious leaders, were rather estranged by the virulence and stupidity of the attacks on what was most obviously a beneficial change, and have, in a majority of cases, testified whole-heartedly in favour of Sunday opening. It has been made quite clear, however, that there are a number of ministers who would be satisfied with nothing short of absolute control of the community on Sunday. Failing that, they would evidently be willing to have the youth of the community exposed to the risks of bored idleness on the streets or the dubious but cheerful company in the public-houses, rather than that they should frequent the picture theatres on Sundays.

Finally, the attack veered, as might have been expected, on to the films themselves. We were told that the pictures which were being shown were tending to demoralise the whole community, and that infamous incitement was being given to riot, robbery, adultery, and bloodshed. In one or two cases it was suggested in court that boy offenders had been encouraged to feats of crude burglary by their having "seen it on the cinematograph." These cases were extensively advertised and a cry raised for censorship; the idea apparently being to emasculate the films if they could not be suppressed, and so bring the entertainment to the innocuous level of a church service. The stupidity of the whole business is self-apparent. If no films of burglaries may be shown for fear of inciting children to such crimes, then novels, police reports, and picture newspapers should be suppressed on the same grounds, and no crime should be permitted to form part of the plot of any novel, newspaper report, or play. Of course, an answer to all this sort of rubbish is to ask why, if these dangers be real, should the minute descriptions which occur in the Bible of every conceivable form of crime be read weekly "before a mixed audience," and thrust into the hands of children to whom these crimes are unknown?

In the meantime, however, fearing that this minority of bigots would, as usual, carry their point through sheer stridency, the film manufacturers in this country appointed a Censor of their own, an appointment which *The Daily News* announced with characteristic smugness as "The very latest moral move for the benefit of the community." A great deal of difficulty was experienced in finding a suitable Censor, and after various gentlemen had been approached, it was decided to appoint Mr G. A. Redford, some of whose exploits as Examiner of Stage Plays have already been referred to in these pages. Mr Redford announced that he hoped "to be able to keep the tremendous number of Cinema theatres throughout the country clean and free from any stigma, *even of vulgarity.*" It will be seen that Mr Redford is shouldering a task which most men would be too modest to accept, since vulgarity is quite as much a matter of the audience as of the performance. Besides, we can imagine some people who would find even Mr Redford's censorship "vulgar," for it is sometimes more vulgar and indecent to cover up ostentatiously the indiscretions of a happy child on the hearth-rug than peaceably to ignore them.

As we dictate these lines the film Censor has not actually started on his career ; but we take from *The Daily News* the following list of things which Mr Redford suggests should be banned :—

"No cremations.

"No final, tear-impelling scenes at funerals, such as lowering the body into the grave, and so on.

"No scenes representing murder, sudden death, or suicide.

" No ' faked ' representations of disasters by sea or land or air.

" No mixed bathing. No ' compromising situations.' No cock fights, no dog fights, and nothing where unnecessary cruelty is brought in, either to man or beast.

" All Biblical scenes to be watched very carefully—particularly anything from the New Testament.

" No Sovereigns, Judges, Ministers, or such high officials of the land to be treated in an unbecoming or undignified or ridiculous manner, and no living individual to be lampooned."

It will be seen that a few subjects for filming are still left to us. There would seem to be no objection to a picture of the Vicar of Little Mumblesea on his lawn or to a Mothers' Sewing Meeting in full swing—if the garments were blotted out. We might even have an inspiring picture of Mr Redford busily censoring films, if it were not for the rule against " tear-impelling " scenes. But, irony apart, we cannot believe that a nation which has for centuries prided itself on its love of sport, its manly virility, and its vigorous independence, will be content with the anæmic dregs from Mr Redford's holy filter. We ask ourselves, Have these rules really been framed for a nation of fighters and manly sportsmen able to do men's work in the world, or had Mr Redford in mind a hospital for anæmic girls of fifteen in the last stage of heart disease ? Have we really reached the stage of senile decrepitude which all this suggests, or is the trouble merely that we are allowing mental and moral invalids too large a share in the control of healthy people ?

This chapter may fittingly be concluded by a short statement as to the present position of dramatic censorship in various foreign countries. Most of these particulars were obtained from His Majesty's Diplomatic Representatives abroad, for the information of the 1909 Select Committee, and appeared as an Appendix to the Report of that Committee.

" *Baden.*—The regulations of theatres and the control over theatrical and other public performances, except in the Grand Ducal Theatre and the National Theatre at Mannheim, which are controlled by an official Censor, are vested in the police, who have power to suppress any performance calculated to give offence or produce disorder.

" *Bavaria.*—Since February 1908 an advisory Censorship Council has been established at Munich in connection with the Directorate of Police. This Council consists of five members, namely, an author, an artist, a schoolmaster, a linguist, and a physician. The Council gives notice to the police, either verbally or in writing, when it is in doubt as to the desirability of allowing the production of any dramatic work. This system is purely local at present.

" *Belgium.*—There is no State censorship of stage plays. The municipal authorities are responsible for the preservation of order in theatres, and have the right to prevent the performance of any play which, in their opinion, might be likely to arouse public feeling.

"*Denmark*.—A licence from the Ministry of Justice is required for the giving of theatrical performances. This licence is granted on condition that the plays produced are first submitted to a Censor appointed by the Ministry of Justice, from whose decisions there is an appeal to the Ministry. In Copenhagen it is also the Censor's duty to supervise performances at music halls, etc., and no song or other kind of entertainment, including cinematograph representations, may be given unless the Censor has approved of it before production. In the provinces the duties of the Censor with regard to the control of music halls, etc., are discharged by the police.

"*France*.—The State censorship of Plays ceased to exist in 1906. At the present time the only restraint upon the performance of a play at a theatre is exercised by the police authorities, who may prosecute the manager if they consider that the play will endanger public order, or is prejudicial to public morals. A 'Commissaire de Police' visits each theatre every evening to take note of the performance.

"Music halls in Paris may only be opened with the authorisation of the police, who may close such establishments summarily if they consider the performances objectionable. In other towns in France the supervision over music halls is exercised by the Prefect of the Department.

"*Hesse*.—There is no actual censorship of stage-plays, etc., but the police may prohibit performances in the interests of the public order, safety, or decency.

"*Holland*.—The control of theatrical and other performances is vested in the Burgomaster of every town by Article 188 of the Municipal Law of 1851. His duty is to watch against anything which is in conflict with public order or morality.

"*Italy*.—The control of theatrical and other public performances is regulated by a statute passed in the year 1889. No public performance of any kind may be given unless the leave of the Public Security Authorities has been obtained. This department is responsible for the safety, etc., of the public in all places of entertainment. In addition to this no opera or stage-play of any kind may be produced without the approval first obtained of the Prefect of the Province in which it is to be performed. The Prefect may withhold his consent to any performance upon grounds of morality or public order. There is an appeal from his decision to the Minister of the Interior.

"*Portugal*.—The censorship of all public performances is vested in the Civil Governor, who, in the outlying townships of his district, delegates his powers to his subordinates. In Lisbon the general powers of the Civil Governor are delegated to the Civil Police, to a branch of which body, viz., the Administrative Police,

belongs the censorship of theatrical performances. The head of this body is practically the
Censor of Stage Plays. From his decisions
there is an appeal to a Committee composed of
three literary men, who receive no payment,
and a superior official of the Ministry of the
Interior. It is open to managers of theatres to
submit the originals of the plays which they
propose to perform to this Committee, but it is
not obligatory for them to do so. If the
approval of the Committee has been obtained
before the production of a play, the police
cannot interfere with its performance, so long
as no alteration is made in the piece. If, however, the approval of the Committee has not
been obtained, the police can order a play to
be stopped at any moment, and all concerned
in its performance are subject to criminal
prosecution.

"As a matter of fact originals of dramatic
works are scarcely ever submitted to the Committee before production, although they are
sometimes shown to the police authorities with
the view of saving the managers from going to
the expense of buying dresses, &c., which might
be disallowed. As a rule, however, the police
will not agree to the performance of a play
simply upon the perusal of the dialogue. An
inspector of police is generally present at the
dress rehearsal of a play and then decides
whether objection must be taken either to the
play itself or to the dresses, make-up, and
gestures of the performers.

"*Saxony.*—A distinction is made between the Royal theatres and theatres under private control. In the former a censorship is exercised over stage plays by an official called the Dramaturg ; in the latter this control is in the hands of the police. The police censorship is conferred upon a high juridicial officer whose duty it is to examine every new play with regard to its moral, political, or religious tendency.

"*Spain.*—The representatives of theatrical companies must supply the Civil Governor, or the Mayor, in towns other than provincial capitals, with two copies of every dramatic work which is to be performed for the first time. Such copies must be signed by the authors, or by representatives of the company, and must be in the hands of the authorities on the same day and at the same hour on which the play is to be performed for the first time. When, in the opinion of the authorities, the performance of a dramatic work involves committing any offence included in the Penal Code, it is at once denounced to a competent court, to which are sent the copies of the play which have been deposited with the Civil Governor. The performance of the play is at once suspended until the decision of the Court of Justice has been given.

"*Sweden.*—There is no longer any State censorship of Plays, but anyone who wishes to give a dramatic, musical, or other public performance is obliged to notify the local police of his intention. When so doing the notifier has to give the authorities all the information which they may require in relation to the nature and purpose of the proposed performance. No special permission from the police authorities is, however, necessary as a rule for giving dramatic and musical performances.

"*Victoria.*—Remarkable steps in the direction of regulating amusements, controlling theatres, and disciplining audiences and performers are foreshadowed in a Theatres Bill which has just been circulated in the State Parliament of Victoria, 14th August 1912. This measure will make a member of the Government an autocrat in command of the pleasures of the people. It contains many wholesome reforms, but alongside them are sections embodying drastic proposals in (to quote the Bill) the interests of ' good manners and decorum.' The Minister is given authority to prohibit any public entertainment, even if produced in a licensed building, should it seem to him desirable to do so. Entertainments on Sunday, Good Friday, and Christmas Day, unless free and of a distinctly religious character, are forbidden. Picture shows are made subject to a censorship, and boxing competitions and circuses are amenable to regulations. Public meetings of many kinds are required to conform to drastic supervision, and only gatherings of a purely charitable or religious nature are exempt from full control.—*Daily Chronicle*, 17th September 1912."

CHAPTER XI

THE feud between the music halls and the regular theatres over the "sketch" problem was brought to an end on the 12th January 1912, when the Lord Chamberlain commenced issuing licences for the performance of stage plays to managers of music halls within the area of his jurisdiction. He announced that he would waive his regulation prohibiting smoking, upon the manager giving him a written undertaking that the programme should consist of not fewer than six items. Managers of theatres could, he said, be placed in a similar position if they wished. The real effect of this concession was rather to strengthen than weaken the control which the Lord Chamberlain exercised over the theatrical world. In any case, the whole question of the "sketch" was a trifling phase in the larger question of censorship; but apart from this one concession no further adjustment of the problem has been arrived at. We have come, then, to the end of our task. A controversial essay on the abolition of the censorship would be both needless and out of place. Every possible argument for or against dramatic censorship has, in recent years, been beaten into fine yarn, and is now ready for weaving into definite legislation. The administrative anomalies of the office have been emphasised, page by page, throughout this book, and in that direction there is little left to be said.

Nevertheless, there are a few loose ends still to be tied up. We have now brought together in coherent form most of the available material relating to this public office, and we shall be justified in making a few broad conclusions. In so doing we should like, if possible, to lift the question as far as may be out of mere topical controversy and personalities, and consider it from a national rather than a purely dramatic standpoint. We have seen how the office had its origin ; how it became legally crystallised, and how it has developed into the thing it now is. As we traced it through the centuries, we were able to discover the motives underlying its activities. First and foremost was the question of personal gain. At no time have its activities been so wide sweeping as when under the control of such men as Herbert and Colman, whose rapacity became a tradition. Throughout its early years, at any rate, the most powerful influence at work was sheer avarice.

There was, even then, however, a more commendable motive. Society was banded to suppress all disruptive elements, and the Censor was only one of a number of court policemen whose duty was to prevent the throwing of intellectual bombs. It is doubtful if such bombs were at that time necessary. The modern bugbear of social unrest was almost unknown, and social conditions were, relatively, not intolerable. Nevertheless, " sedition " was a very practical danger to be guarded against. Anything tending to destroy or challenge the supremacy and authority of Church and State was ruthlessly eliminated. These were poisons the social body could not tolerate, and it promptly purged itself of them. Too much freedom of speech or thought as regards the scope of authority or its exercise could not be permitted. There was jeopardy even in the too careless use of oaths, for to encourage recklessness of speech in the matter of religion would encourage recklessness of speech and of act in other directions. In a word, the Censor was a sort of bodyguard to Authority, and his duty was to see that the people were not indiscreetly encouraged from the stage to make faces at their rulers. Outside these practical limitations dramatists had great freedom ; much greater freedom than is accorded them to-day. Any phase of human activity might be presented on the stage unchecked, and boldness of word as well as of thought was not discouraged.

The third phase came when the office of the Censor resolved itself into a sort of filter of public morals, a phase which has only been noticeable in recent times. In general, however, the Censor has not, until very recent days, set his face against the discussion of sexual problems. By the court the post has consistently been regarded simply as a personal protection, and we have already seen how, when the office was legalised in 1737, it was because the public were criticising, both on and off the stage, a minister whom they regarded as corrupt.

These three phases of censorship have met with varying success. The early Censors were certainly successful in developing the post financially. On the whole, too, they were successful in protecting the throne from seditious plays on the stage. So far as the third phase is concerned, this book has been written in vain if it has not demonstrated that the censorship has not been a serious restraining moral force. We do not wish to recapitulate the hackneyed arguments on this question, but if the Censor is to be regarded as heading any band of moral reformers in the State, we can only say that his sword has done more execution over his shoulder than in front of him.

The Saturday Review excellently summed up this peculiarity when it said :

" In ninety-eight out of every hundred plays submitted to him (this is an official estimate) no question of morals is raised. He has nothing to do but read the play, pocket his two guineas, license the performance, and leave the manager and the author under the impression that he is a very agreeable, unobjectionable person, whose licence is cheap at the price since it relieves everyone of responsibility and makes things pleasant all round. It is not until the two per cent. of plays in which received impressions and hardened prejudices are called in question, and offered for test under the searching rays of the footlights—in other words, the plays on which the whole growth and continued vitality of the theatre depend—that the Censor has his opportunity of showing how much better he is than the public by saying, 'You should listen to these plays, however much they shock you. I have read them, and can certify that they will interest really cultivated people and help to set everybody thinking.' But as the Censor never is any better than the average public, he does exactly the reverse of this. He shares its ignorant intolerance, and its petulance under criticism, and uses his official authority to forbid the performance of the exceptional plays."

But *Blackwood's Magazine*—to take one of the more ardent of the defenders of censorship—has no faith in these exceptional plays. It does not believe we shall again have great or exceptional plays, and when Mr Archer contended that the Censor's standard would have ruled out HAMLET and OTHELLO, it answered, " That is beside the point. The Censor has no control over the works of Shakespeare, and he is not likely to have a modern HAMLET or a modern OTHELLO submitted to him." The senile idiocy of that argument is not worth even anger. Who is to convince us that some Censor has not already contemptuously snuffed out a smaller Shakespeare ? Certainly an author to-day who started on his dramatic career, as Shakespeare did, with a sensual love-song, would have a reception which would send him back to his butcher's block for the rest of his life. The only reason why the Censor has no control over the works of Shakespeare is, as one Censor frankly admitted, that the public would not tolerate interference with those particular works.

Even this particular play of HAMLET has, on occasion, brought to light people who would willingly censor Shakespeare. In Parry's *Life of Macklin* a playbill is to be found, worth reproduction here :

" Bill of Kilkenny Theatre Royal.
By his Majesty's Co. of Comedians,
The last night, because the Co. go tomorrow to Waterford.

On Saturday, May 14*th,* 1793.

Will be performed by command of several respectable people in this learned metropolis, for the benefit of Mr Kearns

THE TRAGEDY OF HAMLET.

Originally written and composed by the celebrated Dan Hayes of Limerick, and inserted in Shakespeare's works.

Hamlet by Mr KEARNS (being his first appearance in that character) who, between the acts, will perform several solos on the patent bagpipes, which play two tunes at the same time.

Ophelia by Mrs PRIOR, who will introduce several favourite airs in character, particularly ' The Lass of Richmond Hill' and 'We'll all be Unhappy Together' from the Rev. Mr Dibdin's ' Oddities.'

The parts of the King and Queen, by the direction of the Rev. Father O'Callaghan, will be omitted, as too immoral for any stage.

Polonius, the comical politician, by a young gentleman, being his first appearance in public.

The Ghost, The Gravedigger, and Laertes, by Mr SAMPSON, the great London comedian.

The characters to be dressed in Roman shapes.

To which will be added an Interlude, in which will be introduced several sleight of hand tricks by Professor HURST.

The whole to conclude with the farce of

MAHOMET THE IMPOSTOR.

Tickets to be had of Mr Kearns, at the sign of the Goat's Beard in Castle Street.

The value of the tickets as usual will be taken (if required) in candles, bacon, soap, butter, cheese, etc., as Mr Kearns wishes in every particular to accommodate the public.

N.B.—No person whatever will be admitted into the boxes without shoes or stockings."

There have been Censors who have confessed how much they would like, with the Rev. Father O'Callaghan, to lick Shakespeare into shape, and if, as *Blackwood's* says, Censors to-day have not that power, it is impotence, and not censorial modesty that has restrained them.

The canons of all this criticism are not difficult to discover. In mentioning a certain play, Mr Barker said that there was one incident in it which he thought might offend the Censor. That incident was the love of a man for his father's young wife. He did not say that was the sole motive of the play; but that it was a part which might have offended the Censor. *Blackwood's* comment was characteristic. "The hardship does not seem to us intolerable, nor does the motive of the play, as described by Mr Barker—the love of a man for his father's young wife—persuade us that a heavy blow would be struck at the art of the drama if it were suppressed." The method of treatment did not interest *Blackwood's* at all, nor the skill in dramatisation; it was not even concerned with the moral standpoint taken. A brief, one-line synopsis was sufficient to convince it that the drama would not suffer a heavy loss if the play were suppressed.

It is worth illustrating this particular method of criticism—which has certain national characteristics—by another specific instance. What, we wonder, would critics of the *Blackwood's Magazine* type say to the following play?

"Here is a distinctly dismal and depressing tale. It tells of the morbid utterances of a half-crazy young prince who has discovered that his father has been murdered by his own brother. This brother has taken the crown, and with it the murdered king's wife. The prince treats his mother as a wanton, and addresses her continually in becomingly coarse language. He kills the father of his betrothed, who goes mad and drowns herself. Eventually the king arranges a little fencing match, with a poisoned foil, and as an extra precaution, has a poisoned drink. The prince gets wounded, then wounds his opponent with the same weapon. All at once an explanation is made, whereupon the prince stabs the king. In the meanwhile the queen drinks the poison and dies. Then the explainer drops, then the king, then the prince, then the curtain." [1]

Blackwood's would have suppressed that play solely on its synopsis ; but that play was HAMLET !

There are one or two broad comments we would make on the relation of the stage to the State. Collier made the cardinal mistake of assuming that the stage had been the cause of the vice it reflected. He lost all sense of proportion, and wrote as though the stage was ten times more evil than the community, and the only vile spot in a nation of virgin innocence. That was exaggeration on one side. We have recently had exaggeration on the other in an effort to show that the Restoration drama, under a tolerant censorship, was not really indecent.

[1] This synopsis, slightly modified, is taken from *The Times*, 11th December 1894, and is by Stanley Weigall.

Neither of these attitudes is fair. The stage has at all times reflected contemporary morality. The Restoration drama was, by modern standards, grossly indecent, but so was the Restoration life and language. What we regard as indecency of speech was not confined to the stage, and was not even confined to the secular masses. It had, as is well known, invaded the pulpits of the time to a notable extent. This indecency of speech—which must not be confused with indecency of morals — when presented on the stage passed unnoticed, because it did not offend the current canons of good taste. We must emphasise this fact. The level of decency in the drama has never varied widely from the level of decency in the street. The public has at all times maintained that drama only which appealed to its tastes.

We shall be asked whether public tastes are to be gratified without check? In that connection we would say that, if the tastes of a nation are toward things which a minority regard as evil, there is no legislative check capable of preventing their gratification. Moreover, if such a check were practicable, what body could be considered competent to say what public tastes might be gratified, and what might not? The Church, to which some might have looked in such a question, has by its official abstention from the stage sacrificed its right to an opinion. It cannot expect to be accepted as an unprejudiced arbiter in a sphere which it has consistently and indiscriminately denounced. Moreover, the Church has shown a voluble impracticability in dealing with any aspect of secular affairs, which rather disheartens the mere spectator. The Bible and hymn-book have been too prominent when affairs of practical public policy have been in question. When called to give relief to a poisoned system, it has too often been inclined to sit down and argue about a state of soul. Social evils are not remedied in that way, and any attempt to control dramatic tastes on those lines would be disastrous.[1]

Ardent and unsophisticated moral reformers instinctively turn to the law for assistance. They would have their patent medicines administered by Act of Parliament, and the results of such a policy are catastrophic, for puritanic laws produce worse evils than those they are intended to cure. We have an illustration to our hand in America. The demoralisation in the New York Police Force is directly traceable to the fact that legislation has been far ahead of what can be enforced. Mr Sidney Brooks, as a result of a careful study of the position, has

[1] The impracticability of the average religious mind when dealing with big social problems has been well illustrated by the recent and sudden outcry over the White Slave Traffic. We do not think it is unfair to comment that, if the Church had produced an army of social workers and not talkers, such phases of that traffic as are curable would have been cured ten years ago. Instead, we have had a sudden clamour for drastic legislation and a demand for the names of those members of Parliament who have dared to hold a contrary opinion, and who have advocated moderation. If this is not the old bigoted spirit which would pillory an honest opponent, we do not understand bigotry. We should whisper two facts: the first is that the Church's belated discovery of an evil so old and extensive as this, is a scathing criticism on its utter detachment from human affairs. The second is that nothing contributes to the success of the White Slave Traffic more directly than the stigma which our conventions, encouraged by the Church, has placed on the outraged girl. In how many churches, one wonders, might such a girl state her wrongs and not be subjected to icy humiliations in comparison with which a life of vice would be attractive.

concluded that such strict puritanical laws, as made by the Legislature, cannot be strictly enforced, and there is, therefore, every temptation to set them aside by common consent. "In the result everybody is satisfied. The law remains on the statute book, a glowing testimonial to the 'morality' of New York; it is not put into action, so nobody feels its inconvenience, and the politicians and the police grow rich on the proceeds of its non-enforcement." When the Mazet Committee sat in 1899 to investigate the police corruption for the second time they came to the same conclusion, and stated that "the police laxity towards certain laws (meaning those aimed at the suppression of vice) inevitably results in laxness towards all criminal offences." It ought, by now, to be axiomatic that legislation enforcing one level in morality is as futile as legislation enforcing one size in hats.

When we come to consider the position in special relation to the stage, we find that it really hinges on different definitions of the permissible limits of liberty. Legislation should tend toward greater liberty. As we grow, rules lose their significance and are superseded by principles; but there seem to be a number of people who would reverse that process and are willing to accept a multiplicity of laws as progress. "Progress" of that kind has two notable results. By putting the morals of a nation in a sort of plaster cast those morals lose their strength and become nerveless. A morality which is hot-pressed between the leaves of a Statute is only the scentless, worthless ruins of virtue.

The second effect is reaction. The vast majority

of the British public is wholly inarticulate, and the articulate and voluble minorities create an effect wholly disproportionate to their numbers. For one bigot who objects to some play or newspaper article there may be five hundred who enjoy it, but would not go to the trouble of writing to say so. Many of us in these matters are phlegmatic optimists, relying, and sometimes relying over-much, on national common-sense to counteract fanatical excesses. We believe it is quite possible that a movement might be set on foot sufficiently vigorous to secure a stricter censorship of plays, largely on account of the inertia of the majority of playgoers. We are, as a nation, easily trodden on ; shamefully indifferent to attacks on our personal liberties. Then, when the burden has become intolerable, we retaliate, and our retaliation is nearly as blind as our indifference was.

Reformers must be urged to face these facts. In conspicuous sincerity they often approach these problems with a flaming enthusiasm which blinds them to all moderation. That has been characteristic of reformers in all ages. Filmer was speaking of the same spirit in his time when he said, " Had those strait-laced partisans of Collier's, with Mr Collier's charitable assistance, once gained their point against plays, we should quickly find them nibbling at most of our other diversions, and giving our ladies as frightful an idea perhaps of Hyde Park or the Mall as Mr Collier has already done of the play-house." Now, as then, it is the people with religious convictions who are the commonest offenders.[1]

---

[1] An example is to be found in the ill-considered outcry raised by some of these people for the closing of the Sunday cinematograph

What then of censorship? How then does it fit in with these broad modern requirements? We have seen how the office came into existence and on what lines it developed. A recent Examiner[1] has placed on record what purports to be the modern official view of the Censor's duties, though we fear he had in mind at the time the dramatic censorship in Utopia:

" It is his business and duty, as the responsible adviser of the Lord Chamberlain, to administer those clauses of the Act which concern his department in the most liberal spirit, with the discernment and discrimination that belong to a wide knowledge of the world, and that cultivated sympathy with literature and art, which is equally regardful of public morality and public decency, and of the freedom and dignity of a liberal profession and a noble art. He does not pretend to be an arbiter of taste, or, as he is jestingly described, a *censor morum*. It is only at the point where public manners affect public morals

theatres. Such a course would almost inevitably provoke a demand for the opening of ordinary as well as picture theatres; but apparently these people prefer to blink the fact for the moment. They have characteristically suggested that after the Sunday licences were withdrawn the churches might do something to present "harmless amusement under proper supervision" on Sunday afternoons! The unconscious impudence of the suggestion is delightful; but whether any large body of citizens would be seen entering the Church to indulge in this mild and "harmless amusement" at the hands of a clerical Censor is to be doubted. If the Church would only distinguish between useless and useful effort, some practical measures might result. We might, for instance, have some picture, as well as ordinary, theatres of a secular and not religious type run solely for young people, where parents might send their children with confidence. Such a venture would be profitable and widely appreciated, and quite legitimately falls within the Church's scope. But we have no hope of seeing so sane a project executed.

[1] E. F. S. Pigott.

that his responsibility begins. The guardianship of abstract morality must always belong to the pulpit. . . . The principles on which the Examiner of Plays consistently acts are to eschew even the faintest semblance of a frivolous or vexatious interference with the managers ; not to fritter away official influence upon details ; to act as much as possible by personal intercourse or confidential correspondence with the managers ; and in some cases even, unofficially, with the authors of the plays ; in short, to avoid all unnecessary friction." The superintendent of the Lord Chamberlain's department, giving evidence before the 1853 Select Committee, said, " the understanding is perfectly clear, unless the matter is *excessively and extravagantly offensive*, that the licence should not be withheld."

We will be moderate and say that censorship has at no time conformed to this specification. Had it done so the present agitation would not have arisen. Instead, we have had a censorship which, in addition to a dozen well-known evils, has steadily weakened the sense of responsibility in the public. Like all such supposed moral " safeguards," it has tended to produce atrophy of the moral sense of the nation. In *The Saturday Review* for 2nd March 1895 you will find interesting corroboration of that assertion. A somewhat puritanical critic wrote a short epitome of an opera, presented at a West End theatre :

" There were two heroines, one a princess. The hero had to marry the princess, though he loved the other heroine. In the second act the stage represented an ante-chamber in the palace of the bride's father on the night of the wedding. The door of the nuptial chamber appeared on the stage. It was guarded by an elderly duenna. The reluctant bridegroom arrived on his way to join his bride. The duenna presented him with the golden key of the chamber. Suddenly it occurred to him that if he were to criminally assault this lady, who was renowned at Court for her austerity, her screams would rouse the Court, and he would be consigned by the outraged monarch to a dungeon, thereby escaping his conjugal obligations. On proceeding to carry out this stratagem he was taken aback by finding the old lady, far from raising an alarm, receive his advances with the utmost ardour. In desperation he threw her to the ground, and was about to escape, when she, making no effort to rise, said, with archly affectionate reproach, ' Don't you see where you've left me, duckie ? ' On this he fled, and presently a young man and a young woman entered and flirted until they were interrupted by the king. He, overhearing a kiss, supposed it to proceed from the bridal chamber of his daughter. He immediately went to the door ; listened at the keyhole ; and, hearing another kiss, remarked, with an ecstatic shiver, that it made him feel young again. If that scene had not been presented to the public under the authority of the Lord Chamberlain, it would be impossible for me to describe it in these columns."

Another proof of the fact that official censorship has tended to destroy the sense of individual responsibility is to be found in the demand, made by a number of people, that a public official should relieve them of their responsibility in connection with the education and moral development of their children. They have made claims which are tantamount to a demand that they shall be able, without the exercise of parental discrimination, to send their children to any theatrical performance in the kingdom. Yet these same people would quickly exercise their own judgment to prevent a girl of ten from wearing an evening dress and a matinee hat, or a boy of eight from ordering a frock coat. Why parental responsibility should be exercised to prevent unfitting precocity in costume and not in morals is hard to understand.

We cannot help asking with Goethe, what are our young girls doing at the theatre, anyway? The stage may be wholly admirable in its influence and yet be an unsuitable browsing ground for an unguided girl of sixteen. Why a parent should insist on his child's music lessons being properly graduated, and yet permit her to learn her moral lessons in any haphazard fashion is not easily answered. The average theatre is intended for people who have reached an intellectual puberty, and to insist on it conforming to the digestive capacity of infants is about as reasonable as for a hostess to expect her guests to dine on milk-sop because the baby must.

Timid people insist that the abolition of the censorship would involve risks. We are glad to think it would. A life without risks is a life without merit. Risks breed virile men and nations, and a nation which dares not to take the risks of freedom is only fit for slavery. With too much confinement and shelter one may easily grow too weak for freedom. But in any case, to purchase freedom of thought with human blood and then delegate its exercise to a Censor at £400 a year is a proceeding which must make the gods laugh.

Let us face the situation frankly and ask ourselves what the risks of abolition are, and whether they are serious enough to justify a humiliating restriction.[1] But there is another question we must consider first. What is the value and strength of the shield it is proposed to abolish? We must point out that the actual censorship has been operating over a comparatively small field. All " private " performances are uncensored. All performances for which no admittance fees are paid are uncensored.[2] All music-hall performances are uncensored, and all old plays including, we must repeat, the most licentious plays which

---

[1] *Blackwood's Magazine* once said that "the fact of the Censor's existing is said to cast a slur upon the good faith and good morals of a respectable class. This cannot be admitted, unless we admit also that the existence of the gallows is an open insult to the peaceful law-abiding citizen." But, with customary brilliance, *Blackwood's* has missed the point of its own simile. It is not a question of the gallows being an open insult to every law-abiding citizen, but of the gallows being specially flaunted in the faces of one small, honourable, and distinguished section. It is in this differentiation that the insult lies.

[2] The Lord Chamberlain cannot exercise any powers over private performances. Edward Lytton Bulwer has reminded us that four of the Kembles once acted together with Mrs Siddons as heroine, in performances for which no admittance fee was charged. Play-bills were, however, circulated, containing this notice : "Nota Bene.—No money taken at the door, but Mr So-and-so (naming a performer) has a very excellent tooth powder at 2s. 1d. a box." Expedients such as these have, as Lord Chesterfield prophesied, been resorted to ever since the passing of the 1737 Act.

have ever been written for the English stage, are also uncensored. Yet there are people who claim that the Censor is a proven necessity. He has spent all his time scrubbing his own little attic floor, and the claim now is that he has kept the whole palace clean.

Not only have the Censor's activities been confined to a small portion of our national stage, but even over that portion his jurisdiction has been imperfect. He has no authority for enforcing such alterations to a play as he may deem necessary. Colman repudiated the idea of his being a spy on the theatre. Pigott also said that he would be very sorry to pursue any manager with a sort of system of espionage which would, he added, be impracticable and worse than arbitrary. In fact, it seems never to have been the practice for succeeding Examiners to take any steps to ascertain whether their prohibitions and emendations had actually been given effect to, though in 1895 the Examiner was informed that he was expected to visit the theatres to see that "the rules of the department" were carried out.

The result has been, of course, that corrections have been acquiesced in for the sake of securing a licence, and afterwards ignored. Mr John Hollingshead has told us of one actor, Mr Wright of the Adelphi, who was such a favourite with the public that he had full liberty to do as he liked, and whatever the Lord Chamberlain struck out of the dialogue he took care to put in again with additions. When the HAPPY LAND was first submitted, it only contained some twenty-four pages, whereas over forty were acted. Mr Redford once censored a play

called THE AGAPEMONE, or THE ABODE OF LOVE,
which was thereupon transferred to the Middlesex
Music Hall, over which he had no jurisdiction.   It
has been freely admitted that it is largely a matter of
chance whether any alterations come to the ear of
the Censor or not, so that in actual practice he has
largely to rely on the good faith and discretion of the
managers and authors.   We believe that in almost
every case in recent times that reliance has been
justified ; but the point to observe is that the actual
protection afforded by the Censor alone (quite apart
from his errors of judgment) has been very slight.

But let us suppose this slight shield abolished.
What are the risks ?   The prompt answer will be
that mushroom managers would be tempted to produce a class of play derogatory to public morals.   As
one journal aptly put it : " If the stage were freed,
managers would immediately produce licentious plays,
actresses would leave off clothing themselves decently,
and the public would sit nightly wallowing in the
obscenity which the Censor now sternly withholds
from them."   If that was the inherent tendency, we
should expect to find that in that part of the stage
which is exempt from the Censor's control the class
of performance steadily has deteriorated.   That is
precisely what has not occurred.   The music-hall
stage, we are told, cannot be censored ; not *ought* not,
but cannot.   Repeatedly it has been stated before the
different Commissions that it would be a physical
impossibility to censor the innumerable sketches,
acts, songs, gags, etc., which are nightly placed
before the audiences in our music halls.   This
enormous mass of matter has therefore gone uncen-

sored, and, so far as music halls are concerned, preventive censorship has not existed.

Nevertheless, both opponents and friends of the censorship have had to admit that the tone of the music hall is steadily rising, that the performances have improved, both in taste and quality, and that the general improvement in the music hall during the last thirty years has been much more rapid and marked than has been the case with the legitimate stage, which has advanced under the censorial wing. The fact is significant. The censorship of the managers themselves, and of the general public, has, over this very large field, proved perfectly efficient. In spite of the extraordinary number of songs, gags, sketches, acts, etc., produced every night in London, only *forty* complaints were received during the four years 1905–9, and out of those the London County Council's inspectors only thought it necessary to take action in respect of *nine*. During the licensing year ending November 1911, only eight complaints were received. In four cases no action was found necessary, and only in one case was the licensee asked to discontinue the performance, and even in that case a modified version was subsequently allowed.[1] No more conclusive answer could be imagined to the claim that the abolition of preventive censorship would result in a lower tone in the theatre.

We have just said something about the efficiency of the censorship exercised by the public itself. We do not wish to go into a discussion of the matter in detail ; but as a fact the public is apt *en masse* to be rather particular as to the liberties which an author

[1] See Appendix.

takes with it. When Boucicault's comedy, OLD HEADS AND YOUNG HEARTS, was produced at the Haymarket in 1844, there was a love scene at the end where Charles Matthews had to say to the lady, "I came to scoff, but I remain to pray," he being on his knees. The public, imagining this innocent expression — really taken from Goldsmith — came out of the Bible, took offence at it and hissed vigorously. When Charles Reade's piece, IT's NEVER TOO LATE TO MEND, was first produced at the Princess Theatre, the public, or at any rate a noisy portion of it, took offence at the prison scene in a rather belligerent manner. Similarly, when THE DEVIL was produced, the gallery objected to certain portions, and called out, "Where is the Censor?" Quite recently, February 1912, Sir Arthur Pinero's play, THE MIND-THE-PAINT GIRL, met with the disapproval of a portion of the audience, who did not hesitate to express it fairly vigorously and to rush into print next day with some very pointed comment on the nature of the piece as judged by them. Mr Redford has admitted that he relied on the unappreciative reception certain plays would receive, to result in their withdrawal, an admission which, from a Censor, is rather like an abdication.

Naturally, in countries where preventive censorship is not in force, the public take their responsibilities more seriously. When Dumas' L'AFFAIRE CLEMEN-CEAU was first produced in America, it caused some excitement. The heroine was represented standing on a pedestal in her husband's studio for a figure of Venus. One of our own Censors in speaking of the piece said, "this statue was to be presented by her, not to her husband, but to her lover, and she was represented in transparent tights." In view of *two* such heinous offences it is not surprising to find that our Censor regarded Dumas' effort as "a most disgusting piece." It was played at a Brooklyn Theatre and caused so much comment that after a time, when all the respectable Press had been denouncing it, the police stepped in and stopped the run. The public sense of decency at that time and place was offended, and in a logical way the play in question was soon brought to an end.

In Sydney, recently, the proprietors of the Adelphi Theatre received an order from the Chief Secretary's Department to eliminate a certain scene from a drama entitled BROUGHT TO RUIN. In this scene a baby—really a doll—is suffocated with a wet towel. Apparently some highly sympathetic spectators thought the baby was a live one, and made representations to the Australian licensing authority. The amusing point about this incident was that Mr OSCAR ASHE, at another theatre in the same city, was nightly strangling his own wife, an obviously flesh-and-blood Desdemona. We can quite easily imagine some managers shuddering at stories such as this. To be placed at the mercy of some ill-balanced cranks will seem a poor exchange perhaps for the eccentricities of the Censor. It seems to us that this is one of the risks which a manager must face, and may legitimately be expected to face. The manager must not, more than any other semi-public man, expect to be protected legally from the attacks of ignorant bigots. Here, again, the solution lies in overcoming the inertia of the sympathetic majority. Individual cranks only succeed in imposing their ideas on the majority, because the majority is intellectually too lazy to get up and shout them down. It is not that these cranks represent the considered opinion of the majority ; but they are voluble and assertive, and in some cases organised. The supporters of the drama must be stung to equal assertion of their rights, and, if necessary, to retaliatory attacks.

For a time, of course, managers would have to face the risks of ignorant and dogmatic criticism ; that self-satisfied, idea-impervious criticism which one witness illustrated when he said, " I should not have the least hesitation myself in deciding whether a play was or was not suitable for production—apart from literary merit or dramatic merit." It will become a virtue to ruffle this irritating complacency, to reduce it to a becoming modesty, and to make it confess that there may be a few ideas in the world which cannot be dismissed " without the least hesitation." In a word, we must have a militant stage, jealous in defence of its rights, secure in its consciousness of public approval, and keen to return word for word and blow for blow.

As we have said, for some time managers must expect a certain crudity of criticism. Till the public works off its first stiffness of judgment, we must expect some awkward and ungainly demonstrations : but very quickly the crudities will disappear and the standard of criticism be raised. The sort of criticism we must look for for a time will be the kind Dr Mosely gave to George Colman, the stage Censor, when the latter read to him his play of INKLE AND YARICO. When Colman had finished the proud reading, he waited for some praise from Dr Mosely, but the doctor obstinately held his tongue. At last Colman ventured the question, " What do you think of it ? " " It won't do at all," snapped the doctor, " It's a lot of stuff and nonsense ! " Colman was amazed and hurt, for everybody so far had expressed themselves as delighted with the play. He begged the doctor to give him his reasons, and at last the latter replied : " I'll tell you why. You say in the finale—

> " ' Now let us dance and sing
>   While all Barbadoe's bells do ring.'

" It won't do at all ! There is only one bell in all the island."

If any reader wishes to study a further instance of bigoted criticism we would refer him to *The Times* controversy of 1894, which practically started the modern censorship agitation. The play in question, which Sir Herbert Tree had produced, was JOHN A DREAMS, by Haddon Chambers. In that play a woman, to save from utter destitution an enfeebled and dying mother, had given herself, without passion or gain of her own, to a detested suitor. Since then her life had been an entirely moral one ; but a number of amiable persons who objected to the play made no scruple of calling her a " harlot "! One virtuous letter-writer protested against " permitting the public glorification of harlotry as a fit subject of entertainment for our wives and daughters," and an Englishwoman wrote to say that "the mere thought and knowledge of sin sullies the pure and innocent mind and heart." There was also in the play a man who, to quote the Rev. H. B. Chapman, was "an idealist, handicapped by a terrible hereditary taint, which he nobly conquers, for the sake of love." This character one amiable critic described as "an opium-drinking sot"; and on these lines the whole genial controversy progressed day by day, with that bigoted distortion, that curious priggish aptitude for calling things spades which are not spades, and that utter lack of humane understanding which characterises so much British criticism. As a nation we seem to have an eccentric fondness for discussing certain questions on stilts, with a mutual understanding that no one shall look lower than his opponent's feet or get down on the solid ground under penalty of ostracism. It is a game which has some mild excitement for the participants; but which is apt to look ridiculous to those who prefer to stand solid on two feet.

We have just said something about the stage being secure in its knowledge of public approval. That approval should be recognised and confirmed in every possible way. The Select Committee of 1832 bluntly stated that one reason of the admitted decline of public taste was the absence of royal encouragement, as well as the slender encouragement afforded to literary talent to devote its labours towards the stage. The royal family in England has varied very largely in different periods in the amount of patronage extended to the stage. It has not always withheld patronage of a kind. The lessee of the Adelphi Theatre told before the 1866 Committee of one

royal Duke who said he would take a private box
for the whole of the year if he was allowed a key
to go behind the scenes. He was quietly told that
that privilege would not be granted him if he took
the whole theatre. Needless to say, it was not
encouragement of this kind to which the 1832
Committee referred. It may be laid down as a
general axiom that just as we look to Royalty to
honour notable achievements in science, discovery,
arms, or sport, by its presence, so we look to Royalty
to honour those who are endeavouring to raise the
intellectual and artistic standing of the nation,
whether it happens personally to sympathise with
them or not.

In so far as the discussion of sexual problems is
concerned, we anticipate that in the near future more
licence will be granted to dramatic authors and freer
general discussion encouraged. We cannot always
hope to hold a veil before our sores ; sooner or later
either the veil must fall or we must. It ought not
to be necessary to plead for the simple virtue of
sincerity. As women assume an increasing part in
public affairs they will enforce more candour in the
discussion of all these questions, and it seems as if
their candour is going to be all the greater because
of the restraint imposed on them in the past. In the
settling of these problems one of the most powerful
mediums will be the stage, both tragic and comic.
Let us take a high and broad view of the position
at once and not be forced to a humiliating series
of niggling compromises. In these matters George
Bernard Shaw has as much right as any minister to
be heard without charge of indecency, and, as a

matter of fact, is probably better fitted for the discussion.

Returning to the fundamental question, the issue would seem to be : are our social evils going to be made worse by talking of them ? If you apply the same question to, say, smallpox, it becomes obviously absurd. If you talk about the terrors of smallpox long enough to persons with any health left, you will provoke them, sooner or later, to get up and wash something. Incidentally, we may remark that the same effect might be achieved even by a funny story about the terrors of smallpox. Then we shall be told that people usually talk neither of smallpox nor of social evils. But that is untrue, and if it were true, it would be unfortunate, for a nation of people talking of smallpox would very quickly discover a remedy. As to the discussion of sex problems, we would say quite moderately that they figure largely in modern conversation. Moreover, they will, in the future, figure more largely than ever before. As women become articulate as a sex, they will, as we have said, insist on the problem being faced with greater candour. No one who has studied the output of women novelists in recent years can be under any illusions on that score. Frankly, we welcome the tendency. We would like to see the whole question faced, disposed of, and relegated to a normal position in human affairs.

Above all, we have got to pinch the public conscience till it shouts. We have got to awaken those public voices which have been hushed into silence by soporific processes such as delegating con-

sciences to a public official. We must do away
with the Public Spokesman, with his tendency to
omniscience and academic cant. We must see that
the voice which is heard is the right voice, and not
the voice of a minority heard simply because it is
strident and organised. Just as we like to see a
youngster thrown on his own resources and made to
think and act and feel for himself, so we would like to
see a nation standing firm on its feet and facing the
winds of life, open-eyed on every side. Those winds
would tear away some of our cherished veils, would
leave some of us breathless and others shouting, both
with fear and with joy. It would, at any rate, be
something gained to have found a voice, and in the
theatre a few healthy, unpremeditated " boos " would
come like a wind from the hills. It is toward this
healthy emancipation, with its risks and rewards,
that our stage has to steer.

Yet, when all this has been said, and said in
earnest sincerity, there comes an uncomfortable
feeling that it is as from the teeth outward ; mere
words divorced from hope. For we have yet to be
convinced that there is in this country any considerable class capable of appreciating the lyrical exaltation
by which all art exists. In poetry, in painting, in
music, especially in sex, that exaltation shocks and
bewilders us, and far from stirring us, as it did the
Greeks, to reverence and humility, it provokes in us
scorn and ridicule and outraged protest. No nation
has set its seal on the earth more solidly than the
English, and on no nation has the earth returned
the compliment with such vindictive savagery. We
have spread roots into this world which shall hold

till the day of doom ; but that kiss of divine fire which would make our harsh gnarled branches bourgeon into gracious flower and mellow fruit seems to be denied us.   Until that coveted fire comes we must nurse our artistic barrenness, perforce content to see that when the first frail buds of promise appear no uncouth hand shall dare to strike them down.

That is the supreme argument against censorship in England.

APPENDICES

Plays Licensed and Refused.

A return, supplied by courtesy of the Lord Chamberlain and now published for the first time, showing the numbers of Stage Plays licensed from the year 1852 to the year 1912, and also the numbers of Plays for which licences were refused (see page 190) :—

Date.	Licences Granted.	Licences Refused.	Date.	Licences Granted.	Licences Refused.
1852	225	2	1883	287	1
1853	204	2	1884	320	0
1854	219	3	1885	288	2
1855	162	0	1886	294	3
1856	176	1	1887	304	3
1857	183	1	1888	348	0
1858	165	2	1889	287	1
1859	202	2	1890	297	0
1860	242	3	1891	244	1
1861	217	1	1892	396	1
1862	201	1	1893	362	0
1863	220	0	1894	433	0
1864	200	0	1895	374	4
1865	181	1	1896	461	2
1866	173	0	1897	481	3
1867	174	0	1898	440	2
1868	159	0	1899	464	6
1869	150	2	1900	466	3
1870	184	2	1901	513	2
1871	263	5	1902	519	2
1872	206	1	1903	538	3
1873	247	0	1904	468	1
1874	178	1	1905	520	2
1875	213	0	1906	579	2
1876	344	0	1907	536	4
1877	272	4	1908	560	4
1878	204	0	1909	577	3
1879	272	0	1910	604	2
1880	252	0	1911	608	6
1881	286	0	1912 (to Oct. 31st).	1070	6
1882	302	0			

COPY OF OATH TAKEN BY EXAMINER OF PLAYS.

You shall swear by the Holy Evangelists, and the contents of that book, to be a true and faithful servant unto our Sovereign Lord George the Fourth of the United Kingdom of Great Britain and Ireland King.

You shall know nothing that may be in any wise hurtful or prejudicial to His Majesty's Royal Person, State, Crown or Dignity, but you shall hinder it all in your power and reveal the same to the Lord Chamberlain or one of His Majesty's most Honourable Privy Council.

You shall serve the King truly and faithfully in the place and quality of Examiner of all plays, tragedies, comedies, operas, farces and interludes or any other entertainment of the stage of what denomination soever.

You shall be obedient to the Lord Chamberlain of His Majesty's household.

[So help you GOD.]

MEMORANDUM ON THE LAW AND PRACTICE AS TO RESTORATION PLAYS.

LORD CHAMBERLAIN'S OFFICE,
ST JAMES'S PALACE, S.W.

The practice has always been to regard plays of this period as not coming under the designation of new stage plays. They are treated in the same category as Shakespear's plays, which are not submitted for licence.

With regard to the law, by a Warrant of the 4th June 1647, issued in consequence of profane plays being brought forward, no new play was to be acted till submitted to the Lord Chamberlain's Secretary.

By the Act 10 George II., cap. 28, to take effect from and after the 24th June 1737, the illegality of producing or acting any new play, &c., without sending a copy to the Lord Chamberlain 14 days at least before its performance was established. The Act also provided that the Lord Chamberlain could, whenever he thought fit, prohibit a performance of "any interlude, tragedy, comedy," &c., or any part thereof.

This Act has been repealed, but the powers are preserved by the Theatres Act of 1843, which requires that any new play, &c., must be submitted to the Lord Chamberlain for licence, and gives him powers, under Section 14, to stop the performance of any play, however old, "in the interests of good manners, docorum or of the public peace."

10th August 1909.

COPY OF THE LICENCE ISSUED BY THE LORD CHAMBERLAIN TO PERMIT THE PERFORMANCE OF A STAGE PLAY.

It having been represented to Me by the Examiner of all Theatrical Entertainments that a

does not in its general tendency contain anything immoral or otherwise improper for the Stage I The Lord Chamberlain of His Majesty's Household do by virtue of my Office and in pursuance of the Act of Parliament in that case provided Allow the Performance of the said   at your
with the exception of all Words and Passages which are specified by the Examiner in the endorsement of this Licence and without any further variations whatsoever.

Given under my hand this   day of   190

Lord Chamberlain.

To the Manager of the

MEM.—The particular attention of the Management is called to the following Regulations, which refer to all Stage Plays licensed by the Lord Chamberlain. The strict observance of these Regulations is to be considered as the condition upon which the Licence is signed.

Notice of the change of title of a piece to be given to the Examiner of Plays.

No profanity or impropriety of language to be permitted on the Stage.

No indecency of dress, dance, or gesture to be permitted on the Stage.

No offensive personalities or representations of living persons to be permitted on the Stage, nor anything calculated to produce riot or breach of the peace.

Copy of Grant made to Thomas Killigrew.

On the 21st of August 1660 the following grant (to Killigrew) against which Sir Henry Herbert had petitioned to be heard, passed the privy signet :

" Charles the Second, by the grace of God, of England, Scotland, France and Ireland, King, defender of the fayth, &c., to all to whome these presents shall come greeting. Whereas we are given to understand that certaine persons in and about our citty of London, or the suburbs thereof, doe frequently assemble for the performing and acting of playes and enterludes for rewards to which divers of our subjects doe for their entertainment resort ; which said playes, as we are informed, doe containe much matter of prophanation, and scurrility, soe that such kind of entertainments, which, if well managed, might serve as morall instructions in humane life, as the same are now used, doe for the most part tende to the debauchinge of the manners of such as are presente at them, and are very scandalous and offensive to all pious and well-disposed persons. We, takeing the premisses into our princely consideration, yett not holding it necessary totally to suppresse the use of theatres, because wee are assured, that, if the evill and scandall in the playes that now are or have bin acted were taken away, the same might serve as innocent and harmless divertisement for many of our subjects ; and having experience of the art and skill of our trusty and well beloved Thomas Killigrew, esq., one of the Groomes of our Bedchamber, and of Sir William Davenant, knight, for the purposes hereafter mentioned, doe hereby give and grante unto the said Thomas Killigrew and Sir William Davenant full power and authority to erect two companies of players, consistinge respectively of such persones as they shall chuse and appoint, and to purchase, builde and erect, or hire at their charge, as they shall thinke fitt, two houses or theatres, with all convenient roomes and other necessaries thereunto appertaininge, for the representation of tragydies, comedyes, playes, operas, and all other entertainments of that nature, in convenient places : and likewise to settle and establish such payments to be paid by those that shall resort to see the said representations performed, as either have bin accustomely given and taken in the like kind, or as shall be reasonable in regard of the great expenses of scenes, musick, and such new decorations as have not been formerly used ; with further power to make such allowances out of that which they shall so receive, to the actors, and other persons employed in the said representations in both houses respectively, as they shall think fitt : the said companies to be under the government and authority of them the said Thomas Killigrew and Sir William Davenant. And in regard of the extraordinary licentiousness, that hath been lately used in things of this nature, our pleasure is, that there shall be no more places of representations, nor companies of actors of playes, or operas, by recitative musick, or representations by danceing and scenes, or any other entertainments on the stage in our citties of London and Westminster, or in the liberties of them, then the two to be now erected by vertue of this authority. Nevertheless wee doe hereby by our authority royal strictly enjoine the said Thomas Killigrew and Sir William Davenant, that they doe not at any time hereafter cause to be acted or represented any play, enterlude or opera, containing any matter of prophanation, scurrility or obscenity. And wee doe further hereby authorize and command them, the said Thomas Killigrew and Sir William Davenant to peruse all playes that have been formerly written, and to expunge all prophanesse and scurrility from the same, before they be represented or acted. And this our grante and authority made to the said Thomas Killigrew and Sir William Davenant, shall be effectuall and remaine in full force and vertue, notwithstanding any former order or direction by us given, for the suppressing of play houses and playes, or any other entertainments of the stage."

Given, &c.,

August 21, 1660.

Lord Chesterfield's Speech in the House of Lords.

My Lords,—The Bill now before you I apprehend to be of a very extraordinary Nature. It seems designed not only as a Restraint on the Licentiousness of the Stage, but it will prove a most arbitrary Restraint on the Liberty of the Stage ; and, I fear, it looks yet farther, I fear, it tends towards a Restraint on the Liberty of the Press, which will be a long Stride towards the Destruction of Liberty itself. It is not only a Bill, my Lords, of a very extraordinary Nature, but it has been brought in at a very extraordinary Season, and pushed with most extraordinary Dispatch. When I consider how near it was to the end of the Session, and how long this Session had been protracted beyond the usual Time of the Year ; when I considered that this Bill passed through the other House with so much Precipitancy, as even to get the Start of a Bill which deserved all the Respect, and all the Dispatch, the Forms of either House of Parliament could admit of, it set me upon inquiring, what could be the reason for introducing this Bill at so unseasonable a time, and pressing it forward in a manner so very singular and uncommon. I have made all possible Inquiry, and as yet, I must confess, I am at a loss to find out the Great Occasion. I have, it is true, learned from common Report, without Doors, that a most seditious, a most heinous Farce had been offered to one of the Theatres, a Farce for which the Authors ought to be punished in the most exemplary Manner. But what was the Consequence? The Master of that Theatre behaved as he was in duty bound, and as common Prudence dictated: He not only refused to bring it upon the Stage, but carried it to a certain honourable Gentleman in the Administration, as the surest Method of having it absolutely suppressed. Could this be the Occasion of introducing such an extraordinary Bill, at such an extraordinary Season, and pushing it in so extraordinary a Manner? Surely no;—The dutiful Behaviour of the Players, the prudent Caution they shewed upon that Occasion, can never be a Reason for subjecting them to such an arbitrary Restraint. It is an Argument in their Favour, and a material one, in my Opinion, against the Bill. Nay, further, if we consider all Circumstances, it is to me a full Proof that the Laws now in being are sufficient for punishing those Players who shall venture to bring any seditious Libel upon the Stage, and consequently sufficient for deterring all Players from acting any thing that may have the least Tendency towards giving a reasonable Offence.

I do not, my Lords, pretend to be a Lawyer; I do not pretend to know perfectly the Power and Extent of our Laws, but I have conversed with those that do, and by them I have been told, that our laws are sufficient for punishing any Person that shall dare to represent upon the Stage what may appear, either by the Words or the Representation, to be blasphemous, seditious, or immoral. I must own, indeed, I have observed of late a remarkable Licentiousness in the Stage. There have but very lately been two Plays acted, which, one would have thought, should have given the greatest Offence, and yet both were suffered to be often represented without Disturbance, without Censure. In one, the Author thought fit to represent the three Great Professions, Religion, Physick, and the Law, as inconsistent with Common Sense. In the other, a most tragical Story was brought upon the Stage, a Catastrophe too recent, too melancholy, and of too solemn a Nature, to be heard of anywhere but from the Pulpit. How these Pieces came to pass unpunished, I do not know : if I am rightly informed, it was not for want of Law but for want of Prosecution, without which no Law can be made effectual. But if there was any Neglect in this Case, I am convinced it was not with a design to Prepare the Minds of the People, and to make them think a new Law necessary.

Our Stage ought certainly, my Lords, to be kept within Bounds, but for this, our Laws as they stand at present are sufficient. We have Precedents, we have Examples of Persons having been punished for Things less criminal than either of the two Pieces I have mentioned. A new Law must therefore be unnecessary, and in the present Case it cannot be unnecessary without being dangerous. Every unnecessary Restraint on Licentiousness is a Fetter upon the Legs, is a Shackle upon the Hands of Liberty. One of the greatest Blessings we enjoy, one of the Greatest Blessings a People, my Lords, can enjoy, is Liberty,—but every Good in this Life has its Allay of Evil—Licentiousness is the Allay of Liberty, it is an Ebullition, an Excrescence—it is a Speck upon the Eye of the Political Body, which I can never touch but with a gentle—with a trembling Hand, lest I destroy the Body, lest I injure the Eye upon which it is apt to appear. If the Stage becomes at any Time licentious, if a play appears to be a Libel upon the Government, or upon any particular Man, the King's Courts are open, the Laws are sufficient for punishing the Offender ; and in this Case the Person injured has a singular Advantage ; he can be under no Difficulty to prove who is the Publisher ; the Players themselves are the Publishers, and there can be no want of Evidence to convict them.

But, my Lords, suppose it is true, that the Laws now in being are not sufficient for putting a Check to or preventing the Licentiousness of the Stage ; suppose it absolutely necessary some new Law should be made for that purpose ; yet it must be granted that such a Law ought to be maturely considered, and every Clause, every Sentence, nay, every Word of it well weighed and examined, lest under some of those Methods, presumed or pretended to be necessary for restraining licentiousness, a Power should be concealed, which might be afterwards made use of for giving a dangerous Wound to Liberty. Such a Law ought not to be introduced at the Close of a Session, nor ought we, in the passing of such a Law, to depart from any of the Forms prescribed by our Ancestors for preventing Deceit and Surprise. There is such a Connection between licentiousness and Liberty, that it is not easy to correct the one, without dangerously wounding the other.   It is extremely hard to distinguish the true limit between them like a changeable silk, we can easily see there are two different Colours, but we cannot easily discover where the one ends, or where the other begins.   There can be no great or immediate Danger from the licentiousness of the Stage ; I hope it will not be pretended that our Government may, before next Winter, be overturned by such licentiousness, even though our Stage were at present under no sort of legal Controul.   Why then may we not delay till next Session passing any Law against the Licentiousness of the Stage ?   Neither our Government can be altered, nor our Constitution overturned by such a Delay ; but by passing a Law rashly and inadvisedly, our Constitution may at once be destroyed, and our Government rendered arbitrary.   Can we then put a small, a short-lived inconvenience in the Ballance with perpetual Slavery ?   Can it be supposed that a Parliament of Great Britain will so much as risque the latter, for the sake of avoiding the former ?

Surely, my Lords, this is not to be expected, were the licentiousness of the stage much greater than it is, were the insufficiency of our Laws more obvious than can be pretended ; but when we complain of the licentiousness of the Stage, and of the insufficiency of our Laws, I fear we have more Reason to complain of bad measures in our Polity, and a general Decay of Virtue and Morality among the People.   In publick as well as private Life, the only way to prevent being ridiculed or censured, is to avoid all ridiculous or wicked Measures, and to pursue such only as are virtuous and worthy.   The People never endeavour to ridicule those they love and esteem, nor will they suffer them to be ridiculed.   If anyone attempts it, the Ridicule returns upon the Author : he makes himself only the Object of publick Hatred and Contempt.   The Actions or Behaviour of a private Man may pass unobserved, and consequently unapplauded, uncensured ; but the Actions of those in high Stations, can neither pass without Notice, nor without censure or Applause ; and therefore an Administration without Esteem, without Authority among the People, let their Power be never so great, let their Power be never so arbitrary, they will be ridiculed.   The severest Edicts, the most terrible Punishments, cannot entirely prevent it.   If any Man therefore thinks he has been censured ; if any Man thinks he has been ridiculed upon any of our Public Theatres, let him examine his Actions—he will find the Cause ; let him alter his Conduct—he will find a Remedy.   As no Man is perfect, as no Man is infallible, the greatest may err, the most circumspect may be guilty of some piece of ridiculous Behaviour. It is not Licentiousness, it is an useful Liberty always indulged the Stage in a free Country, that some Men may there meet with a just Reproof, which none of their friends will be free enough, or rather faithful enough to give them. Of this we have a famous instance in the *Roman* History. The great *Pompey*, after the many Victories he had obtained, and the great conquests he had made, had certainly a good Title to the Esteem of the People of Rome ; yet that great man, by some Error in his Conduct, became an Object of general Dislike ; and therefore in the Representation of an old Play, when *Diphilus*, the Actor, came to repeat these Words, *Nostra Miseria tu es Magnus*, the Audience immediately applied them to *Pompey*, who at that time was as well known by the name *Magnus* as by the name *Pompey* ; and were so highly pleased with the Satyr, that, as *Cicero* says, they made the Actor repeat the Words an hundred times over. An Account of this was immediately sent to *Pompey* who, instead of resenting it as an Injury, was so wise as to take it for a just Reproof. He examined his Conduct, he altered his Measures, he regained by degrees the Esteem of the People and then he neither feared the Wit, nor felt the Satyr of the Stage. This is an example which ought to be followed by great Men in all Countries. Such Accidents will often happen in every free Country, and many such would probably have afterwards happened at Rome, if they had continued to enjoy their Liberty ; but this sort of Liberty on the Stage came soon after, I suppose, to be called Licentiousness, for we are told that Agustus, after having established his Empire, restored Order in Rome by restraining Licentiousness. God forbid we should, in this Country have Order restored and Licentiousness restrained, at so dear a Rate as the People of Rome paid for it to Augustus.

In the Case I have mentioned, my Lords, it was not the Poet that wrote, for it was an old play, nor the Players that acted, for they only repeated the Words of the play ; it was the People who pointed the Satyr, and the Case will always be the same. When a Man has the Misfortune to incur the Hatred or Contempt of the People, when public Measures are despised the audience will apply what never was, what could not be designed as a Satyr, on the present Times. Nay, even though the people should not apply, those who are conscious of guilt, those who are conscious of the Wickedness or Weakness of their own Conduct, will take to themselves what the author never designed. A public thief is as apt to take the Satyr as he is apt to take the Money, which was never designed for him. We have an instance of this in the Case of a famous Comedian of the last Age, a Comedian who was not only a good Poet but an honest Man and a quiet and good Subject ; the famous Molière, where he wrote his *Turtuffe*, which is certainly an excellent and a good moral Comedy, did not design to satirize any great Man of that Age ; yet a great Man in France at that Time took it to himself, and fancied the Author had taken him as a Model for one of the principal and one of the worst characters in that Comedy. By good Luck he was not the Licenser, otherwise the Kingdom of France had never had the Pleasure, the Happiness I may say, of seeing that Play acted ; but when the Players first proposed to act it at Paris, he had Interest enough to get it forbid. Molière, who knew himself Innocent of what was laid to his Charge, complained to his Patron the Prince of Conti, that as his Play was designed only to expose Hypocrisy, and a false Pretence to Religion, it was very hard it should be forbid being acted, when at the same time they were suffered to expose Religion itself every Night publicly upon the Italian Stage. To which the Prince wittily answered, *'Tis true*, Molière, *Harlequin ridicules Heaven, and exposes Religion ; but you have done much worse—you have ridiculed the first Minister of Religion.*

I am as much for restraining the Licentiousness of the Stage, and every other sort of Licentiousness, as any of your Lordships can be ; but, my Lords, I am, I shall always be, extremely cautious and fearful of making the least Encroachment upon Liberty ; and therefore, when a new Law is proposed against Licentiousness, I shall always be for considering it deliberately and maturely, before I venture to give my consent to it being passed. This is a sufficient Reason for my being against passing this Bill at so unseasonable a Time, and in so extraordinary a Manner ; but I have my Reasons for being against the Bill itself, some of which I shall beg leave to explain to your Lordships. The Bill, my Lords, at first view, may seem to be designed only against the Stage, but to me it plainly appears to point somewhere else. It is an Arrow that does but glance upon the Stage, the Mortal Wound seems designed against the Liberty of the Press. By this Bill you prevent a Play's being acted, but you do not prevent its being printed ; therefore, if a Licence should be refused for its being acted, we may depend on it the Play will be printed. It will be printed and published, my Lords, with the refusal in capital letters on the Title Page. People are always fond of what is forbidden. *Libri prohibiti* are in all Countries diligently and generally sought after. It will be much easier to procure a Refusal, than it ever was to procure a good House or a good sale. Therefore, we may expect, that plays will be wrote on purpose to have a Refusal. This will certainly procure a good Sale. Thus will Satyrs be spread and dispersed through the whole Nation, and thus every Man in the Kingdom may, and probably will, read for Sixpence, what a few only could have seen acted, and that not under the expense of half-a-Crown. We shall then be told, What! Will you allow an infamous Libel to be printed and dispersed, which you would not allow to be acted? You have agreed to a Law for preventing its being acted, can you refuse your Assent to a Law for preventing its being printed and published? I should really, my Lords, be glad to hear what Excuse, what Reason, one could give for being against the latter, after having agreed to the former; for I protest, I cannot suggest to myself the least Shadow of an excuse. If we agree to the Bill now before us, we must perhaps, next Session, agree to a Bill preventing any Plays being printed without a Licence. The Satyrs will be wrote by way of Novels, secret Histories, Dialogues, or under some such Title, and thereupon we shall be told, What! will you allow an infamous Libel to be printed and dispersed only because it does not bear the Title of a Play? Thus, my Lords, from the Precedent now before us, we shall be induced, nay we can find no Reason for refusing to lay the Press under a general Licence, and then we may bid adieu to the Liberties of *Great Britain*.

But suppose, my Lords, it were necessary to make a new Law, for restraining the Licentiousness of the Stage, which I am very far from granting, yet I shall never be for establishing such a Power as is proposed by this Bill. If Poets and Players are to be restrained, let them be restrained as other Subjects are, by the known Laws of their Country; if they offend, let them be tried as every *Englishman* ought to be, by God and their Country. Do not let us subject them to the arbitrary Will and Pleasure of any one Man. A Power lodged in the hands of one single Man, to judge and determine, without any Limitation, without any Controul or Appeal, is a sort of Power unknown to our Laws, inconsistent with our Constitution. It is a higher, a more absolute Power than we trust even to the King himself; and therefore I must think, we ought not to vest any such Power in his Majesty's Lord Chamberlain. When I say this, I am sure I do not mean to give the least, the most distant Offence to the noble Duke who now fills the Post of

Lord Chamberlain. His natural Candour and love of Justice, would not, I know, permit him to exercise any Power but with the strictest regard to the Rules of Justice and Humanity. Were we sure his Successors in that high Office would always be Persons of such distinguished Merit, even the Power to be established by this Bill could give me no farther Alarm, than lest it should be made a Precedent for introducing other new Powers of the same Nature. This, indeed, is an Alarm which cannot be avoided, which cannot be prevented by any Hope, by any Consideration; it is an Alarm which, I think, every man must take, who has a due Regard to the Constitution and Liberties of his Country.

I shall admit, my Lords, that the stage ought not, upon any Occasion to meddle with Politics, and for this very Reason, among the rest, I am against the Bill now before us. This Bill will be so far from preventing the Stage's meddling with Politics, that I fear it will be the Occasion of its meddling with nothing else; but then it will be a political Stage *ex parte*. It will be made subservient to the Politics and Schemes of the Court only. The Licentiousness of the Stage will be encouraged instead of being restrained; but, like Court journalists, it will be licentious only against the Patrons of Liberty, and the Protectors of the People. Whatever Man, whatever Party opposes the Court in any of their most distinctive Schemes, will, upon the Stage be represented in the most ridiculous Light the Hirelings of a Court can contrive. True Patriotism and Love of Public Good will be represented a Madness, or as a Cloak for Envy, Disappointment, and Malice; while the most flagitious Crimes, the most extravagant Vices and Follies, if they are fashionable at Court, will be disguised and dressed up in the Habit of the most amiable Virtues. This has formerly been the Case:—In King *Charles* IId.'s Days the Play-House was under a Licence. What was the Consequence? — The Play-House retaled nothing but the Politics, the Vices, and the Follies of the Court. Not to expose them; no—but to recommend them; tho' it must be granted their Politics were often as bad as their Vices, and much more pernicious than their other Follies. 'Tis true, the Court had, at that Time, a great deal of Wit; it was then, indeed, full of Men of true Wit and great Humour; but it was the more dangerous; for the courtiers did then, as thorough-faced Courtiers always will do, they sacrificed their Honour, by making their Wit and their Humour subservient to the Court only; and what made it still more dangerous, no Man could appear upon the Stage against them. We know that *Dryden*, the Poet Laureate of that Reign, always represents the Cavaliers as honest, brave, merry Fellows, and fine Gentlemen. Indeed, his fine Gentleman, as he generally draws him, is an atheistical, lewd, abandoned Fellow, which was at that Time, it seems, the fashionable Character at Court. On the other Hand, he always represents the Dissenters as hypocritical, dissembling Rogues, or stupid senseless Boobies. When the Court had a mind to fall out with the *Dutch*, he wrote his *Amboyne*, in which he represents the *Dutch* as a Pack of avaritious, cruel, ungrateful Rascals. And when the Exclusion Bill was moved in Parliament, he wrote his *Duke of Guise*, in which those who were for securing the Religion of their Country, were exposed, under the Character of the Duke of *Guise* and his Party, who leagued together, for excluding *Henry IV.* of France from the Throne, on account of his Religion. The City of *London*, too, was made to feel the partial and mercenary Licentiousness of the Stage at that Time ; for the Citizens having at that Time, as well as now, a great deal of Property, they had a mind to preserve that Property, and therefore they opposed some of the arbitrary Measures which were then begun, but pursued more openly in the following Reign ; for which Reason they were then always represented upon the Stage, as a Parcel of designing Knaves, dissembling Hypocrites, griping Usurpers, and—Cuckolds into the Bargain.

My Lords, the proper Business of the Stage, and that for which only it is useful, is to expose those Vices and Follies, which the Laws cannot lay hold of, and to recommend those Beauties and Virtues, which Ministers and Courtiers seldom either imitate or reward ; but by laying it under a Licence, and under an arbitrary Court-licence, too, you will, in my Opinion, intirely pervert its Use ; for though I have the greatest Esteem for that noble Duke, in whose Hands this Power is at present designed to fall, tho' I have an intire Confidence in his Judgment and Impartiality ; yet I may suppose that a leaning towards the Fashions of a Court is sometimes hard to be avoided. It may be very difficult to make one, who is every Day at Court believe that to be a Vice or Folly, which he sees daily practised by those he loves and esteems. By Custom even Deformity itself becomes familiar, and at last agreeable. To such a Person, let his natural Impartiality be never so great, that may appear a Libel against the Court, which is only a most just and a most necessary Satyr upon the fashionable Vices and Follies of the Court. Courtiers, my Lord, are too polite to reprove one another ; the only Place where they can meet with any just Reproof, is a free, tho' not a licentious Stage ; and as every Sort of Vice and Folly, generally in all Countries, begins at Court, and from thence spreads thro' the Country, by laying the Stage under an arbitrary Court-licence, instead of leaving it what it is, and always ought to be, a gentle Scourge for the Vices of Great Men and Courtiers, you will make it a Canal for propogating and conveying their Vices and Follies thro' the whole Kingdom.

From hence, my Lords, I think it must appear, that the Bill now before us cannot so properly be called a Bill for restraining the Licentiousness, as it may be called a Bill for restraining the Liberty of the Stage, and for restraining it too in that Branch which in all Countries has been the most useful : therefore I must look upon the Bill as a most dangerous Encroachment on Liberty in general. Nay, further, my Lords, it is not only an Encroachment upon Liberty, but it is likewise an Encroachment on Property. Wit, my Lord, is a Sort of Property. It is the Property of those that have it, and too often the only Property they have to depend on. It is, indeed, but a precarious Dependence. Thank God ! We—my Lords, have a Dependence of another Kind ; we have a much less precarious Support, and therefore cannot feel the inconveniences of the Bill now before us ; but it is our duty to encourage and protect Wit, whosoever's Property it may be. Those Gentlemen who have any such Property, are all, I hope, our Friends : Do not let us subject them to any unnecessary or arbitrary Restraint. I must own, I cannot easily agree to the laying of any tax upon Wit ; but by this Bill it is to be heavily taxed,—it is to be excised ;—for if this Bill passes, it cannot be retaled in a proper Way without a Permit ; and the Lord Chamberlain is to have the Honour of being chief Gauger, Supervisor, Commissioner, Judge and Jury : But what is still more hard, tho' the poor Author, the Proprietor, I should say, cannot perhaps dine till he has found out and agreed with a Purchaser ; yet before he can seek for a Purchaser, he must patiently submit to have his Goods rummaged at this new Excise-office, where they may be detained for fourteen Days, and even then he may find them returned as prohibited Goods, by which his Chief and best Market will be for ever shut against him ; and that without any Cause, without the least Shadow of Reason, either from the Laws and his Country, or the Laws of the Stage.

These Hardships, this Hazard, which every Gentleman will be exposed to who writes anything for the Stage, must certainly prevent every Man of a generous and free Spirit from attempting anything in that way ; and as the Stage has always been the proper

Channel for Wit and Humour, therefore, my Lords, when I speak, against this Bill, I must think I plead the Cause of Wit, I plead the Cause of Humour, I plead the Cause of the *British* Stage, and of every Gentleman of taste in the Kingdom. But it is not, my Lords, for the Sake of Wit only ; even for the Sake of his Majesty's Lord Chamberlain, I must be against this Bill. The noble Duke who has now the Honour to execute that Office, has, I am sure, as little Inclination to disoblige as any Man ; but if this Bill passes, he may disoblige, he must disoblige some of his most intimate friends. It is impossible to write a Play, but some of the Characters, or some of the Satyr, may be interpreted so as to point at some Person or other, perhaps at some Person in an eminent Station. When it comes to be acted the People will make the Application, and the Person against whom the Application is made, will think himself injured, and will, at least privately, resent it. At present this Resentment can only be directed against the Author, but when an Author's Play appears with my Lord Chamberlain's Passport, every such Resentment will be turned from the Author, and pointed directly against the Lord Chamberlain, who by his Stamp made the Piece current. What an unthankful Office are we therefore by this Bill to put upon his Majesty's Lord Chamberlain ! an Office which can no way contribute to his Honour or Profit, and yet such a one as must necessarily gain him a great deal of ill-will, and create him a number of enemies.

The last Reason I shall trouble your Lordships with for my being against the Bill, is that, in my Opinion, it will no way answer the End proposed : I mean the End openly proposed, and, I am sure, the only End which your Lordships propose. To prevent the acting of a Play which has any tendency to Blasphemy, Immorality, Sedition, or private Scandal, can signify nothing, unless you can likewise prevent its being printed and published. On the contrary, if you prevent its being acted, and admit of its being printed and published, you will propagate the Mischief. Your Prohibition will prove a Bellows which will blow up the fire you intend to extinguish. This Bill can therefore be of no Use for preventing either the publick or the private Injury intended by such a Play ; and consequently can be of no manner of Use, unless it be designed as a Precedent, as a leading Step towards another, for subjecting the Press likewise to a Licenser. For such a wicked Purpose it may, indeed be of great Use ; and in that Light, it may most properly be called a Step towards arbitrary Power.

Let us consider, my Lords, that arbitrary power has seldom or

never been introduced into any country at once. It must be introduced by slow degrees, and as it were step by step, lest the people
should perceive its approach. The barriers and fences of the people's
liberty must be plucked up one by one, and some plausible pretence
must be found for removing or hood-winking, one after another,
those sentries who are posted by the constitution of every free
country for warning the people of their danger. When these pre-
paratory Steps are once made, the People may then, indeed with
Regret, see Slavery and arbitrary Power making long Strides over
their Land, but it will then be too late to think of preventing or
avoiding the impending Ruin. The Stage, my Lords, and the
Press, are two of our Out-sentries; if we remove them—if we
hood-wink them—if we throw them in Fetters—the Enemy may
surprize us. Therefore I must look upon the Bill now before us as
a Step, and a most necessary Step too, for introducing arbitrary
Power into this Kingdom : It is a Step so necessary, that, if ever
any future ambitious King, or guilty Minister, should form to himself so wicked a Design, he will have reason to thank us for having
done so much of the work to his Hand ; but such Thanks, or
Thanks for such a Man, I am convinced every one of your Lordships would blush to receive—and scorn to deserve.

THE THEATRES ACT OF 1737.

2 George II., c. 28 (1737).

*An Act to explain so much of an act made in the twelfth year of the
reign of Queen* Anne, *intituled,* An act for reducing the laws relating
to rogues, vagabonds, sturdy beggers, and vagrants, into one act of
parliament ; and for the more effectual punishing such rogues, vagabonds, sturdy beggars, and vagrants, and sending them whither they
ought to be sent, *as relates to common players of interludes.*

*Whereas by an act of parliament made in the twelfth year of the
reign of her late majesty Queen* Anne, *intituled,* An act for reducing
the laws relating to rogues, vagabonds, sturdy beggars, and vagrants,
into one act of parliament, and for the more effectual punishing such
rogues, vagabonds, sturdy beggars, and vagrants, and sending them
whither they ought to be sent, it was enacted, *That all persons
pretending themselves to be patent gatherers or collectors for prisons, gaols,
or hospitals, and wandering abroad for that purpose, all fencers, bear-*

wards, common players of interludes, and other persons therein named and expressed, shall be deemed rogues and vagabonds, and whereas some doubts have arisen concerning so much of the said act as relates to common players of interludes : now for explaining and amending the same, be it declared and enacted by the King's most excellent majesty, by and with the consent of the lords spiritual and temporal, and commons in this present parliament assembled, and by the authority of the same, That from and after the twenty-fourth day of *June* one thousand seven hundred and thirty-seven, every person who shall, for hire, gain, or reward, act, represent, or perform, or cause to be acted, represented, or performed any interlude, tragedy, comedy, opera, play, farce, or other entertainment of the stage, or any part or parts therein, in case such person shall not have any legal settlement in the place where the same shall be acted, represented, or performed, without authority by virtue of letters patent from his Majesty, his heirs, successors, or predecessors, or without licence from the lord chamberlain of his Majesty's household for the time being, shall be deemed to be a rogue and a vagabond within the intent and meaning of the said recited act, and shall be liable and subject to all such penalties and punishments, and by such methods of conviction, as are inflicted on or appointed by the said act for the punishment of rogues and vagabonds who shall be found wandering, begging, and misordering themselves, within the intent and meaning of the said recited act. *[marginal note: Persons acting plays, etc., in any place where they have not a settlement or without authority, etc., to be deemed vagabonds]*

II. And be it further enacted by the authority aforesaid, That if any person having or not having a legal settlement as aforesaid shall, without such authority or licence as aforesaid, act, represent, or perform, or cause to be acted, represented, or performed, for hire, gain, or reward, any interlude, tragedy, comedy, opera, play, farce, or other entertainment of the stage, or any part or parts therein, every such person shall for every such offence forfeit the sum of fifty pounds ; and in case the said sum of fifty pounds shall be paid, levied, or recovered, such offender shall not for the same offence suffer any of the pains and penalties inflicted by the said recited act. *[marginal note: and forfeit 50l]*

III. And be it further enacted by the authority aforesaid, That from and after the said twenty-fourth day of *June*, one thousand seven hundred and thirty-seven, no person shall for hire, gain, or reward, act, perform, represent, or cause to be acted, performed, or represented, any new interlude, tragedy, comedy, opera, play, farce, or other entertainment of the stage, or any part or parts therein, or any new prologue, or epilogue, unless a true copy thereof be sent to the lord chamberlain of the King's household for the time being *[marginal note: No new plays, or additions to old ones, to be acted, unless a copy thereof be sent to the chamberlain, etc.,]* fourteen days at least before the acting, representing, or performing thereof, together with an account of the playhouse or other place where the same shall be, and the time when the same is intended to be first acted, represented, or performed, signed by the master or manager, or one of the masters or managers of such playhouse, or place, or company of actors therein.

IV. And be it enacted by the authority aforesaid, That from and after the said twenty-fourth day of *June*, one thousand seven hundred and thirty-seven, it shall and may be lawful to and for the said lord chamberlain, for the time being, from time to time, and when, and as often as he shall think fit, to prohibit the acting, performing, or representing, any interlude, tragedy, comedy, opera, play, farce, or other entertainment of the stage, or any act, scene, or part thereof, or any prologue, or epilogue ; and in case any person or persons shall for hire, gain, or reward, act, perform, or represent, or cause to be acted, performed, or represented, any new interlude, tragedy, comedy, opera, play, farce, or other entertainment of the stage, and per- or any act, scene, or part thereof, or any new prologue or epilogue, sons acting before a copy thereof shall be sent as aforesaid with such account as against his aforesaid, or shall for hire, gain, or reward, act, perform, or repre- prohibi- sent, or cause to be acted, performed, or represented, any interlude, tion, etc., tragedy, comedy, opera, play, farce, or other entertainment of the to forfeit stage, or any act, scene, or part thereof, or any prologue or epilogue, 5ol. and contrary to such prohibition as aforesaid ; every person so offending their licence. shall for every such offence forfeit the sum of fifty pounds, and every grant, licence, and authority (in case there be any such) by or under which the said master or masters or manager or managers set up, formed, or continued such playhouse, or such company of actors, shall cease, determine, and become absolutely void to all intents and purposes whatsoever.

V. Provided always, That no person or persons shall be No plays authorized by virtue of any letters patent from his Majesty, his to be acted heirs, successors, or predecessors, or by the licence of the lord but in chamberlain of his Majesty's household for the time being, to act, West- minster or represent, or perform, for hire, gain, or reward, any interlude, places of tragedy, comedy, opera, play, farce, or other entertainment of the his stage, or any part or parts therein, in any part of *Great Britain*, Majesty's residence. except in the city of *Westminster*, and within the liberties thereof, and in such places where his Majesty, his heirs or successors, shall in their royal persons reside, and during such residence only; anything in this act contained to the contrary in any wise notwithstanding.

VI. And be it further enacted by the authority aforesaid,

That all the pecuniary penalties inflicted by this act for offences Penalties committed within that part of *Great Britain*, called *England*, *Wales*, how to be recovered, and the town of *Berwick* upon *Tweed*, shall be recovered by bill, etc. plaint or information, in any of his Majesty's courts of record at *Westminster*, in which no essoin, protection, or wager of law shall be allowed ; and for the offences committed in that part of *Great Britain* called *Scotland*, by action or summary complaint before the court of session or justiciary there ; or for offences committed in any part of *Great Britain* in a summary way before two justices of the peace for any county, stewartry, riding, division, or liberty, where any such offence shall be committed, by the oath or oaths of one or more credible witness or witnesses, or by the confession of the offender, the same to be levied by distress and sale of the offender's goods and chattels, rendering the overplus to such offender, if there be any above the penalty and charge of distress ; and for want of sufficient distress the offender shall be committed to any house of correction in any such county, stewartry, riding, or liberty, for any time not exceeding six months, there to remain without bail or main prize ; and if any person or persons shall think him, her, or themselves aggrieved by the order or orders of such justices of the peace, it shall and may be lawful for such person or persons to appeal therefrom to the next general quarter sessions to be held for the said county, stewartry, riding, or liberty, whose order therein shall be final and conclusive ; and the said penalties for any offence against this act shall belong, one moiety thereof to the informer or person suing or prosecuting for the same, the other moiety to the poor of the parish, where such offence shall be committed.

VII. And be it further enacted by the authority aforesaid, That if any interlude, tragedy, comedy, opera, play, farce, or other enter- Persons tainment of the stage, or any act, scene, or part thereof, shall be acting in publick-acted, represented, or performed in any house or place where wine, houses ale, beer, or other liquors shall be sold or retaled, the same shall be included deemed to be acted, represented, and performed for gain, hire, and in this act. reward.

VIII. And be it further enacted by the authority aforesaid, That no person shall be liable to be prosecuted for any offence Limitation against this act, unless such prosecution shall be commenced within of actions. the space of six calendar months after the offence committed ; and if any action, or suit, shall be commenced or brought against any justice of the peace or any other person for doing, or causing to be done, any thing in pursuance of this act, such action or suit shall be commenced within six calendar months next after the fact done ;

General
issue.

and the defendant or defendants in such action or suit shall and may plead the general issue, and give the special matter in evidence ; and if upon such action or suit, a verdict shall be given for the defendant or defendants, or the plaintiff or plaintiffs or prosecutor shall become nonsuit, or shall not prosecute his, or their said action or suit, then

Treble
costs.

the defendant or defendants shall have treble costs, and shall have the like remedy for the same, as any defendant or defendants have in other cases by law.

Colman's Appointment as Examiner.

Stamp, £25.

Whereas in consequence of an Act of Parliament made in the tenth year of the reign of His late Majesty King George the Second, for the better regulation of the stage I am empowered to constitute, nominate and appoint an officer to examine all plays, tragedies, comedies, operas, farces, interludes and any other entertainment of the stage of what denomination soever. These are therefore to require you to swear and admit George Colman esquire into the place and quality of Examiner of all and every the above recited plays, tragedies, comedies, operas, farces, interludes and other entertainments of the stage, of what denomination soever, in the room of John Larpent esquire deceased, to have hold, exercise and enjoy the same, together with all salaries, fees and other emoluments to the said office that may arise or in any way legally appertain ; and for so doing this shall be your Warrant

[Given under my hand and seal this 19th day of January 1824 in the fourth year of His Majesty's reign.]

[Signed] Montrose. (Seal.)

Relevant Clauses from the Act for Regulating Theatres, 22nd August 1843.

No new
Plays or
Additions
to old ones
to be acted

XII. And be it enacted, That One Copy of every new Stage Play, and of every new Act, Scene, or other Part added to any old Stage Play, and of every new Prologue or Epilogue, and of every new Part added to an old Prologue or Epilogue, intended to be produced and acted for Hire at any Theatre in *Great Britain*, shall be sent to the Lord Chamberlain of Her Majesty's Household for the Time being, Seven Days at least before the first acting or presenting thereof, with an Account of the Theatre where and the Time when the same is intended to be first acted or presented, signed by the Master or Manager, or One of the Masters or Managers, of such Theatre ; and during the said Seven Days no Person shall for Hire act or present the same, or cause the same to be acted or presented ; and in case the Lord Chamberlain, either before or after the Expiration of the said Period of Seven Days, shall disallow any Play, or any Act, Scene, or Part thereof, or any Prologue or Epilogue, or any Part thereof, it shall not be lawful for any Person to act or present the same, or cause the same to be acted or presented, contrary to such Disallowance. *until submitted to the Lord Chamberlain.*

XIII. And be it enacted, That it shall be lawful for the Lord Chamberlain to charge such Fees for the Examination of the Plays, Prologues, and Epilogues, or Parts thereof, which shall be sent to him for Examination, as to him from Time to Time shall seem fit, according to a Scale which shall be fixed by him, such Fee not being in any Case more than Two Guineas, and such Fees shall be paid at the Time when such Plays, Prologues, and Epilogues, or Parts thereof, shall be sent to the Lord Chamberlain ; and the said Period of Seven Days shall not begin to run in any Case until the said Fee shall have been paid to the Lord Chamberlain or to some Officer deputed by him to receive the same. *Fees to be paid for Examination of Plays, etc.*

XIV. And be it enacted, That it shall be lawful for the Lord Chamberlain for the Time being, whenever he shall be of opinion that it is fitting for the Preservation of good Manners, Decorum, or of the public Peace so to do, to forbid the acting or presenting any Stage Play, or any Act, Scene, or Part thereof, or any Prologue or Epilogue, or any Part thereof, anywhere in *Great Britain*, or in such Theatres as he shall specify, and either absolutely or for such Time as he shall think fit. *The Lord Chamberlain may forbid any Play.*

XV. And be it enacted, That every Person who for Hire shall act or present, or cause to be acted or presented, any new Stage Play, or any Act, Scene, or Part thereof, or any new Prologue or Epilogue, or any part thereof, until the same shall have been allowed by Lord Chamberlain, or which shall have been disallowed by him, and also every Person who for Hire shall act or present, or cause to be acted or presented, any Stage Play, or any Act, Scene, or Part thereof, or any Prologue or Epilogue, or any Part thereof, contrary to such Prohibition as aforesaid, shall for every such Offence forfeit *Penalty for acting Plays before they are allowed or after they have been disallowed.*

such Sum as shall be awarded by the Court in which or the Justices by whom he shall be convicted, not exceeding the Sum of Fifty Pounds ; and every Licence (in Case there be any such) by or under which the Theatre was opened, in which such Offence shall have been committed, shall become absolutely void.

What shall be Evidence of acting for Hire.

XVI. And be it enacted, That in every Case in which any Money or other Reward shall be taken or charged, directly or indirectly, or in which the Purchase of any Article is made a Condition for the Admission of any Person into any Theatre to see any Stage Play, and also in every Case in which any Stage Play shall be acted or presented in any House, Room, or Place in which distilled or fermented Exciseable Liquor shall be sold, every Actor therein shall be deemed to be acting for Hire.

Text of Petition to the King.

June 11th, 1912.

May it please your Majesty,

We, your undersigned humble petitioners, beg leave to call attention to the grave injury inflicted on the art of the drama, and the obstacles placed in the way of its further development, by the present administration of the functions of the Censorship of Plays under the Department of your Majesty's Lord Chamberlain.

Your petitioners submit :

That during recent years a development has taken place in the British drama which is proving so fertile that among the subjects of your gracious Majesty there is now a group of native dramatists which, in point of literary culture, dramatic power, and intellectual quality, cannot be matched by any similar group since the days of the unparalleled outburst of drama in the time of Shakespeare. The production and publication of plays if permitted to attain their natural development will cause the British drama to become one of the chief artistic glories of your most gracious Majesty's reign. At present, however, this natural development is being hampered and checked by the methods and principles of administration exercised by officials of your Majesty's Household in the department of the Lord Chamberlain—methods and principles which had they existed in the days of your Majesty's predecessor, Queen Elizabeth, would have deprived the English-speaking world of some of the chief glories of its literature, namely, " Hamlet," and most of the historical plays of William Shakespeare.

That the Lord Chamberlain's department—in pursuance of a custom that has neither the sanction of statute nor of the common law, and that acquires authority only from the fact that in acting upon it the officials are not subject to the control either of your Majesty's Courts of Justice or of the Houses of Parliament—has largely extended the bounds prescribed by Statute for the exercise of the power of refusing to grant licenses to plays, and has prohibited some plays and forced authors to make changes in others for reasons that are purely arbitrary and unwarranted by the Statutes regulating the office, with the result that dramatists either avoid the treatment of many of the vital problems of human life or approach them with a timidity which gravely injures their work. In consequence the theatre which could and should be one of the greatest educational forces of the time threatens to fall short of the accomplishment of that part of its mission.

"GROSSLY UNJUST."

That the Lord Chamberlain's Department by working on custom and not on ascertainable results has been grossly unjust to managers, authors, and the public, and has cast discredit on the administration of the Department by its treatment of classical plays, and of plays in which Scriptural characters appear, as may be instanced by the repeated refusals to many managers of a license for Sophocles' great play ŒDIPUS REX, which now, at last permitted, has been produced with every indication of public approval. . . .

That since the Report of the Joint Select Committee of the House of Lords and the House of Commons on the Stage Plays (Censorship) was ordered by the House of Commons on November 8, 1909, to be printed, no steps have been taken by your Majesty's Government to bring before either of the Houses of Parliament the recommendations of the Committee that serious alterations in the manner of licensing stage plays should be made.

That since that date the Lord Chamberlain's department has rendered its office more burdensome and grievous than it was before to the dramatists and managers of your Majesty's kingdom by appointing a number of private individuals to act as a so-called advisory board, for the existence of which no warrant of any kind can be found in the laws of your Majesty's realm, and by referring to such board plays submitted in confidence for private perusal by the Lord Chamberlain and his own officials; with the result that the statutory period of seven days within which it is his duty to grant or refuse a license is frequently exceeded, and that managers, relying upon the propriety of the works submitted for sanction considerably more than seven days before the day fixed for production, have been unable to obtain a license from the Lord Chamberlain until a few hours before such day, or in some cases until after such day.

Still More Oppressive.

That since the date of the said report, the Lord Chamberlain has exercised his powers of refusing to license plays far more oppressively than before, and that several of the plays which he has refused to license have been published in book form and been regarded almost universally as fit for production.

That since the date of the said report, the Lord Chamberlain has granted permission to the music halls of your Majesty's metropolis to present stage plays upon the condition that they produce no such works not licensed by him, with the result that an indefensible situation has been created by which managers of places of entertainment are under the censorship of the Lord Chamberlain's Department for a portion of their entertainment, whilst free, subject only to the ex-post facto control of the local licensing authority, to exercise their own sense of responsibility as to the fitness for public representation of the remainder.

That for the reasons here stated, among others, there exists a great amount of dissatisfaction with the present administration of the Lord Chamberlain's Department in its relations with the drama, which is the more regrettable in so much as it is due to the operations of officials of your Majesty's Household.

That in view of the danger that these conditions " may hinder the growth of a great and serious national drama, and of the grave injury that such hindrance would do to the development of thought and of art "

Your petitioners most humbly pray that your Most Excellent Majesty will be pleased to take this petition into your most gracious consideration, and to take such steps in the premises as to your Majesty, in your great wisdom, shall seem meet.

And your petitioners, as in duty bound, will ever pray, &c.

[The petition, which had an impressive list of signatures, was signed by more than sixty dramatists, among them being J. M. Barrie, Arnold Bennett, Granville Barker, Rudolf Besier, George Calderon, W. L. Courtney, Joseph Conrad, H. V. Esmond, J. B.

Fagan, Frederick Fenn, C. B. Fernald, H. Hamilton Fyfe, John Galsworthy, Edward Garnett, Miss Cicely Hamilton, Maurice Hewlett, Roy Horniman, Laurence Housman, Henry James, Jerome K. Jerome, Henry Arthur Jones, Cosmo Gordon Lennox, W. J. Locke, Mrs Alfred Lyttelton, Miss Margaret Macnamara, John Masefield, Justin Huntly M'Carthy, Charles M'Evoy, George Moore, T. Sturge Moore, Gilbert Murray, Alfred Noyes, Sir Gilbert Parker, George Paston, H. M. Paull, Eden Phillpotts, Sir Arthur Pinero, John Pollock, Cecil Raleigh, Miss Elizabeth Robins, Arthur Symons, H. M. Walbrook, H. G. Wells, Mrs Cornwallis West, Anthony Wharton and W. B. Yeats.

Among the signatories of representatives of Repertory Theatres, Dramatic Societies, Dramatic critics, and others immediately associated with the Theatre were : William Archer, E. A. Baughan, Harold Child, Anthony L. Ellis, Charles Frohman, Miss A. E. F. Horniman, Miss Gertrude Kingston, S. R. Littlewood, Miss Lillah M'Carthy, Herbert Trench, Alfred Wareing, Frederick Whelen, and R. H. M. Spooner and H. W. Sandham, Honorary Secretaries of the Censorship Petition Committee. The signatories also include representatives of the Incorporated Stage Society, the Manchester Repertory Theatre, the Liverpool Repertory Theatre, the Glasgow Repertory Theatre, the Manchester Playgoers' Society, the Leeds Playgoers' Society, the Sheffield Playgoers' Society, the Stockport Garrick Society, and other provincial societies.

The signatories also included many musicians, artists, professors, members of Parliament, editors, authors, and others, among them being Granville Bantock, Harold Begbie, Robert Anning Bell, J. M. Bulloch, George Clausen, Walter Crane, Frank Danby, Sidney Dark, Robert Donald, James Douglas, Lord Farrer, Mrs Fawcett, A. G. Gardiner, Patrick Geddes, Edmund Gosse, R. B. Cunninghame Graham, Sarah Grand, Mrs J. R. Green, Sir James Guthrie, *P*.R.S.A., the Hon. Walter Guinness, Stephen Gwynne, Beatrice Harraden, Austin Harrison, Frederic Harrison, Lucas Malet, Sir H. H. Johnston, Sir Alexander Kennedy, Sir Oliver Lodge, Lord Lytton, H. W. Massingham, Mortimer Menpes, Dr Chalmers Mitchell, Sir Alfred Mond, Felix Moscheles, H. W. Nevinson, Henry Newbolt, T. P. O'Connor, Rt. Hon. Sir Frederick Pollock, Sir Arthur Quiller Couch, Rt. Hon. Russell Rea, Lord Redesdale, Morley Roberts, F. Cayley Robinson, Albert Rothenstein, Dr C. W. Saleeby, the Hon. Lord Salvesen, Professor Sauter, Charles Shannon, Clement K. Shorter, Joseph Simpson, J. St Loe Strachey, William Strang, Hamo Thornycroft, G. M. Trevelyan, T. Fisher Unwin, Professor A. W. Verrall, Professor Paul Vinogradoff, Arnold White, Richard Whiteing, Norman Wilkinson, Sir Henry Wood, Mrs Margaret L. Woods, the Master of the Temple, Filson Young, and Sir J. H. Yoxall.]

LETTER TO THE KING.

29th February 1912.

YOUR MAJESTY,—In view of a petition which it is proposed to send to your Majesty, protesting against the censorship of plays, we, the undersigned managers of theatres, and actors, whilst claiming the fullest freedom for the stage, desire to assert the necessity for such a censorship as a protection to ourselves and to the public.

We cannot help feeling that were such a censorship abolished, not only might undesirable plays be presented to the public, but that the interference of the police, of municipal bodies, and various vigilance societies would render the conduct of theatres most irksome, and would be detrimental to the best interests of the drama. In this spirit we desire to express our confidence in the censorship as exercised under the Lord Chamberlain's supervision.—We are,

Your Majesty's loyal and devoted servants.

Albert Archdeacon, Miss Lena Ashwell, Lady Bancroft, J. H. Barnes, George Barrett, Rutland Barrington, George Bellamy, J. D. Beveridge, Alfred Bishop, B. Blaiberg, Acton Bond, J. W. Boughton, Arthur Bourchier, Mrs Patrick Campbell, Miss Alexandra Carlisle, R. Holman Clark, Robert Loraine, Malcolm Cherry, C. F. Collings, Miss Compton, G. A. Cookson, Sydney Cooper, Robert Courtneidge, Joseph Coyne, Philip Cunningham, E. Dagnall, S. F. Davidson, E. Domville, Ernest Dottridge, Kenneth Douglas, Gerald du Maurier, George Edwardes, Charles Elphinstone, Miss Winifred Emery, James Fernandez, Loring Fernie, Miss Rosina Filippi, Norman Forbes, A. E. George, George Grossmith, jun., Weedon Grossmith, Edmund Gwenn, Oscar Hammerstein, Sir John Hare, Arthur Hardy, Frederick Harrison, Charles Hawtrey, J. R. Huddlestone, Percy Hutchison, W. W. Kelly, Mrs Kendal, W. H. Kendal, Mrs Langtry, Gerald Lawrence, Miss Marie Lohr, James W. Mathews, A. E. Matthews, Miss Margery Maude, Cyril Maude, Charles Maude,

Edmund Maurice, Miss Julia Neilson, Harry Nicholls, Walter Nightingale, Edmund Payne, H. A. Saintsbury, Edward Sass, C. W. Somerset, Ernest Stevens, Athol Stewart, Miss Ellaline Terriss, Lady Tree, Sir Herbert Tree, Miss Violet Vanbrugh, E. S. Willard, Arthur Wontner.

[The above letter, though published in the daily papers, with the list of signatures, was not received by the Home Secretary, though we understand that another petition, signed by Sir Herbert Tree and other managers, was submitted later.]

MUSIC-HALL INSPECTIONS MADE BY THE LONDON COUNTY COUNCIL DURING THE LICENSING YEAR ENDED 24TH NOVEMBER 1911, WITH PARTICULARS OF ACTION TAKEN.

Date of inspection.	Place of entertainment.	Nature of performances.	Action (if any) taken by Committee.
1911. 10th Feb. .	London Coliseum	Wordless play entitled " Sumurun "	No action.
18th Feb. .	Paragon Music Hall	Boxing	,,
14th June .	London Palladium	Songs by George Robey	,,
24th June .	New Kilburn Empire	Sketch entitled "The Girl who lost her Honeymoon," played by Arthur Roberts	Licensee asked to have certain passages modified.
27th Oct. .	London Coliseum	Wordless play entitled " Rialon "	Licensee informed that the performance was one to which considerable objection might not unreasonably be taken.
13th Nov. .	London Palladium	Wordless sketch entitled "The Dawn of Love "	Licensee asked to discontinue performance. Modified version subsequently allowed.
29th Nov. .	New Kilburn Empire	Oriental dance by " Ular Api "	Licensee informed that the continuance of performances of this nature was undesirable, and asked not to allow the performance at any of the other halls under his control.
21st Nov. .	Palace Theatre	Oriental dance by Mademoiselle Napierkowska	No action.

INDEX